SEXUALITY AND THE RISE OF CHINA

SEXUALITY AND
THE RISE OF CHINA

THE POST-1990S GAY GENERATION IN HONG KONG, TAIWAN, AND MAINLAND CHINA

Travis S. K. Kong

DUKE UNIVERSITY PRESS
Durham and London
2023

Printed in the United States of America on acid-free paper ∞
Designed by A. Mattson Gallagher
Project Editor: Ihsan Taylor
Typeset in SangBleu Republic and TheSans
by Westchester Publishing Services

Library of Congress Cataloging-in-Publication Data
Names: Kong, Travis, author.
Title: Sexuality and the rise of China : the post-1990s gay generation
in Hong Kong, Taiwan, and mainland China / Travis S. K. Kong.
Description: Durham : Duke University Press, 2023. | Includes
bibliographical references and index.
Identifiers: LCCN 2022043149 (print)
LCCN 2022043150 (ebook)
ISBN 9781478019862 (paperback)
ISBN 9781478017165 (hardcover)
ISBN 9781478024439 (ebook)
Subjects: LCSH: Gay culture—Asia. | Gay community—Asia. | Gay
men—Asia—Social conditions. | BISAC: SOCIAL SCIENCE / LGBTQ
Studies / General | SOCIAL SCIENCE / Sociology / General
Classification: LCC HQ76.3.A78 K66 2023 (print) | LCC HQ76.3.A78
(ebook) | DDC 306.76/62095—dc23/eng/20230111
LC record available at https://lccn.loc.gov/2022043149
LC ebook record available at https://lccn.loc.gov/2022043150

Cover art: Miao Xiaochun, *Some hours are lightning fast*
(detail), 2019. 3D print photopolymer resin, 14¼ × 13¾ × 13¾
inches (36 × 35 × 35 cm). Courtesy of the artist and Eli Klein
Gallery. © Miao Xiaochun.

*In loving memory of Ken Plummer (1946–2022) and
for all who fight for love, equality, and respect*

CONTENTS

CCP	Chinese Communist Party
DPP	Democratic Progressive Party
ELAB	Extradition Law Amendment Bill
HKLGFF	Hong Kong Lesbian and Gay Film Festival
HKSAR	Hong Kong Special Administrative Region
IDAHOT	International Day against Homophobia, Transphobia and Biphobia
KMT	Kuomintang (Chinese Nationalist Party)
LGBT+	Lesbian, gay, bisexual, transgender, and other related nonnormative genders and sexualities
NGO	Nongovernmental organization
PFLAG	Parents, Families, and Friends of Lesbians and Gays
PRC	People's Republic of China
ROC	Republic of China

All non-English terms are Chinese unless stated otherwise, and I italicize them throughout the book. I do not use English plural markers (e.g., *tongzhi* instead of *tongzhis*). The Romanization of Chinese characters follows the *Hanyu Pinyin* system, or *pinyin*, which is the official Romanization system for standard Mandarin Chinese in mainland China (and to some extent in Taiwan). It is widely used in English-language scholarly publications. Cantonese Romanization is marked with the specification "Cant." (e.g., *nanshen* [Cant.]). The Wade-Giles system is used in this book for the translation of some Taiwanese authors' names if they have no English translation or if they used that system in their previous publications.

PREFACE AND ACKNOWLEDGMENTS

I am increasingly interested in the topic of generational sexualities (Plummer 2010), as it links sexual identity to the sexual life cycle, age and sexual cohorts, and generational sexual worlds. One of the major issues we are currently facing in East Asia is an aging population, with most affected countries seeking ways to care for that population and increase birth rates. At the same time, I am also confronted with my own aging and how it connects to my sexual identity and sexual life cycle. More than these issues, however, the topic has made me consider the positionality of the generations before and after me and the challenges we have all faced as gay men in a Chinese society.

In 2009, I started an oral history project on older gay men in Hong Kong, men born before 1950. I later published a book (Kong 2014 in Chinese, with a translation in English [2019a]) to capture the complexities of their lives intertwined with the history of Hong Kong society. These men, part of what I call the first *tongzhi* (local parlance for LGBT+) generation, were born between 1920 and 1950 in Hong Kong or came to Hong Kong from mainland China as refugees or migrants, living with their parents and siblings in squatter settlements, huts, or overcrowded and unsanitary tenements in postwar Hong Kong. With little support from the government, they lived in close-knit family networks that defined social roles, offered career possibilities, arranged marriages, and provided social security. Homosexuality, largely a taboo subject, was criminalized and seen as a form of mental illness or social deviance or simply as an unhealthy lifestyle. In such an environment, there was little room for these men to explore their same-sex desires. Most of them married women and found largely fleeting sexual, romantic, and social liaisons in public toilets.

I am part of a later generation, born in the late 1960s and raised in a working-class family, living with my parents and four elder siblings in a tiny apartment in a public housing estate in Hong Kong. Postwar Hong Kong was undergoing a transformation from an industrial society to an international financial center, from extreme poverty and working-class dominance to affluence and an expanded middle class, and from deprivation to adequate social-service provision. When I was a teenager in the 1980s, Hong Kong society was still conservative and homophobic. Over time, however, increasing numbers of gay men and lesbians started to come out (especially those who had studied overseas and returned to Hong Kong), and the *tongzhi* world has slowly developed with the establishment of fairly substantial yet quite Western expatriate-dominated gay communities, increasing visibility in popular culture, and the emergence of underground *tongzhi* social groups. Like most young gay men at that time, I dated girls and thought that being gay was just a phase, although I secretly tried to explore my puzzling desires. Hong Kong seemed to be too small for me, or at least that's what I thought at the time. With a burning desire to see the world and explore my repressed sexuality, I moved to the United Kingdom in the 1990s to study for my master's and PhD at the University of Essex. I was excited to learn cutting-edge ideas and theories from renowned scholars in sociology and was challenged by the arrival of queer theory from the humanities. I lived in London. Although I regularly complained about the bad weather, technological backwardness, and inefficiencies of everyday life, I embraced the city's cosmopolitan culture and well-established queer world. I enjoyed and benefited from both the society at large and the white-dominated queer community, but at the same time I felt strongly that it was not my place, as I was always seen as a racial and sexual minority.

In late 1999, I came back to Hong Kong to teach and began engaging with queer pedagogy and *tongzhi* activism. I have since come to know more and more young gay men, first in Hong Kong and later in mainland China and Taiwan. They live in a very different era than those of previous generations. Homosexuality is no longer seen as a crime and/or mental illness. Moreover, there is a substantial infrastructure of *tongzhi* consumer markets, various burgeoning offline and online communities and "scenes" and emergent activism. My bigger project is to compare and contrast different gay generations in Hong Kong, Taiwan, and mainland China, but this book has a more modest aim: to compare and contrast the lives of the post-'90s generation in these three Chinese locales based on ninety life stories. My key question is: How might we understand these young gay men's lives? They share a common Chinese/Confucian cultural heritage but live in very different social, economic, cultural, and political circumstances. This question is especially crucial at this specific historical moment characterized by the rise of China—especially the rise of Chinese nationalism—which has tended to obscure the heterogeneous transformations in Hong Kong and Taiwan. In recent years, I have been much concerned with young people. In Hong Kong, they experienced one of the most turbulent periods of social unrest in the city's history, first by the Umbrella Movement in 2014, and then the protests against the proposed extradition law in 2019. In Taiwan, they (mainly students) led and engaged heavily and passionately with the Sunflower Movement in 2014 and stood proud as Taiwanese when same-sex marriage legislation passed in 2019, despite living under the constant threat of mainland China declaring war on Taiwan. In mainland China, they have sought ways to survive under the rise of the Xi Jinping regime, with its strong state and strict control and censorship of civil society, including the *tongzhi* community, since 2012.

Over the years, I have critically engaged with Western theories in understanding notions of identity, masculinity, the body, and intimacy in contemporary Chinese communities in the context of global cultures, and I sought dialogue across disciplines in understanding human sexualities. In this book, I propose what I call *transnational queer sociology* to compare and contrast the intricate and complicated relations of young gay sexualities in Hong Kong, Taiwan, and mainland China during the latest era of globalization. Such sociology acknowledges the West's historically dominant, yet not totalizing, role in shaping experiences in non-Western (in my case, Chinese) societies while acknowledging local and interregional specificities, thereby engaging in critical dialogue with the West and within the non-West. I see my work as part of the decolonizing sexualities program and, more specifically, the emergent discipline of queer Asian studies, which seeks to understand the complex process of Western, local, and interregional knowledge systems in shaping experiences, identities, and desires in specific sites within Asia.

My use of transnational queer sociology to understand the complexity of Chinese male gay sexualities is inspired by three "missing revolutions" in sociology. In Stacey and Thorne's (1985) critique of the "missing feminist revolution" in sociology, they argue that mainstream sociology, with its legacy of functionalism, quantitative treatment of gender as a variable, and the sexism of Marxism, has prevented feminist scholars from transforming the discipline's theoretical and conceptual frameworks. Almost a decade later, Stein and Plummer (1994) identified a "missing sexual revolution" in sociology, urging sociologists to take sexuality (at that time, queer theory) seriously. Scholars advancing queer theory have not asked simply for a theory of queers but sought to make theory queer, thereby transforming homosexuality as a minority theory into a general theory and challenging the hetero/homo binary embedded in the knowledge and social systems (sexual or not) that construct selves, identities, and practices. Although feminism and queer studies within sociology have incorporated women and "the sexual self" in the past two decades or so, Bhambra (2007) has criticized the discipline's "missing post-colonial revolution," as feminism and queer studies, as well as postcolonialism, have in her view failed to challenge the constitution of sociology and its founding categories of modernity. However, the development of the three revolutions has tended to be compartmentalized. What we need is critical dialogue on a transnational scale that enables sociology to take feminism, queer studies, and postcolonialism more seriously and incorporate the intersection of gender, sexuality, and race/ethnicity in the basic conceptual framework used to formulate sociological knowledge (see Wharton 2006).

I would argue that the three missing revolutions have failed in differing degrees in terms of epistemic exclusion in sociology (i.e., the exclusion of gender studies, queer studies, and postcolonial studies) in Hong Kong, Taiwan, and mainland China. Comparatively speaking, the inclusion of gender studies has experienced the greatest success in sociology departments in the three Chinese societies, although many gender studies courses and programs were recently closed down in mainland China. The inclusion of sexuality studies and postcolonial studies in sociology remains rare, as they are often seen as marginal, niche, and/or improper, although they are well received in arts and humanities departments (e.g., comparative literature, language, and cultural studies).

In the course of my writing and research, I often encounter common obstacles, such as the seeming incompatibility between poststructuralism and sociology (e.g., mainstream sociologists believing Foucault is incompatible with sociology; claims that queer theory is not sociology), sociology's neglect of postcolonial literature, the geopolitics of knowledge production (e.g., theory generated from the West being used to elucidate non-Western experiences), and interdisciplinary boundaries (e.g., sociologists not much interested in the humanities, and the humanities not much interested in sociology). Despite these obstacles, I still see this book as part of a continuing effort to decenter Western knowledge of genders and sexualities. Through the lens of transnational queer sociology, I hope to offer a better understanding of Chinese gay male sexualities.

This book would not have been possible without the generosity, support, and kindheartedness of friends, colleagues, and students. The book is based on a research project funded by a General Research Fund grant from the Research Grants Council of the Hong Kong Special Administrative Region, China (HKU 17613316). I would like to thank the following individuals and organizations for their generous help in completing this project: coinvestigators Lin Chwen-der (Taiwan), Frank Wang Tsen-yung (Taiwan), and Wei Wei (mainland China); research assistants Darren Fung Tsz-hin (Hong Kong), Eva Li Cheuk-yin (Hong Kong), Chen Wei-hong (Taiwan), and He Ji-yu (mainland China); and organizations such as AIDS Concern (Hong Kong), the AIDS Foundation (Hong Kong), Midnight Blue (Hong Kong), the Boys' & Girls' Clubs Association of Hong Kong (Hong Kong), the Taiwan Tongzhi (LGBTQ+) Hotline Association (Taiwan, especially Cheng Chi-wei and Peng Chih-liu), and PFLAG China (later changed to Trueself, mainland China, especially Aqiang and Ah Shan) for referring interviewees. I would also like to thank Ken Wissoker of Duke University Press, who encouraged me to turn this project into a book and gave his unstinting support throughout the process. I am grateful to three other individuals from Duke: Joshua Gutterman Tranen for his general assistance, Alejandra Mejía for her excellent administrative help, and Ihsan Taylor for his dedicated support during the book's production, as well as to the two anonymous reviewers who strengthened the book with their extremely positive comments and helpful suggestions. I also thank Erika Hebblethwaite for editing the manuscript, and Laura Helper for working closely with me to shape the manuscript into a book. In the course of writing, my research assistants Trevor Ma Yuk-tung (Hong Kong), Chen Wei-hong (Taiwan), and Gong Jin (mainland China) offered excellent and timely support, for which I thank them. I was fortunate to present parts of the chapters at the following universities and thank those who invited me. I enjoyed my conversations with the attendees: the Department of Sociology and Center for China Studies, Rutgers University, United States (thanks to Louise Schein and Arlene Stein), March 2018; Global Asia Research Center, College of Social Science, National Taiwan University, Taiwan (thanks to Lan Pei-chia), April 2018; the Department of Sociology, the Chinese University of Hong Kong, Hong Kong (thanks to Luo Muyuan), May 2018; the Department of Communication and New

Media, the National University of Singapore, Singapore (thanks to Michelle Ho and Audrey Yu), June 2019; the Amsterdam Research Centre for Gender and Sexuality, University of Amsterdam, the Netherlands (thanks to Jeroen de Kloet and Rachel Spronk), November 2019; and the Graduate Institute of Social Work, National Chengchi University, Taiwan (thanks to Frank Wang Tsen-yung), November 2020. Earlier versions of chapters 1 and 5 and portions of the introduction have been published previously in the *British Journal of Sociology* (Kong 2019b), the *Journal of Homosexuality* (Kong 2022), and *The Oxford Encyclopedia of LGBT Politics and Policy* (Kong et al. 2021). I owe a particular debt to the following individuals who read the book proposal and/ or drafts of the book and gave me extremely generous, inspiring, and useful feedback despite their busy schedules: Chris Berry, James Farrer, Fung Ka-keung, Ho Sik-ying, Stevi Jackson, Karen Joe-Laidler, Ken Plummer, Lisa Rofel, and Denise Tang. I am particularly grateful to Ken Plummer, who was my PhD supervisor and who passed away in November 2022. He was a walking encyclopedia of sociology, an inspiring and caring mentor, and a long-term friend. He taught me that sociology should stem from precarious human experiences and should be fun and showed me how to live as an out gay academic with pride and integrity. I thank the following organizations or individual for their permission to reprint the figures in the book: BigLove Alliance (fig. 1.1), the Hong Kong Lesbian and Gay Film Festival (fig. 1.2), the Taiwan Tongzhi (LGBTQ+) Hotline Association (fig. 1.3 and fig. 5.1), the Taiwan Gender Equity Education Association (fig. 1.4), a Shanghai participant (fig. 1.5), Trueself (fig. 1.6), Vibranium (fig. 3.1), and ShanghaiPRIDE (fig. 3.2). I also thank JC for offering his unfailing love and support and my best friends who have always been here with me: Chan Ka-kei (K), Hung Keung, Teresa Kwong, Bobo Lee, Olive Leung, Fion Ng, and Sikay Tang. I miss K very much after his untimely death in 2020 at the young age of forty-six. If he were still alive, he would have helped me with the book cover design. My deepest debt is to the participants, whom I met in Hong Kong, Taiwan, and mainland China. They appear in the text under pseudonyms. They shared with me their insights about their lives for little in return. I hope I have done justice to their stories. This book is dedicated to the post-'90s generation, whose members are living with a difficult social and political climate and the ongoing COVID-19 epidemic while struggling for love, freedom, and equality.

Travis Kong
Hong Kong
December 2022

Introduction

Yifan was born in 1990 in a small village in Shaanxi in mainland China and is one of the left-behind, or stay-at-home, children common in rural areas of China, raised by his grandparents after his parents left home to find work in an urban area. After graduating from a university in Guilin, he took up a position in an overseas trading company in Shanghai, which is where we first met in 2017. Yifan moved to Hangzhou in 2018 and then to Shenzhen in 2020, where he lives with his boyfriend but remains deeply closeted. When his sister once came to visit him in Shenzhen, he slept separately from his boyfriend and pretended that they were flatmates, although he thinks his sister knew otherwise. He is still thinking of getting married to please his parents. Yifan is tall and lean and dresses well.

When I first interviewed him in 2017, Yifan applauded the fast pace of Chinese economic achievement, which from his point of view "only took us forty years" while "countries like France and the U.S. [took] a couple hundred years." Yifan was well aware of the accusations of human rights violations in mainland China by the international press but argued that "democracy . . . is improving. The government has a lot of considerations . . . [and] economic developments will lead to democracy." His political stance remained the same when I last spoke to him in 2020. Like many of the young gay men I talked to in mainland China, Yifan has a strong Chinese national identity and agrees with the One China policy. Living under a government that is not considered "democratic" by most Western countries, these young men still have faith that economic pluralism will eventually lead to political pluralism.

However, they recognize that mainland China may never have the same kind of democracy as that in the West but rather "democracy with Chinese characteristics." In our conversations, Yifan and others regularly make an interesting comparison: we don't have Facebook, but we have *weibo*. We don't have WhatsApp, but we have WeChat. We don't use iPhones, but we have Huawei and Xiaomi, which are even better than iPhones, or at least much cheaper. If the post-'80s generation in mainland China was eager to see the world and join the track of the world, the post-'90s generation proudly proclaims that China is the world! If you want to see the world, come to China. They are self-confident and pragmatic but also politically conservative and reluctant to do anything that could be deemed politically radical. In their private lives, most members of the generation are primarily concerned with their education and securing a good job. Most of them, like Yifan, still struggle with their sexual identity, with some attempting to hide their sexuality and/or thinking about getting married to either a straight woman or a *lala* (lesbian) to please their parents. In the meantime, browsing and dating apps such as Blued seem to be the only way to connect with others, as the gay world in mainland China is heavily censored, regulated, and subject to surveillance.

Born in Hong Kong in 1993, Bobby is the only son of a working-class family. He works at a health-associated nongovernmental organization (NGO) but is constantly looking for a better job. He lives with his parents in public housing and shares a bunkbed with his mother. Bobby is out to his parents, even though they still want him to get married. He is a bit chubby but likes to go to the gym. He is quite desperate to find a boyfriend but finds it difficult to maintain an intimate relationship. He is currently single, although he has ambiguous relationships with several men. He strongly identifies as a Hongkonger, not as a *Zhongguoren* (Chinese national). In 2019, Bobby was heavily involved in the protests against the Extradition Law Amendment Bill (ELAB), which would have allowed the extradition of criminal suspects to mainland China. He only dates guys from the yellow-ribbon camp (crudely seen as prodemocracy), eschewing those from the blue-ribbon camp (who are seen as progovernment, pro-police, or pro-Beijing). When I talked to him in 2020, he said, "Even if he is a *nanshen* [Cant., male god] who fulfills all my fantasies, I would reject him if he were blue ribbon." He thinks the future will be grim; he is very unhappy and feels powerless. Because of his social class and financial status, and because he is the caregiver for his parents, he is stuck in Hong Kong. Bobby, like other young gay men I talked to in Hong Kong, participated in the social protests in 2019 to varying degrees. They feel angry, anguished, depressed, and hopeless. With a strong sense of being a Hongkonger, they have fashioned a different kind of Chineseness and cry for freedom and autonomy. In their private lives, they are still concerned about education and work. Finding a boyfriend is a paramount concern, but political affiliation has become an important criterion in choosing one. They are generally comfortable with their sexual identity, and most have come out to their families. However, they are quite pessimistic about Hong Kong's future and its political situation. By extension, they are concerned about the stagnant development of the fight for gender and sexual equality.

Born in 1996 in Taipei, Hao is the only son in his family. He lives with his mother; his father passed away during his first year at university. He has a handsome face, a lean body, and pale skin. He is in the second year of a master's program and working part time as a teaching assistant. His mother runs a small boutique but has encountered financial difficulty due to COVID-19. He has thought of suspending his studies and working full time, but his mother insists that he should complete his education. Hao is out to his family and out at work. He is currently going out with a young man whom his mother likes very much. He has a very strong sense of Taiwanese identity and is proud of Taiwan. When I interviewed him in 2017, he told me that Taiwan "is a pluralistic society [with a] Chinese culture, Taiwanese culture, indigenous culture, and East Asian culture" and, most importantly, is "a land of freedom and equality." When we spoke again in 2020, he cited the previous year's legalization of same-sex marriage as an example of the latter. The young gay men I talked to in Taiwan, like Hao, are proud of being Taiwanese, not just because Taiwan was the first Asian society to legalize same-sex marriage, in May 2019, making that the notable event of 2019 for the Taiwanese, but also because of their determination that Taiwan remain independent and because of their commitment to universal values such as democracy, freedom of speech, and human rights. Although they have difficulty finding jobs or are forced to accept low salaries despite their impressive educational qualifications, they are generally accepting of their sexual identity, have come out to their parents, and engage with gay communities and in gay activism to different degrees.

This book examines the socioeconomic and political transformations in Hong Kong, Taiwan, and mainland China over the past few decades, with a particular focus on the changing nature of same-sex identities, communities, and cultures.[1] Drawing on the life stories of ninety young gay men born in or after 1990 in these three locales, this book investigates the changing meanings of gender and sexuality in terms of the ways in which these young men see themselves (identity), come out to their parents (family), and connect with one another (community) as well as how they love (intimacy) and do politics (activism). I am particularly interested in examining the interplay between the personal biographies of young gay men and their engagement with social institutions in the three Chinese societies—including the state, the market, mass media, the Internet, NGOs, religion, school, the workplace, and the family—and the ways in which they devise various tactics, be it resistance, redefinition, or accommodation, to negotiate a range of possibilities for the gender and sexual practices that inform their lives. More broadly, I show how these gay men create their own definitions of what it means to be gay by selectively incorporating, revising, or rejecting Western constructions of gayness but at the same time comparing and referencing the idea of being gay among Chinese and other Asian locales. There are significant commonalities among the three Chinese societies under study: they broadly share similar social values and cultural norms with a family-centered culture rooted in Confucianism. Although done at different rates, they have embraced neoliberalism and developmentalism and have come to exhibit strong neoliberal values of success, competition, and performance in such social institutions as the state, the family, education, and work. They have all become affluent societies with established pink economies (a term to describe the purchasing power of the LGBT+ community) and *tongzhi* worlds and a relatively positive sexual identity among members of the young gay generation. However, each of the three societies exhibits a distinct way of being a young Chinese gay man, resulting less from generalized Western queer culture, rhetoric, and processes such as coming out, community building, and queer activism and more from the increasingly inter-Asian influences and their own specific socioeconomic and political contexts under the hegemonic rise-of-China discourse in the latest globalization era. These distinctive pathways demonstrate a complex interplay among history, state, market, and civil society in the three locales, characterized less by the trajectory of Western modernity and more by the logic of polychronic modernities (Eisenlohr, Kramer, and Lanhenohl 2019). In this introduction, I explain why it is important to understand young Chinese gay men at this particular historical moment. I propose a transnational queer sociological approach that has the strength to compare and contrast the specificities of different Chinese locales and, by extension, the lived experiences of the young gay men in each. I then spell out the methods of investigation used in this study and briefly introduce the following chapters.

The New Era of Globalization: The Rise of China and the Post-'90s *Tongzhi* Generation

Young gay men who were born in or after 1990 are living in a new era of globalization that has dramatically changed the dynamics of mainland China's role in world politics and its relations with Hong Kong and Taiwan. Previous eras of globalization featured the traffic "from the West to the rest" (Hall 1992), with successive Western countries as global hegemonic powers in different waves of globalization: notably, various European superpowers and imperialism from the sixteenth to the early twentieth century (Portugal, the Netherlands, Great Britain) and the United States in the post–World War II era (Therborn 2011). The hallmark of the new era, in contrast, is the rise of Asia, with growing economic development and Asian regionalism. More specifically, mainland China has experienced rapid economic growth, expanded its economic and political power to Asia and beyond, and is in the process of constructing a new social, political, and cultural world order (Arase 2016; Chan, Lee, and Chan 2011; Choi 2018; Fong, Wu, and Nathan 2021). The resulting new geopolitical alignments are thus not only driving new traffic from "the rest to the West" but also traffic among the rest. Dai Jinhua (2018) has argued that a "post-post–Cold War era" began sometime around 2008 with the global financial crisis of neoliberal capitalism, the Beijing Olympic games, and China's emergence as the United States' largest creditor. Meanwhile, authoritarianism and fascism have risen in reaction to that financial crisis and, more broadly, neoliberal globalization in the early twenty-first century, with increasing recognition of the need for human rights protection (Berberoglu 2021). There is growing anxiety globally about the rise of China, especially about its shift from "soft power" to "sharp power" (Walker and Ludwig 2017), sparked in particular by the country's launch of a China-centered global trading network under the Belt and Road Initiative in 2013. China is also accused of using its economic clout to silence challenges from other countries in recent years (Roth 2020).

How has the rise of China specifically affected the relationship among Hong Kong, Taiwan, and mainland China? The historical division in 1949 between the People's Republic of China (PRC) and Republic of China (ROC) has shaped the postwar development of all three societies, but the enormous social, economic, and political transformations that have taken place over the past few decades have tied them together culturally and politically in unprecedentedly intimate and constraining ways. Hong Kong was formerly a British colony (1842–1997). It underwent rapid industrialization and urbanization from the 1950s onward and separated itself from mainland China under the sway of both Cold War ideology and its British colonial status, developing a distinctive Hong Kong identity. It then successfully transformed itself from a colonial city into an international financial center, with a strong middle class emerging in the 1970s. Hong Kong has made significant economic contributions to mainland China, particularly in the early reform period of the 1980s, contributions that have led to the restructuring of its own economy. Since Hong Kong's return to Chinese sovereignty in 1997 under the one country, two systems political framework, the new government, the Hong Kong Special Administrative Region (HKSAR) has rebranded Hong Kong as "Asia's world city." As Mathews (1997) has argued, after the handover, Hong Kong found itself in the new position of being "a part of China" but also "apart from China," owing to its distinct social, cultural, and political features such as cosmopolitanism, colonialism, and the rule of law. The dilemma is how to maintain its own unique position without falling into nationalization (Hong Kong as just another Chinese city) or localization (an independent Hong Kong) (So 2002; Wong and So 2020). In recent years, however, Hong Kong has experienced political turmoil, first with the Umbrella Movement protests calling for universal suffrage in 2014 and then the large-scale anti-ELAB protests in 2019, culminating in the introduction of a new national security law proposed by the Beijing government in 2020.[2]

Taiwan has taken a somewhat different path. Although the ROC was formed on mainland China in 1911, Chiang Kai-shek's Kuomintang (KMT) relocated the government to Taiwan after Chiang's defeat by Mao Zedong in 1949. Taiwan experienced rapid economic growth from the 1970s onward with aid from the United States. After its transition from authoritarian KMT rule to representative democracy in 1996, it developed a strong and distinctive Taiwanese identity. Taiwan also contributed to China's economy, especially in the 1980s and 1990s. Although Taiwan is a world leader in the manufacture of electronic components and devices, its economy lags behind those of both Hong Kong and mainland China, and Taiwan is politically marginalized on the international stage due to the One China policy insisted on by the Beijing government and adopted by the United Nations and many countries. In her victory speech following her second election as president in 2020, Tsai Ing-wen asked China to "face the reality" of Taiwan's independence.[3]

The PRC celebrated its seventieth anniversary in 2019, marking the seventy years that had passed since its founding by the Chinese Communist Party (CCP) in 1949. China's economic reforms and its opening up in the late 1970s reconfigured both the state and the market, leading to a shift from Maoism/socialism to a postreform China that since the late 1990s can be characterized as late socialism or state capitalism.[4] However, the Beijing government under President Xi Jinping's leadership continues to exert strong control. It has tightened regulations over various sectors of society, with the Internet, activists, and many NGOs subject to surveillance. Issues related to freedom of speech and human rights are highly sensitive subjects. The One China policy is manifesting itself in the government's attempts to unify different races and ethnicities within China, including Tibetans and Uyghurs as well as Taiwanese, Hongkongers, and Macanese. Using "imperialist center-periphery theories," Fong (2021, 5) conceptualizes mainland China as the center in East Asia, with Hong Kong seen as having "peripheral autonomy" (6) and Taiwan as a "peripheral contested state" (6).

These sociopolitical transformations in the three locales have had major impacts on everyday life, including sexual life, and the young generations have been particularly affected. Since the 1980s, all three societies have relaxed restrictive standards of sexual morality and have seen an increase in sexual permissiveness; increases in premarital sex, abortion, and divorce; the burgeoning of pornography and the sex industry; and the emergence of new sexual identities, including *tongzhi* (which literally means "common will," although it is often translated as "comrade," and is the local parlance for LGBT+) (Davis and Freedman 2014; Ho et al. 2018; Huang 2011; Jeffreys and Yu 2015; Pan 2006).[5] These developments have nurtured the emergence of new forms of sexual subjectivity, marking a turn from colonial subjectivity (Hong Kong), politically repressed subjectivity (Taiwan), and Maoist collective subjectivity (mainland China) to cosmopolitan, transnational, neoliberal, or desiring subjectivity.[6]

In particular, young gay men in Hong Kong, Taiwan, and mainland China who were born in or after 1990 are living in a markedly different era of sexuality from that of previous gay generations. The Western medical model that had long constructed homosexuals as mental patients or social deviants[7] is now far less influential in the three locales, although it still carries power, and the laws governing homosexual acts were changed in all three societies in the 1990s.[8] In Hong Kong, male homosexual acts were criminalized in 1842 under British rule but then decriminalized by the colonial government in 1991. Homosexuality was never a criminal offense in Taiwan, but gay men were often charged with offenses against *shangliang fengsu* ("virtuous customs") under the Police Offense Law, which was replaced by the Social Order Maintenance Law in 1991 (Huang 2011). In mainland China, *liumangzui* ("hooliganism," the offense used to arrest homosexuals) was deleted from the country's criminal law in 1997, and the Chinese Psychiatric Association has not considered homosexuality a mental illness since 2001. The consumer infrastructure of the pink economy is now firmly in place, characterized by such visible and often Westernized "gay ghettos" as Lan Kwai Fong in Hong Kong and the Red House in Taipei and the gay scenes of major cities in mainland China (Beijing, Shanghai, Shenzhen, Chengdu). Originating in North America, circuit parties (large-scale dance parties targeting mainly gay and bisexual men) have now spread to metropolitan cities worldwide, with an increasing trend in Asia. There were more than fifty-four globally identified weekend circuit parties held in metropolitan areas in 2015, twenty-three of them in Asia (Cheung et al. 2015); for example, SongKran (April, Bangkok), Ageha or Gtopia (July, Tokyo), I am (August, Seoul), and Parade Party (October, Taipei).[9] Although attended by gay men from across Asia, they are dominated by gay men from Hong Kong, Taiwan, and mainland China. *Tongzhi* communities and social groups, as well as social media and dating apps, have burgeoned. Finally, the 2000s saw the emergence of *tongzhi* activism, inspired by the rise of the sexual citizenship and queer political movements in the West—for example, International Day against Homophobia (2005–), the Pride Parade (2008–), and Pink Dot (2014–) in Hong Kong; LGBT Pride in Taiwan; and Shanghai Pride (2009–2020) in mainland China (Kong, Lau, and Li 2015; Kong et al. 2021). Same-sex marriage legislation was passed in Taiwan in 2019, and the next Gay Games will be held in Hong Kong in 2023. Transnational Christian/evangelical groups in Hong Kong, Taiwan, South Korea, and Singapore are the main opposing forces to the *tongzhi* movement in Hong Kong (Wong 2013) and Taiwan (Ho 2008; Huang 2017; Lee 2017), whereas in mainland China, it is the government (Engebretsen and Schroeder 2015).

It is at this particular historical juncture that we see generalized but differential Western influences still impinging on each locale but also witness interinfluences among the three. Chinese gay men are increasingly taking their references on what it means to be gay less from the West and more from themselves and from other East and Southeast Asian countries such as Japan, South Korea, Thailand, and Singapore. At the same time, the heterogeneous transformations mean that men in Hong Kong and Taiwan exhibit very different ways of being gay from those in mainland China, and young gay men in those two societies are thus implicitly resisting the domination of the rise-of-China discourse and the emergence of a homogeneous Chinese or Sinophone gay identity. Why do we need a comparative framework? It is because the terms *Chinese, young, gay*, and *man*, among others, hold such different meanings in Hong Kong, Taiwan, and mainland China, which is why I now turn to my proposed approach: transnational queer sociology.

Transnational Queer Sociology

The sociology of homosexuality and queer theory are the two dominant models for understanding contemporary nonnormative sexual identities. However, they are drawn primarily from the theorization of Western queer identities, cultures, and communities. Western theories are often universalized, with non-Western experiences serving merely as empirical data for validation. Engaging with the emerging field of queer Asian studies, I call for a "transnational" turn in the sociology of homosexuality, proposing a new theoretical approach that I call *transnational queer sociology*, which advances the literature in three major respects. First, it resists the dominance of Western models in elucidating non-Western, nonnormative sexualities. It does not completely reject Western theories but rather provincializes them through critical application (Chakrabarty 2000). Second, it goes beyond the usual binary and essentialist ways of framing research and analysis to cultivate a glocal queer understanding and critique of globalization by examining cross-national and cross-cultural similarities and differences to produce mutually referenced experiences to inform gender and sexuality studies. Third, it engages sociology with queer theory by paying equal attention to the materiality and practices of social institutions as well as to discourses and culture in shaping genders and sexualities.

Because transnational queer sociology is built on the sociology of homosexuality and queer theory, a brief history is needed. Here I outline the history of the sociology of homosexuality and queer theory in understanding nonnormative genders and sexualities and discuss how these two approaches have made a global turn and how queer Asian studies has become an important school of thought to understand nonnormative, non-Western genders and sexualities. Before we start, a note on terminology. I use the term *West* or *Western* for convenience and treat it as a cultural construction rather than a geographical absolute (Jackson and Ho 2020). *West* is a contested term; it is not homogeneous but usually refers collectively to the social and political constructs of the Anglo- and Euro-American cultures and traditions of North America and Western Europe and also extends to Northern and Southern Europe as well as to Australia and New Zealand. The term *non-West* refers broadly to "the rest of the world" (Hall 1992) and, like the term *West*, it is a cultural construction with its own heterogeneity. In this book, it refers specifically to Asian societies, and its nuanced differences are shown through the case studies of three Chinese societies—namely, Hong Kong, Taiwan, and mainland China.

Sociology originated as a discipline preoccupied with European modernity. Its emergence between the 1880s and World War I coincided with the heyday of Western imperialism, when Britain, Germany, France, and the United States exercised control over broad swathes of Asia and Africa (Seidman 1996a). In classical (or Comtean) sociology, "progress" was generally used to highlight the difference between metropole and colony; the status of women, evolution of sexuality, and changing forms of family and marriage were themes of great interest in measuring societal progress. However, classical sociologists in both Europe and the United States also concerned themselves with the great problems of modernity. Examples include Karl Marx's class struggle-based critique of "ill" capitalism, Max Weber's thesis on rationalization and the bureaucratization of modern life, and Emile Durkheim's division of labor as conducive to social growth. Sociology should be seen as part of the development of empire itself, which shaped sociological thinking on what counts as knowledge and who can produce it and who cannot (Go 2020). In the story that early sociologists told, there was little room for gender, sexuality, or race (Connell 2014; Seidman 1996b).

In examining the modern "social," sociology has traditionally neglected homosexuality, dismissing it as belonging to the realm of nature (as illness), and thus to the fields of sexology, psychology, and psychiatry. The 1960s and 1970s saw sociology take up the study of sexuality (e.g., sexual scripts [Gagnon and Simon 1974]), but it generally subsumed it under gender within feminism (e.g., sex roles in Parsonian sociology [see, e.g., Parsons 1942]), whereas homosexuality fell largely into the sociology of deviance.[10] In the 1970s and 1980s, social constructionism became the major framework for understanding gender and sexuality, especially in explaining sexual identities (Stein and Plummer 1994). These new (homo)sexuality studies signified a new paradigm, deeming human sexuality to be socially produced, organized, maintained, and transformed (Plummer 1998). They examined the sociohistorical conditions that gave rise to the "making" of homosexual identity and explored that identity in terms of the coming-out process of individuals, thereby linking identity to politics (Seidman 1996b).[11]

Although social constructionism argues that gender and sexual identities are historically contingent, it tends to view identities, once formed, as neatly fixed, binary categories. The arrival of queer theory in the early 1990s heralded a discursive or poststructuralist turn in the study of sexuality (e.g., Butler 1990; Sedgwick 1990; Warner 1993). Queer theory is indeed poststructuralism applied to genders and sexualities. Queer theory rethinks identity by focusing on "deviant" cases that do not align neatly with sex, gender, and sexuality and views identity as interlocking with other social divisions such as gender, class, race, and ethnicity, rendering identity permanently multiple, open, hybrid, and in flux (Seidman 1996b; Valocchi 2005); this resonates with the symbolic interactionist tradition in sociology, which also views the self as emergent, processual, and transformative. Queer theory also challenges mainstream homosexuality-as-minority theory for its dependence on conceptual dualisms (male/female gender models, natural/cultural systems, essentialist/constructionist frameworks) that reinforce the notion of minority as other; these binary oppositions leave the center (read *heterosexuality*) intact and unquestioned (Stein and Plummer 1994). By exposing the hetero/homosexual binary as a master framework for constructing the self, knowledge, and social structures, queer theory opens up homosexual theory as a general social theory and critique (Seidman 1996b).

Rooted primarily in philosophy and literary criticism, queer theory tends to ignore both the materiality of sociostructural configurations that makes cultural discourses and analyses possible and the lived experiences, habitus, and practices of queer lives. Sociology and queer theory are thus at odds with each other—but some changes are reconciling them. For example, some sociologists have called for the "queering of sociology" to address the gap between sociology and queer theory (e.g., Green 2002; Seidman 1996b; Stein and Plummer 1994; Valocchi 2005), whereas others have advanced a new approach called "queer materialism" or the materialist analysis of sexuality (e.g., Alldred and Fox 2015; Tapley 2012). Queer theorist Love (2021) recently acknowledged the importance of the post–World War II social science tradition, especially the sociology of deviance, in understanding the history of (homo)sexuality and linked that tradition to queer theory. Transnational queer sociology builds on the history of sociology but is sensitive to its Eurocentric narrative of modernity. It also draws on the long history of both the sociology of homosexuality, for its strength in offering sociomaterialist analysis and narrative tradition to understand

and interpret social action, and queer theory, for its strength in offering discursive analysis and a creative critique of binary thinking. Transnational queer sociology thus joins the aforementioned efforts. It acknowledges the contributions of each discipline and attempts to bridge the two.

However, the sociology of homosexuality and canonical queer theory offer little on non-Western (homo)sexualities. Such sexualities were initially studied in history and literature (e.g., *The Immoralist* by André Gide) and in anthropology (e.g., Herdt 1981; Malinowski 1922; Mead 1952; Weston 1993) and were then later addressed by the sociology of homosexuality and queer theory when they took a global turn in the late 1990s.[12] Transnational queer sociology is thus situated in these later developments. Since the late 1990s, the Western model of sexual identity and emancipation has provided the dominant explanations of same-sex desires and practices in both academia and politics across the globe. Building on the coming-out model, the discussion of sexual identity has shifted toward the formation of sexual citizenship: the sexual citizen has distinct rights concerning conduct, identity, and relationships (Richardson 2000, 2017). This model has manifested in an equal rights/assimilation-based LGBT+ political movement, urban and consumption-based queer enclaves alongside homonormative mainstream assimilation, and a "global gay identity" (Altman 1997) or "gay International" (Massad 2002) in which the West is culturally represented as the origin of gayness.[13] Western theories of sexual knowledge have become universal in explaining non-Western, nonnormative genders and sexualities. Two broad strands of sexuality studies address this global turn. The first is what Plummer (2012) calls "critical sexualities studies." Primarily sociological or social science-based, they seek to understand the complex relationships among sexual selves, meanings, cultures, structures, conflicts, and regulations within the wider process of globalization, glocalization, and transnationalism. The second is what Manalansan (2003) calls "new queer studies." Based on canonical queer theory and the humanities, their aim is to provide a "more nuanced understanding of the traffic and travel of competing systems of desire in a transnational frame" (Gopinath 1998, 117). Later developments of this second approach expand queer theory to "address issues of US empire, race, immigration, diaspora, militarization, surveillance, and related concerns in the wake of 9/11 and its political aftermath" (Eng and Puar 2020, 1) and most recently to "explore how emergent theoretical debates in debility, indigeneity, and trans revise and rework subjectless critique, histories of materialism, and queer studies as American exceptionalism" (2).[14]

Neither strand has produced a single mode of inquiry in the study of genders and sexualities in the interconnected global world. Martin and colleagues (2008) articulate three approaches. "Global homogenization," the dominant approach, is a direct, linear process of sexual Westernization on a global scale. "Local essentialism," in contrast, which constitutes an opposing thesis, uses local sexual experiences to reify "authentic" sexual cultures and traditions that are unpolluted by and resist the West. Both approaches have been criticized as overly simplistic, failing to explore the complexity of non-Western sexual cultures in an increasingly interconnected world. For example, the first approach sees theory itself as Western, and thus universal. Non-Western experiences are used merely as empirical data to validate such Western theories as social constructionism and Foucault or queer theory. As Chen (2010, 226) argues, Foucault's *The History of Sexuality* is usually seen not just as an account of European sexual experiences but as a history of *all* human sexual experiences. The notion of "global queering" (Altman 1997), which has been criticized as privileging the Western origin story of gay liberation, posits "a *white* gay male gaze" (Manalansan 2003, 6), rendering, for example, Asian gay men "forever in the place of deferred arrival" (Rofel 2007, 91). The second, opposing approach assumes an indigenous selfhood and culture untouched by the West. Chou's (2000) distinction between Western "confrontational" queer politics and Chinese "silent" and "non-confrontational" *tongzhi* politics, for example, has been criticized for essentializing Chinese cultures (Liu and Ding 2005). Martin and colleagues (2008) thus propose a third approach, what they call the "queer hybridization model," in which "*both* Western and non-Western cultures of gender and sexuality have been, and continue to be, mutually transformed through their encounters with transnationally mobile forms of sexual knowledge" (6, emphasis in the original). This approach forces the study of globalization and sexuality to acknowledge a transnational understanding of global sexualities and examine the complexity of sexuality and culture as they intersect with race, class, gender, capital, and nation (e.g., Cruz-Malave and Manalansan 2002). Fascinating work has been done across the globe, such as in Mexico (Carrillo 2017), the Arab States (Massad 2007), and Africa (Epprecht 2004). Queer Asian studies, emerging sometime in the early 2000s (Wilson 2006), manifest this third approach, which can be further divided into two main camps. One camp is part of the queer-of-color critique (e.g., Ferguson 2004) and queer diasporic studies (e.g., Manalansan 2003), especially in the North American context, in which queer scholars of Asian origin examine the complex diasporic queer experiences in Western cultures (e.g., Eng 2001; Han 2015; Leong 1996; Lim 2014; Nguyen 2014). The other, "critical regionalism" (Johnson, Jackson, and Herdt 2000; see also Chiang and Wong 2016), conceptualizes queer life in the complex modernities of Asia as centers of transnational queer critique and analysis (e.g., Berry, Martin, and Yue 2003; Chu and Martin 2007; Ho and Blackwood 2022; McLelland and Mackie 2015), with some scholars focusing specifically on a comparison of Hong Kong, Taiwan, and/or mainland China.[15]

With this very short history, I have shown that transnational queer sociology draws on the strengths of both sociology and queer theory in offering nuanced understandings of non-Western, nonnormative genders and sexualities; this history also situates transnational queer sociology in global studies of sexualities in general, and queer Asian studies in particular. So what does a transnational queer sociology look like? Another note on terminology is in order, specifically the words *transnational*, *queer*, and *sociology*. The word *transnational* is used strategically. Transnationalism usually means above and beyond nations and is used mainly in economics (e.g., transnational corporations) and politics (transnational social movements and activism). However, it also means "from below" and is used mainly in relation to individuals (especially immigrants) and civil society, such as transnational civil society or international NGOs (Tedeschi, Vorobeva, and Jauhiainen 2020). I use transnationalism in a broad sense to examine connections and flows of people, capital, cultural reproduction, and politics that traverse a variety of locations and to show how different locales are exposed to and adapt wider translocal, interregional, and cross-national social, cultural, economic, and political influences. Transnationalism is thus a form of consciousness and identity, a mode of cultural reproduction, an avenue of capital, a form of political engagement, and a basis to reconsider the meaning of "place" (Watson 2017). The word *queer* is used in this book less as a sexual identity marker (an umbrella term for LGBT+) and more as a verb (to queer), an adjective (queer feeling), an attitude, an enduring practice of unsettling or challenging normativity, and a continual effort to embrace the potentiality of gender, sexuality, bodies, desires, and affects (Ahmed 2016; Butler 1990; Moussawi and Vidal-Ortiz 2020; Somerville 2014). I understand the term *queer*, in a Foucauldian sense, has its disciplinary effect, and in a postcolonial sense, its colonizing effect. I mainly use *queer* in the first sense when I talk about LGBT+ people in Western countries or in Asia as a whole. When I talk about LGBT+ people in Hong Kong, Taiwan, or mainland China, I generally use *tongzhi*. I use *gay* to refer to the study participants, as it is the identification in which most of them choose to identify. I use *queer* in the second sense when I talk about the general LGBT+ state of being (queer activism, queer feeling), although I sometimes use it interchangeably with *tongzhi* (*tongzhi* activism). The word *queer* should be distinguished from queer theory, which refers to a specific theory that originated in North American humanities universities (e.g., works by Eve Kosofsky Sedgwick, Michael Warner, Judith Butler, and Lauren Berlant) but later became an important theory for conceptualizing the lives of LGBT+ (e.g., work by Jack Halberstam, Lisa Duggan, and Heather Love), and some studies go beyond the West (e.g., David Eng, Roderick Ferguson, Jasbir Puar, and José Esteban Muñoz). Moreover, queer is also different from queer studies, a broader emerging school of thought that incorporates queer theory, feminism, postcolonialism, and other critical theories to understand the multifarious lives of LGBT+. Queer Asian studies is part of this new school of thought. And the word *sociology* signifies that this approach is sociological in nature, as it stems from earlier works on the sociology of homosexuality and efforts to combine sociology with queer theory (e.g., Stein and Plummer 1994; Valocchi 2005). In contrast with the textual analysis of literary works and films as the main method of investigation in queer theory, my work is an important intervention, using traditional sociological methods (in this case, ethnography, in-depth interviews, life stories) to provide insight into lived experiences, habitats, and practices of queer people—that is, insight that sociology can best offer.

My proposed sociology has a particular theoretical orientation. I situate myself in the "mobilities paradigm" (Sheller and Urry 2006), which calls for a "sociology beyond societies" in the age of mobilities. This paradigm emphasizes the mobility and fluidity of social processes and movements of people, capital, information, and images, which have effectively replaced geoculturally bounded societies, thereby transforming the static (or "sedentarist" to use the authors' term) view of sociology. More specifically, I engage with transnational studies (e.g., Hannerz 1996, 6; Ong 1999, 4–8; Grewal and Kaplan 1994, 1–33), which calls for "transnational" rather than globalization study, as transnational analysis addresses the asymmetric nature of the globalization process. I am indebted to transnational sexualities studies that address questions of "globalization, race, political economy, immigration, migration, and geopolitics" (Grewal and Kaplan 2001, 666) and conceptualize the complex terrain of sexual politics as "at once national, regional, local, even 'cross-cultural' and hybrid" (663). I am also indebted to transnational feminist studies (Alexander and Mohanty 1997; Grewal and Kaplan 1994). In particular, I have gained insight from Kim-Puri's (2005) transnational feminist sociology, which bridges discursive and material analyses, highlights the importance of social structures and the state, examines linkages across cultural contexts, and stresses the role of empirical research as well as from the transnational feminist queer methodologies of Browne and colleagues (2017), which engage with the multiplicities of "many many" lives and recognize local specificities and the complexities— parallels, divergences, linkages—of lives within transnational research.

Transnational queer sociology does not simply involve the transnationalism of sexualities. Rather, it seeks to analyze how general processes impinge upon national practices while *comparing* different nations at any given time. Such a sociology rejects both the top-down approach of applying Western theories to understand non-Western local experiences (global homogenization) and the separationist approach of reifying authentic traditional cultures (local essentialism). The task is to seek ways of understanding the complex processes of Western, local, and interregional knowledge systems in shaping experiences at specific sites and engaging in critical dialogue with the West and within the non-West. The approach goes beyond the usual binary queer flows between the global and local (as well as other binary imageries such as East-West, modernity-tradition, power-resistance) to examine the glocal queer flows among and within non-Western societies that constitute, inform, and shape queer identities, desires, and practices. The approach thus rejects the teleological trajectory of the linear development of Western modernity and engages with the logic of polychronic modernities (Eisenlohr, Kramer, and Lanhenohl 2019), which could be characterized as disjunctive modernities (Appadurai 1996); discrepant modernity (Rofel 1999); or compressed modernity (Chang 2010).

Transnational queer sociology embraces a power-resistance paradigm that is based on a politics of difference about identity within the matrix of domination and maps it onto a transnational time/space geography of sexuality.[16] Such sociology refutes the essentialist or unified notion of identity and understands that identities, rather than identity, are always multiply formed, with various identity components or categories of difference (e.g., class, gender, sexuality, race and ethnicity, nationality, etc.) intersecting and combining with one another.[17] A matrix of identities gives rise to a matrix of oppression. This politics of difference rejects the system of oppression as separate but points to the intersections and interconnectedness, such as the "intersectionality" (Collins 1990; Crenshaw 1991) of how interlocking systems of oppression structure the experience of individuals—in the case of this book—of young (age), gay (sexuality) men (gender) in three Chinese (race/ethnicity) locales in any given sociohistorical context (political-economy). While an intersectional model of identity may presume components as separable analytics, an assemblage is "more attuned to interwoven forces that merge and dissipate time, space, and body against linearity, coherency, and permanency" (Puar 2007, 212). To understand identity as assemblage is to acknowledge identity not as an attribute of individuals but rather as "an event or action, whereby a multitude of factors such as historical context, geographic location, and social context contribute to the experience of 'identity'" (Warner, Kurtis, and Adya 2020, 266). Whether intersectionality or assemblage, such a reformulation of subjectivity that suspends or moves away from identity does not intend to abandon identity but to acknowledge that "queer" has no fixed political referent (Eng and Puar 2020, 2).[18] Identity formation and assemblage are a part of the disciplinary and regulatory structures that frame the self, body, desires, practices, and social relations. Heteronormativity—the major form of oppression of sexuality—works with other multiple fluid and complex forms of domination (patriarchy, sexism, racism, nationalism, neoliberalism, developmentalism), which form "scattered hegemonies" (Grewal and Kaplan 1994, 7) that construct our identities, desires, and practices in a transversal space. This web of dominations actively administers, regulates, and reifies sexuality on different levels—the systemic, the community, and the personal—in our everyday lives and on a transnational scale. It is through these disciplining gazes of surveillance at all levels that we are constituted as sexual subjects (Foucault 1982). At the same time, these sites of domination are potential sites of resistance (Foucault 1980), and the scope of domination and scale of resistance are both subject to the political, social, and cultural circumstances of a particular locale as well as to the position of the subject, who possesses different intersectional categories or assemblages. Such an understanding of identity avoids essentializing a category called "Chinese gay man" by paying special attention to the personal and interpersonal levels, social structures, material and discursive practices, geographical location, and particular historical moments that constitute what it means to be a Chinese gay man. It is this "decolonial intersectionality" (Warner, Kurtis, and Adya 2020) that challenges the Western world (including the Western epistemological position) in discussing identity and subjectivity, oppression and domination, and liberation and emancipation.

Transnational queer sociology is interdisciplinary in nature. It engages sociology with queer theory and highlights the importance of both material/structural and textual/discursive analyses. Discourse and materiality should be seen as two sides of the same coin (Moussawi and Vidal-Ortiz 2020). Transnational queer sociology acknowledges not only that social structures and relations are mediated and (re)produced through cultural representations and discourses but also that discourses are embedded in particular sociostructural configurations that make such cultural discourses and analyses possible. More specifically, it stresses the role of material analysis of such social structures as the state, the market, and civil society, thereby revealing how identities, social structures, and cultural discourses are mutually constituted (cf. Kim-Puri 2005; see also Alldred and Fox 2015). It is thus grounded in material conditions and political economies as well as in discursive formations and cultural representations, centering the multifarious display of power relations in the personal, social/interpersonal, and institutional aspects of everyday life.

Finally, transnational queer sociology draws on various strategies from sociology and cultural studies for comparing different societies. Skocpol's (1979) comparative historical analysis is useful: it examines the specificities of different national/cultural contexts through a comparative lens to highlight cross-national similarities and differences, such as comparing and contrasting the different paths of the homosexual cultures in Hong Kong, Singapore, and India, all of which were British colonies in which the penal code pertaining to homosexual conduct was (or still is) enforced, thereby highlighting the role of sociomaterial conditions in shaping sexualities and subjectivities on a transnational level. Chakrabarty's (2000) and Go's (2020) "provincializing" strategy of European history and sociology, respectively, is also important, as it highlights the epistemic exclusion of non-Western studies and emphasizes that genders and sexualities in Europe and North America are as provincial, specific, and local as those in China, Japan, and India.[19] Chen (2010) proposes "Asia as method" as an imaginary anchoring point that provides multiple frames of reference among Asian societies to transform existing knowledge structures and ourselves, thereby offering alternative horizons and perspectives to advance a different understanding of world history. De Kloet, Chow, and Chong (2019) propose a trans-Asia-as-method project that aims to examine human mobilities, media cultural flows, and connections across Asia and beyond. Ong's (2011) notion of worlding Asian cities suggests comparing Asian cities using different modes to understand metropolitan transformation: "modeling," which refers to the replicability of urbanism that does not find its ultimate reference in the West; "inter-referencing," which refers to the "practices of citation, allusion, aspiration, comparison, and competition" (17) among Asian locales;

and "new solidarities," which refers to the "symbiosis between neoliberal calculations and social activism" (21). Of the three, "inter-Asia referencing" is particularly important to transnational queer sociology, as it makes "concepts and theories derived from Asian experiences translocally relevant and shared" (Iwabuchi 2014, 44) and thus leads to a nuanced comprehension of Asian experiences through a reciprocal learning process—although we should be mindful that comparison may lead to hierarchical competition (Chong, Chow, and de Kloet 2019). Transnational queer sociology constitutes a response to Chiang and Wong's (2016) call for "queering the transnational turn" to consider what critical edge "regionalism" might afford investigations of queer modernities in Asia and to Yue and Leung's (2017) "queer Asia as method," which aims to provincialize Western queer knowledge production and initiate critical conversations.

Generational Sexualities and Life Stories

This research is qualitative in nature. Although I appreciate the merits of quantitative sociology (e.g., surveys), which can sketch out a general pattern (attitudes, behavior, practices) of a population, the complexity of the life experience of individuals—the meaning, context, and constraints they face—is best captured by qualitative sociology such as life stories. A sociology of stories focuses on the social role of stories: "the ways they are produced, the ways they are read, the work they perform in the wider social order, how they change, and their role in the political process" (Plummer 1995, 19). My basic premise is that human beings make personal and social meaning by constructing stories that make experience sensible (Hammack and Cohler 2009, 2011; Plummer 2010). Individuals make meaning of social and political environments through the construction of stories. Such stories are particularly important for sexual minorities who have to negotiate with a master narrative that negates their thoughts, feelings, and actions to produce their own counternarrative or resistance narrative (Hammack and Cohler 2011). Stories, especially sexual stories (Plummer 1995), are important, as they are personal and powerful, sometimes therapeutic and empowering, and challenge and transform societal domination and oppression. Different generations have different stories to tell. Situating the study within the emergent field of generational sexualities studies (Plummer 2010), I understand young gay men as occupying a specific generational position. I view generation not only in terms of biological age, age cycle, or age cohort but also as a socially constructed and symbolically grounded position (Mannheim 1952; Plummer

2010). Age is therefore a result of a "nexus of social pathways, developmental trajectories, and social change" (Elder, Johnson, and Crosnoe 2003, 10) in a life-course approach (e.g., Elder 1975). A life-course approach to the study of young gay male identity can reveal the interplay between individual life stories and larger social and historical forces.

Western work draws on a range of terms to describe the young (and queer) generations: Millennial (1981–1996), Generation Y (mid-1980s to mid-1990s), Generation Z (late-1990s and into the new millennium), and similar terms (e.g., Howe and Strauss 2000; McCrindle 2014; Marshall et al. 2019). In the Chinese context, the term *post-'90s generation* (*jiu ling hou*) was first used to describe the second generation of Chinese people who grew up as only children in the post-Tiananmen era and the first generation born after the Tiananmen protests. The term is sometimes used interchangeably with the post-'80s generation and millennial generation to refer to the young generation in China (Li 2021; de Kloet and Fung 2017). People in Hong Kong began using the term *post-'90s generation* largely after the publication of a Chinese book called *Hong Kong Children* (Huang 2009), which describes the post-'90s children in Hong Kong who were raised by overprotective and indulgent parents (Chan and Lee 2014). In Taiwan, the "strawberry generation" refers to the post-'80s generation (e.g., Jheng 2018) while the "collapsing generation" (Lin et al. 2011) is used to refer to the young generation in a more general sense. Nevertheless, the post-'90s generation in the three sites grew up in different sociopolitical eras: mainland China entered a postreform era in 1990 following the suppression of the democratic movement in 1989, Hong Kong ratified the Basic Law in 1990 and was returned to China in 1997, and Taiwan overturned martial law in 1987 and had its first democratic presidential election in 1996. In all three sites, the post-'90s generation has enjoyed a more affluent and consumption-oriented lifestyle than prior generations and faced a highly competitive education and work environment. More specifically, the post-'90s gay generation, whose adolescence and young adulthood was in the 2000s and 2010s, live lives that are qualitatively different from those of previous gay generations, owing to changes in the laws governing homosexuality, the establishment of the pink economy, and the emergence of *tongzhi* activism since the 1990s.

Between 2017 and 2019, I conducted in-depth interviews with Han Chinese men who were born in or after 1990 and were at least eighteen (i.e., members of the post-'90s generation). All of the participants self-identified as gay (or another sexual identity label indicating same-sex desires/experiences or emotional attachment to members of the same sex) and had been born in or were currently living in Hong Kong (n = 30), Taipei (n = 30), or Shanghai (n = 30). Ninety interviews were conducted, thirty in each site. During the 2017–2019 period, I made numerous field trips to Taipei and Shanghai but could no longer travel from 2020 onward because of the COVID-19 pandemic.[20] In 2020 and 2021, I updated their stories by conducting follow-up interviews with half of the interviewees in each site, most conducted online. I have also closely followed some of the men over the years and with whom I have had informal conversations from time to time, and whose stories appear in the various chapters as ongoing, focused case studies. Hong Kong, Taipei, and Shanghai were chosen as study sites to facilitate comparison. Hong Kong is a uniquely cosmopolitan city owing to its British colonial history and special "one country, two systems" constitutional principle. Historically it has had the most well-established pink economy of the three sites. Shanghai is the largest and most populous city in China, attracts the greatest amount of foreign investment, and exemplifies a strong market economy that encompasses both state-owned corporations and small, privately owned businesses fostered by the state. It also has a lively *tongzhi* scene. Taipei, the capital of Taiwan, is also a cosmopolitan city, it is the hub of social movements and *tongzhi* activism, and it has a large and vibrant *tongzhi* life. The three cities are all urban, cosmopolitan, and populous cities with thriving *tongzhi* activities and differing degrees of activism that may exhibit the strong presence of metronormativity (Halberstam 2005). I recognize that other cities (especially in rural areas) may have different governing strategies and patterns of hetero/homonormativities, and the gay men therein may have different lived experiences. I chose the Han Chinese, the major ethnic group in all three cities, for ease of comparison. Other ethnic groups such as South Asians in Hong Kong, indigenous people in Taiwan, or Uyghurs and Tibetans in China, who may well exhibit a different sense of belonging and a different life trajectory, were excluded. The interviewees were recruited via nonprobability (purposive) sampling, such as personal and NGO referrals, publicity in social media (Facebook), and the snowball sampling technique. I do not claim that my participants are representative of the post-'90s gay generations in Hong Kong, Taiwan, and mainland China, but I tried to compile a sample that was as demographically diverse as possible in terms of class, education, occupation, relationship status, religion, health status, sexual experiences, living conditions, and social activism.[21]

I have developed standard interview guidelines over the years that use a life-course approach to capture the life stories of participants, with a particular focus on their same-sex experiences: (1) participants' realization of their same-sex desires as well as their sexual practices, romantic experiences, and intimate relationships; (2) their coming-out experiences to their families, schools, workplaces, churches, and other social institutions; (3) their participation in the gay scene or community and *tongzhi*/queer activism (if any); (4) their opinions about the three societies as a whole and their *tongzhi* communities in particular; and (5) their understanding of the meaning of life and of what it means to be young, Chinese, gay, and a man. As a self-identified Chinese gay male researcher who was born and raised in Hong Kong and educated in Hong Kong and Britain, I was able to establish rapport with the interviewees quite easily based on shared gender (male), sexuality (gay), ethnicity (Chinese), and language (I speak both Cantonese, the major language in Hong Kong, and Mandarin, the major language in mainland China and Taiwan). The interviews were conducted at my office and in hotels, NGO offices, and the interviewees' homes. I am well aware of the power differential and other issues embedded within the insider/outsider dilemma in social research (Denzin and Lincoln 1994) and of intersectionality issues in queer studies (Kong 2011, 208–11; Kong 2018; Rahman 2010). I followed other self-identified queer researchers (see Lewin and Leap 1996) in being "out" in the field and often declared my own sexual orientation at the beginning of the interviews to collapse the split between the subject/researcher and the object/researched (Kong, Plummer, and Mahoney 2002). In this sense, I am an insider. I am studying something that is as much a part of me as it is of the people I interview, and what I have learned has contributed as much to my own self-understanding as it has to a social understanding. It was also easy to establish rapport with and gain trust and acceptance from the participants because they saw themselves in me and because I have a well-known, decades-long track record of researching Chinese (homo)sexuality. I am also an outsider, not just because of the age difference (I am in my early fifties), but also because of such intersectional differences as education, class, and cultural upbringing. Ethical approval was obtained from my university's institutional review board. The nature of the study was carefully explained to all interviewees, and they were assured of confidentiality and anonymity. A small honorarium was provided to cover transportation and other expenses. All names appearing in this book are pseudonyms, and minor alterations have been made to the interviewees' biographies to protect their identities. Their written consent was sought before audio-recording the interviews. Spoken Cantonese or Mandarin was transcribed verbatim, with all quotes translated into English by me. Each interview is a story of its time and space. I treat interviews as a site of storytelling and as both text and lived experience. I offer a discursive analysis of the interviews and a sociomaterial analysis that links the participants' stories with broader sociohistorical and political changes. Guided by the grounded-theory approach (Strauss and Corbin 1997), the analysis of these stories included identifying themes, building codebooks, and marking texts (Ryan and Bernard 2000). Themes were initially based on the interview guidelines and findings, and the analyses were then compared with the local and international literature. Due to space limitations, each data chapter generally presents two focused cases for each locale. The two cases chosen are generally contrasting and entail theoretical diversity of the samples. They are also selected in consideration of the comparisons across the three locales (i.e., Hong Kong, Taiwan, and mainland China). The three locales appear in different order in each chapter, subject to the respective chronological or theoretical dynamics of the argument. The main aim is to reveal the intercategorical differences among young gay men in the three locales rather than the intracategorical differences within each locale. This book thus brings my encounters with these young men to life by telling their stories about coming out, about their families, about connecting with people, about love and sex, and about their love and hate relationships with their societies.[22]

Outline of the Book

The overarching aim of *Sexuality and the Rise of China* is to examine Hong Kong, Taiwan, and mainland China—their past, present, and future—with a particular focus on age, sexualities, families, love, and community under the new socioeconomic and political world order. Chapter 1 examines the historical formation of contemporary *tongzhi* identities and cultures in Hong Kong and Taiwan (1980s to 1990s) and mainland China (late 1990s–early 2000s) and tracks the effects of recent socioeconomic and political transformations. The chapter offers a social-material analysis that conceptualizes the state, the market economy, and civil society (family, religion, NGOs, popular culture) as sites of both governance and resistance wherein different *tongzhi* generations are being made and are self-making as sexual subjects. It also demonstrates that the birth of contemporary *tongzhi* identities is the result of both the differential impacts of the West and mutually referencing effects among the three locales. This background chapter provides context to inform the subsequent chapters, which focus on members of the post-'90s generation.

Four major aspects of the lives of these young gay men are investigated in this book. In chapter 2, I examine how the participants came out to their families, if they indeed have come out. There is a double closet in the Chinese context, characterized by the tension between heterosexuality and homosexuality and the tension between performing and not performing a traditional familial role (a filial son/daughter who gets married and has children). They have devised a range of coming-out strategies in response to both their parents' and their own expectations of what it means to be a son within this double closet. Instead of viewing coming out as identity politics, I argue that it is better viewed as relational politics. Through their stories of coming out, we see the changes in family, parenting culture, and the parent-child relationship as well as the shifting meaning of masculinity and filial piety in the three Chinese societies.

In chapter 3, I examine how these young men connect with one another. I show that the participants exhibit three rather different trajectories of *tongzhi* community engagement under the societies' particular forms of neoliberal development and state governance: cross-national economic/consumption engagement in Hong Kong, fragmented/mainly online engagement in mainland China, and diffuse engagement in Taiwan. No matter whether they engage with large-scale collectivities or small-scale personal communities or commons, what is important are the affective/emotional and imaginative/translocal components of engagement as well as the encountering of what I call "homonormative masculinity"—a combination of hegemonic masculinity (Connell 1995) and homonormativity (Duggan 2002)—under neoliberalism, cosmopolitanism, and nascent consumerism.

In chapter 4, I examine the young men's love and sex lives. I argue that they view monogamy as a major component of a good adult life, which is an example of Berlant's (2011) notion of "cruel optimism": "Something you desire is actually an obstacle to your flourishing" (1). Accordingly, they have developed various strategies for negotiating with the monogamy ideal—for example, venturing out, either together or separately, openly or in secret, and with explicit or implicit rules, to form different kinds of relationships. However, this particular type of love story is complicated by the specific socioeconomic and political circumstances of each society: family co-residence, political unrest, and the ethics of the self under the COVID-19 pandemic in Hong Kong; marriage pressure, a fragmented gay world, and the precarity of labor in mainland China; and a democratic environment, well-established gay world, and optimism after the Sunflower Movement in Taiwan.[23]

In chapter 5, I examine the participants' cultural/national identities and their engagement with civic-political activism. I show that the three governments exert both enabling and restricting effects on (homo)sexuality, revealing three versions of "homonationalism" (Puar 2007): incorporative homonationalism in Taiwan, deficient homonationalism in Hong Kong, and pragmatic homonationalism in mainland China. The three distinctive cultural/national identities (Taiwanese, Hongkonger, and Chinese national) give rise to three different identifications with (homo)nationalism, resulting in three different forms of civic-political activism that align with or contradict the state's position on homosexuality.

Sexuality and the Rise of China offers a nuanced analysis of Chinese queer identities, practices, and cultures in which we can simultaneously see the generalized Western queer culture, rhetoric, and processes that have impinged upon Hong Kong, Taiwan, and mainland China as well as the differential negotiations of subject formation owing to their particular social, historical, political, economic, and cultural circumstances. What we gain is an understanding of the mutually referenced, commonly shared, and translocally influenced queer experiences among different locales that are often neglected in studies of the globalization of sexuality. Moreover, the subject-formation of identity is intimately connected with the personal, interpersonal, and institutional levels that link social structures and practices such as the family (chapter 2); the gay community and pink economy (chapter 3); intimate relationships, marriage, and monogamy (chapter 4); and the state (chapter 5), allowing an emphasis on the mutually constitutive relationship between sexuality and intersubjectivity, institutional structures, social practices, and discourses. Through the narratives of the post-'90s gay generation in Hong Kong, Taiwan, and mainland China, *Sexuality and the Rise of China* is part of the emerging decolonizing sexualities program (e.g., Bakshi, Jivraj, and Posocco 2016), an ongoing effort to provincialize Western knowledge of sexualities.

Queering Hong Kong, Taiwan, and Mainland China

This chapter examines the historical formations of contemporary LGBT+ (or *tongzhi*) identities, cultures, and communities in Hong Kong, Taiwan, and mainland China and traces their recent development. Although these three Chinese societies share common social and cultural norms rooted in Confucian values and heteropatriarchal family ideals, they have experienced distinct political and economic trajectories since 1949 that have created very different possibilities and paths of development in terms of gender and sexuality. Scholars have reviewed the development of Chinese *tongzhi* identities but usually focusing on one or two but not all three societies and more on the cultural and literary aspects of *tongzhi* life. Notable examples are Bao (2018, 2020) on mainland China, Liu (2015) on mainland China and Taiwan, and Martin (2003) and Huang (2011) on Taiwan. Chou's (2000) work, which offers a three-way discussion of same-sex identities in mainland China, Hong Kong, and Taiwan is important, but his analysis focuses on the cultural specificity of same-sex eroticism and tends to essentialize Chinese cultures, especially when it comes to *tongzhi* activism. Building on my previous transnational sociomaterialistic analysis of the United Kingdom, mainland China, and Hong Kong (Kong 2011), the current transnational three-way comparative study of the *tongzhi* histories and contemporary contexts of Hong Kong, Taiwan, and mainland China serves two purposes: it acknowledges that the three Chinese locales are deeply marked by different political histories, local cultures, civic traditions, and social structures, but it also treats them as intimately connected and explicitly articulates their mutually influencing paths along with their exposure to and adaptation of wider global and intra-Asian influences to differing degrees (thus "transnational" rather than "translocal"). It offers a sociohistorical and material analysis in which social institutions and sexuality are mutually constituted.

More specifically, I articulate the state, the market, and civil society (such as family, religion, popular culture, NGOs) as sites of governance and resistance that have formed different assemblages at different times, with various generations undergoing a dual process of subjectification in which they are both being made and self-making as subjects (Foucault 1980, 1982): from pathological or social-deviant subject to cosmopolitan, liberal, or consumerist *tongzhi* subject, and from earlier generations characterized as criminal, sick, shameful, and closeted to later generations that can be characterized as coming out, proud, liberal, cosmopolitan, digital, and virtually normal. Claims from LGBT+ citizens for sexual citizenship, as manifested in the fight for three domains of rights—conduct-based, identity-based, and relationship-based (Richardson 2000, 2017)—have undergone different developments in the three societies. This chapter challenges the teleological approach to understanding the development of sexual identity and citizenship. Rather than ranking the three societies on a scale ranging from more closed to more open and equating openness with progressiveness, it instead emphasizes their similarities and divergences. It acknowledges the shared histories that create significant commonalities across the three sites while underscoring the striking differences in their *tongzhi* citizens' ability to claim diverse rights and protections under the umbrella of a multifaceted form of sexual citizenship. The chapter serves as background to inform the discussions in subsequent chapters.

The Birth of the Homosexual in Modern China and the 1949 Division

Ancient China had a rich literature of relative tolerance for same-sex love between both men (Hinsch 1990; Ruan and Tsai 1987; Samshasha 1997; van Gulik 1961, 62–63) and women (Ruan and Bullough 1992, 218–21; Sang 2003). Male homosexuality was not seen as a threat to traditional masculinity (Louie 2002). Same-sex sexual conduct was never criminalized in ancient China, although codes against male rape and sodomy were introduced in the Qing dynasty, emphasizing status differences for accepting or outlawing same-sex sexual relations (Sommer 1997).[1] Homoerotic practices enjoyed a long history, ending only with modernity (Hinsch 1990). Republican-era China (1912–1949) was a period of intense nationalism and state-building under the threat of both internal political warfare and Western imperial power. Inspired by social Darwinism and a belief that scientism and democracy could save the nation, many Chinese intellectuals in the early twentieth century were eager to import Western ideas and criticize traditional Chinese thought such as Confucianism. Sexuality was a heated subject for Chinese intellectuals and the general public alike (e.g., Dikötter 1995; Kang 2009). Major Western sexological texts (such as those of Richard von Krafft-Ebing, Edward Carpenter, Sigmund Freud, Havelock Ellis, and Magnus Hirschfeld), often mediated through Japanese translations, were also translated into Chinese during the period. The terms *sex* and *homosexuality* were translated from Western sexology through the Japanese translations *sei* and *doseiai* into *xing* and *tongxing'ai* (*tongxing lian'ai* or *tongxing lian*), respectively (Sang 1999, 278). It was believed that medical science could help to bring about the nation's revival by disciplining individual sexual desire, eliminating evil habits, and regulating sexual behavior (Dikötter 1995). It is in this context that homosexuality was scrutinized, notably in the discussions of the 1930s, with intellectuals debating whether homosexuality was right or wrong, whether it was a personal or social problem, and whether it could be cured (Chiang 2010; Kang 2009).[2] Female same-sex love was seen as abnormal and a threat to patriarchal power on the one hand and as an example of intense affectionate attachments between women on the other (Sang 2003; Hershatter 2007, 40–41). However, it was English sexologist Havelock Ellis's medical theory of homosexuality, especially his book *Psychology of Sex* (1933), which viewed homosexuality as sexual inversion and dichotomized sexual normality and deviation, that gained recognition among Chinese intellectuals through repeated citation and translation, notably after Pan Guangdan's Chinese translation of the book in 1946.[3] Although Ellis viewed homosexuality not as a crime or disease but as an inversion (an inborn gender anomaly), his biomedical model of deviance/normality became the orthodox understanding of male homosexuality in modern China (Kang 2009; Sang 1999, 2003).[4]

The conception of homosexuality was then shaped by the postwar development of Hong Kong, Taiwan, and mainland China with the historical division in 1949 that split China into the People's Republic of China (PRC) and the Republic of China (ROC). Following the division, all three entered the Cold War milieu, whether under British colonial rule (Hong Kong), martial law (Taiwan), or Maoist socialism (China), which defined acceptable gender and sexual expression through heteronormative reproductive roles and marginalized, or even criminalized, practices seen as challenging sexual normativity. Although *tongxinglian* subcultures have always been present, and even seemed to flourish in the post–Second World War period, it was only in the late 1980s (Hong Kong and Taiwan) and late 1990s (mainland China) that the three societies witnessed the blossoming of visible, explicitly LGBT+ cultural production, commercial venues, and political activism, together with a more distinctive gay, lesbian, or *tongzhi* identity, among other self-identified labels.[5] *Tongzhi* identities and communities slowly emerged, along with vigorous social, legal, economic, and cultural developments.

Hong Kong: From British Colonialism to the Hong Kong Special Administrative Region and from the Criminal to Cosmopolitan and Consumerist *Tongzhi* Subject

Hong Kong was a British colony from 1842 to 1997. After the historical 1949 division splitting China, an influx of immigrants and refugees, primarily from southeast China, doubled the Hong Kong population. Development in the 1950s and 1960s was characterized by rapid industrialization and urbanization under a colonial government that externally aligned Hong Kong with the capitalist West, internally limited political expression, and emphasized the rule of law, economic entrepreneurship, and cultural expression. In the early 1970s, the colonial government rebranded Hong Kong in contrast to Communist China as a modern, cosmopolitan, Westernized city with an ethos of economic rationality and nurtured an apolitical economic citizenry (Ma 2012), transforming it into an international financial center with the emergence of the middle class.

The history of the governmental response to same-sex sexuality begins with British colonial rule in 1842 when buggery was made a crime, following English law. The colonial government refused to follow suit when the United Kingdom's Sexual Offences Act of 1967 decriminalized male homosexual conduct in private for three reasons: (1) homosexuality was not perceived as a social problem by the population, and thus the government considered such legal reform too radical; (2) Chinese homosexuals were very discreet, as seen from the low number of reported arrests; and (3) the few visible homosexuals were mainly Europeans, who were usually sent home upon discovery with their contracts unrenewed or encouraged to resign (Lethbridge 1976). By contrast, there have never been laws governing female homosexual conduct in Hong Kong. This legal landscape existed in tandem with a dominant social understanding of homosexuality that, in accordance with the Western medical model of sexual deviance, viewed it as a form of mental illness or social deviance. Many Hong Kong people believed in Chinese folk religion or secular Buddhism and Taoism. These religions are ambivalent toward homosexuality (Ruan 1991). Christians, who only accounted for 10 percent of the population in 1962 (Hong Kong Government 1963), played an important role in Hong Kong's moral and sexual culture owing to early missionary endeavors that made Christian institutions the principal providers of educational, medical, and social welfare services; they defined homosexuality as a sin, an unhealthy lifestyle, and unnatural behavior (Wong 2013). Although the proportion of Christians today is higher at about 16 percent of the total population, their influence remains embedded in varying degrees in these sectors.[6] Meanwhile, the family was the main social institution governing gay male and lesbian lives in postwar Hong Kong because the colonial government constructed colonial subjects with minimal civil, political, and social rights (Ku and Pun 2004; So 2002) and treated social welfare as a residual concept based on charity and benevolence. Owing to high land prices, most families lived in densely populated public housing estates and relied on their personal family and neighbor networks or voluntary agencies for protection, social security, marriage arrangement, and career advancement. The Hong Kong family was thus a close-knit network that put particular pressure on men (and women) with same-sex desires (Kong 2012a, 2014, 2019a, 2021). The first *tongzhi* generation (born between 1920 and 1950) complied with parental wishes to marry, continue the family bloodline, and do nothing to harm the family's status and reputation.[7] The idea of a same-sex relationship outside the marriage institution was unimaginable, so these men commonly sought sexual release in public spaces. This early generation has been characterized as criminal, sick, and shameful with a gay identity that had yet to develop (Kong 2012a, 2014, 2019a, 2021).

The historical formation of contemporary gay and lesbian identities, cultures, and communities slowly emerged during the 1980s and 1990s in conjunction with the birth of the second (born in the 1950s and 1960s) and third (born in the 1970s and 1980s) *tongzhi* generations. Such a formation is the result of the interplay between the state, the market economy, and civil society (particularly the rise of a postwar queer elite intelligentsia), within which three factors are significant: legal reform, the emergence of the "pink economy," and *tongzhi* cultural development. Public debate about homosexuality surfaced in 1980 when a Scottish gay police inspector named

John MacLennan, who had been charged with gross indecency, was found dead in his police quarters. In response to suspicions of a police cover-up and widespread media attention, the colonial government reviewed the laws governing male homosexual conduct and subsequently made moves to decriminalize it in 1983 (Collett 2018). Those moves, together with the first HIV case reported in 1984, sparked heated public debate over homosexuality. Religion (Christianity in particular) and Chinese traditions (in the name of the Chinese family) were the two major weapons wielded by those in favor of the continued criminalization of homosexual sexual acts, while those who supported decriminalization couched their arguments in the rhetoric of democracy and human rights (Ho 1997).[8] After nearly a decade of intense public debate, the government finally decriminalized male homosexual conduct in 1991 but made it clear that such a move did not constitute a recognition of gay rights or a gay lifestyle but simply an endorsement of an individual's right to choice (Ho 1997; see also Chan 2007, 2008). The government primarily viewed homosexuality as a public health issue, with male homosexuals seen as a high-risk group for HIV/ AIDS transmission.

Apart from this legal reform, a pink economy slowly emerged in the context of a larger burgeoning entertainment scene and has been crucial to the development of *tongzhi* subculture. British colonialism had suppressed political participation and mobilization but encouraged economic growth and development. This resulted in general affluence and the concomitant popularity of a consumption-oriented culture, hallmarked by the emergence of Lan Kwai Fong, a central district where expatriates and overseas Chinese have been drinking, clubbing, and dining since the early 1980s (Cheng 2001). A hidden pink economy featuring straight bars/clubs with a substantial gay clientele emerged. This Westernized consumption culture facilitated a distinctive colonial byproduct—that is, intimate interracial relationships between older, financially secure Western expatriates, some of whom used money and status to attract younger local Chinese men for love and sex. These Chinese men, for their part, looked up to Westerners as signifiers of social status, privilege, upward mobility, and modernity (Ho and Tsang 2000; Kong 2002). Although these developments nurtured local gay identities and cultures, they also rendered those identities prone to capitalism, cosmopolitanism, and Westernization.

A third factor relevant to shaping sexual identity and culture involves the increased cultural activism around homosexuality—articulated in popular culture (magazines, newsletters, novels, plays, and artworks). The second *tongzhi* generation—postwar baby boomers, especially the middle class with a Western education from abroad—formed a transnational network of queer intelligentsia that facilitated the emergence of visibly queer elite subcultures in the media and popular culture. Notable examples are US-educated Samshasha, who wrote a gay column in the middle-class lifestyle magazine *City Magazine* and published a newsletter called *Pink Triangle Magazine*, and the Hong Kong Lesbian and Gay Film Festival (HKLGFF), an Asian first, which debuted in 1989 (Kong 2011, 64–67).

These three factors (legal, economic, and cultural) have contributed to the formation and flourishing of Hong Kong gay/*tongzhi* identities, cultures, and communities since the 1990s, with four distinct developments transforming homosexuals from deviant/mental patients/social outcasts into cosmopolitan consumerist subjects. The first was the creation of the homosexual as a distinct social group encompassing gay (e.g., *gei* [Cant.] and *memba*) and lesbian (lesi, TB, and TBG) and other nonnormative identities (Ho and Tsang 2004; Kong 2011; Tang 2011).[9] When the first HKLGFF was dubbed the Hong Kong Tongzhi Film Festival, *tongzhi* became an umbrella term for people with nonnormative genders and sexualities or a synonym for LGBT+. The terms *tong* (meaning "same") and *zhi* (meaning "ideal" or "inspiration") exist separately in classical Chinese literature but were used in combination in 1911 to refer to *comrade* (meaning "common will"), a term signifying a revolutionary and political subjectivity, widely used in Republican and Maoist China. The term gained widespread popularity in LGBT+ and straight circles, first in Hong Kong, then in Taiwan, and finally in mainland China in the early 1990s.[10] *Tongzhi* thus carries the dual connotation of being a political subject and sexual subject. *Tongzhi* was the first Chinese translation of the term *queer*, which was later translated as *ku'er* ("cool child"), but *ku'er* is popular only in academia and has never been taken up by the LGBT+ or straight population in Hong Kong.[11]

The second development was the mushrooming of *tongzhi* social groups focused on self-help and community-service provision with the aim of nurturing a positive self-identity, downplaying the sexual aspects of *tongzhi* identity, and stressing the similarities between heterosexuals and homosexuals.[12] These groups came together in the late 1990s (1996–1998) to organize the Chinese Tongzhi Conference, the first transnational event of its kind, which drew roughly two hundred Chinese *tongzhi* from across the region (Taiwan, mainland China, Malaysia, and Singapore) to discuss *tongzhi*-related issues, including arts and culture, social services, HIV/AIDS, the family, and activism.

The third development was the burgeoning of a pink consumer culture through bars, clubs, saunas, and massage parlors, which shifted the public image of homosexuals as social outcasts or sexual perverts to consumer citizens who exhibit salient features of cosmopolitanism, conspicuous consumption, and Westernization (Kong 2011, 73–93). This consumer culture has grown in conjunction with the fourth development—namely, the growing visibility of *tongzhi* in popular culture, including films, theater plays, novels, and many other cultural and art works.[13] Over the past three decades, these cultural productions have successfully reframed the stereotypical image of gay men and lesbians associated with rigid gender roles, HIV/AIDS, and crime and pathology by providing a more realistic representation of *tongzhi* life in relation to individuals' inner worlds, family life, intimate relationships, and efforts to combat social stigma (Kong 2005; Kong 2011, 59–67; Kong, Lau, and Li 2015; Leung 2008; Tang 2011).

Since Hong Kong's return to China in 1997, have *tongzhi* cultures and communities flourished or diminished? What are the main features of the *tongzhi* landscape today? Hong Kong has witnessed varied *tongzhi* identities, cultures, and communities, including (1) three major annual public *tongzhi* events with widespread media attention, the International Day against Homophobia (IDAHO) beginning in 2005, the Hong Kong Pride Parade beginning in 2008, and the Pink Dot Hong Kong beginning in 2014;[14] (2) the mushrooming of *tongzhi* groups and organizations,[15] some politically inclined and others more lifestyle- and leisure-oriented (e.g., BDSM, bear, chemsex, sports, music, comics, and animation);[16] (3) the expansion of Hong Kong's pink economy;[17] (4) the continued growth of the aforementioned *tongzhi*-identified venues (and the rise of same-sex male prostitution, particularly following the influx of young men from mainland China providing commercial sex services for men, who are known as "money boys");[18] (5) the increasing visibility of queer/*tongzhi* representation in media and culture, notably the annual HKLGFF;[19] (6) the burgeoning of university gender and sexuality courses; and (7) an online virtual world, chatrooms, various social media, and smartphone dating apps. The end result is a self-confident generation of *tongzhi* who fight for their rights and have made themselves into new cosmopolitan queer subjects, in turn reshaping sexual and gender norms.

This development of *tongzhi* identities, cultures, communities, and movements should again be understood within a sociomaterialist framework. The state, the market, and civil society are the three major sites of governance and resistance that form different assemblages to shape the contours of such development—in particular, the government's approach to homosexual rights,

FIG. 1.1. Pinkdot Hong Kong 2018 (source: BigLove Alliance).

the strategy of *tongzhi* activism, and the new logic governing the *tongzhi*, especially gay community. First, the Hong Kong Special Administrative Region (HKSAR) government, together with its subtle and strategic alliance with family and religion, is the main assemblage confining the (legal) development of *tongzhi* identities, rights, and movements. A new generation of evangelical Christian groups established after 1997 have taken up the mission of protecting the privileged position of the heterosexual nuclear family to restore social order and public morality.[20] The HKSAR government, with its close relationship with evangelical Christianity (three-quarters of the top administrative positions are held by Christians), has exhibited gradual accommodation and delaying (rather than repressive) tactics toward *tongzhi* rights (Wong 2013; see also Huang 2017). The government is also indifferent about capitalizing on either the pink dollar for economic gain or the gay index for building a creative city. In 2004, the government abandoned an equal opportunity bill outlawing discrimination on the grounds of sexual orientation (the Sexual Orientation Discrimination Ordinance, or SODO) after the Hong Kong Alliance for Family posted a four-page advertisement in a local newspaper with ten thousand signatures opposing the proposed legislation, a move that triggered the launch of the first IDAHO Hong Kong Parade in 2005. In the same year, in *Leung T. C. William Roy v. Secretary for Justice* ([2005] 3 HKLRD 657 [CFI], [2006] 4 HKLRD 211 [CA]), the high

FIG. 1.2. Cover of the Hong Kong Lesbian and Gay Film Festival 2020 program (source: Hong Kong Lesbian and Gay Film Festival; cover credit: Vivian Ho).

court ruled that it was unconstitutional to impose different ages of consent on homosexuals (twenty-one) and heterosexuals (sixteen), although then chief executive Donald Tsang, himself a Catholic, publicly opposed that decision. In 2007, the government set up the Family Council to promote "family core values as a main driver for social harmony" (Family Council 2021), using the heterosexual nuclear family as a policy prototype. In 2009, the government enacted an antidomestic violence law, but, under pressure from evangelical and pro-family protesters, changed its name from the Domestic Violence Ordinance to the Domestic and Cohabitation Relationship Violence Ordinance to distinguish marriage from same-sex and other cohabiting couple relationships. In subsequent years, there were a few legal victories that recognized postoperative gender rather than biological sex at birth as the basis for marriage (*W v. Registrar of Marriages* 2013) and allowed spousal benefits and tax assessment of same-sex civil partners or same-sex couples married overseas (*QT v. Director of Immigration* 2018 and *Leung Chun Kwong v. the Secretary for the Civil Service and Commissioner of Inland Revenue* 2019).[21] However, these landmark judgments have been interpreted as challenging both institutionalized Christian marriage and its civil equivalent, although the government has reiterated that the cases should not be seen as challenges to the Marriage Ordnance but only as affecting immigration policy. Hong Kong is no closer to same-sex marriage legislation. When Hong Kong was announced as the first Asian host city for the 2022 (now postponed to 2023) eleventh Gay Games, a nine-day-long international diversity festival with sports, arts, and cultural events organized by the LGBT+ community, the government and then chief executive Carrie Lam offered a lukewarm response. Despite Hong Kong's status as an international city, the government prefers to render *tongzhi* perspectives invisible in terms of social policy (Kong, Lau, and Li 2015).

Second, *tongzhi* activism is a site of resistance, tied to wider social movements fighting for social justice, equality, and democracy before those movements were recently forced into stalemate. Local pop stars Anthony Wong and Denise Ho (a.k.a. HOCC), and legislator Raymond Chan Chi-chuen came out publicly in 2012. They and others established the *tongzhi* group BigLove Alliance. These public figures were actively involved in the 2014 Umbrella Movement and the antiextradition bill protests (2019–2020), thereby forging closer connections between the *tongzhi* movement and larger democratic movements. The antiextradition bill protests triggered a landmark victory for the pro-democracy camp in the 2019 district council elections, with electoral victories by three openly lesbian and gay pro-democracy candidates (Wei Siu-lik, Jimmy Sham, who is also the convener of the Civil Human Rights Front, and Cheung Kam-hung) symbolizing the gradual acceptance of lesbian/gay politicians by the general public. However, since the introduction of the National Security Law in 2020, many prodemocracy legislators have been arrested, including Jimmy Sham, and many district council members have been disqualified by the government or resigned, either because of worry that the government might disqualify them or because they do not want to follow the new oath-taking legislation requiring them to pledge allegiance to the government and uphold the Basic Law, which now includes the new security law.[22]

Third, the *tongzhi* (or, more specifically, gay) community is heavily subjected to the logic of neoliberalism and the market (pink) economy, owing to their economic rather than political participation. Accordingly, conspicuous consumption has been a key means for social inclusion and cultural citizenship for Hong Kong *tongzhi* in the past (Kong 2011, 73–93). The result is a hybrid form of hetero/homonormativity that can be seen as "new homonormativity"—that is, "a politics that does not contest dominant heteronormative assumptions and institutions but upholds and sustains them while promising the possibility of a demobilized gay constituency and a privatized, depoliticized gay culture anchored in domesticity and consumption" (Duggan 2002, 179). Heteronormativity functions to create a hierarchy of good and bad sexual citizens by privileging heterosexuals and stigmatizing homosexuals, with the new homonormativity differentiating good, normal, healthy, and decent *tongzhi*, who are inevitably middle class, educated, cosmopolitan, and supportive of dominant heteronormative values, from their bad, radical, dangerous, and shameful counterparts. A derivative that I call *homonormative masculinity* will be discussed in detail in chapter 3.

The younger (post-'90s) *tongzhi* generation was born into this new dynamic. In contrast to previous *tongzhi* generations, they acquired a clear sexual identity through social interactions at school, with the mass media and social media, and/or the Internet. Having benefited from well-established gay communities, they have been quick to transform their same-sex desires into such socially recognized identities as homosexual, gay, *tongzhi*, and *memba*. They espouse a strong gay identity, considering it as normal as a straight identity and view themselves as normal citizens. Unlike some of their counterparts in the United States (e.g., Savin-William 2005), they treat sexuality as a master identity for organizing their lives.

Taiwan: From Authoritarian to Democratic Taiwan and from Crystal Boys to Democratic Liberal *Tongzhi* Subjects

Taiwan has a different and complicated colonial history. The indigenous inhabitants of Taiwan were first colonialized by Europeans in 1624, first by the Dutch who took the South and then, in 1626, by the Spanish who took the North before being ousted by the Dutch in 1642. It was then colonized by the Chinese when Cheng Chenggong took the South in 1661. After defeating the Dutch in 1662, Cheng formed the Cheng kingdom in the same year but was defeated by Qing forces in 1683. The Qing empire then ruled Taiwan for the next two hundred years, until 1895, when it was ceded to Japan at the end of the Sino-Japanese War. In 1945, following Japan's defeat in the Second World War, Chiang Kai-shek, together with his Kuomintang (KMT) army and allies, took over Taiwan and launched his own project of

Han Chinese nationalism. During the Cold War, KMT military modernization was closely linked with cultural Americanization owing to Taiwan's reliance on US military and economic aid. Taiwanese modernity was thus heavily influenced by "Japanese colonialism, Chinese Republican culture, the US military presence and economic aid, and KMT Cold War political and cultural practice" (Martin 2003, 11).

This complex colonial history is reflected in the treatment of homosexuality. Neither the Japanese colonizers (1895–1945) nor the KMT military administration (1945–1987) made any reference to homosexuality or sodomy in their legal codes. In the mid-1950s, the KMT government launched the "mental hygiene movement" to "deploy the language of mental hygiene to tackle new 'social problems' in a rapidly industrialising society" (Huang 2011, 35) and promote "normal and moral" behaviors. The movement was tolerant of homosexuality and did not categorize it as a type of perversion or abnormal sexuality but rather as *pi* (obsession), a self-indulgent sexual addiction resulting from excessive masturbation that could be cured by endocrine therapy (Huang 2011). However, Taiwan's intellectual culture absorbed many aspects of Chinese Republican modernity, including such European scientific discourses as sexology and Freudian psychoanalytic theory (Martin 2003). The Western (primarily the US) medical and scientific model of mental hygiene was long the dominant model for understanding male homosexuality and was reinforced by the onset of HIV in the mid-1980s (Damm 2017; Huang 2011).[23] Gay men had frequented public spaces like parks, railway stations, and cinemas since the 1950s. The most famous was Taipei New Park (later called 228 Peace Memorial Park). Bar culture slowly developed in conjunction with US army bases since the 1970s (Chao 2001), although its development was checked under martial law (1949–1987), the primary aim of which was to suppress communist activities. The police repeatedly raided public spaces and venues frequented by gay men, charging those arrested with offenses against *shangliang fengsu* ("virtuous customs") under the Police Offense Law, later replaced by the Social Order Maintenance Law in 1991 (Huang 2011).

Christianity was relatively silent on homosexuality before the 2000s (Huang 2017). During the martial-law era under KMT rule, most Christian churches maintained a pro-state attitude (partly because Chiang Kei-shek and his wife were Christians), alienating themselves from politics but supporting the state's anti-communist moral crusade. The major site of governance was thus the Chinese family in which filial piety was the organizing principle, manifested by producing an heir to continue the paternal line.

Like their counterparts in Hong Kong, most of the first *tongzhi* generation (born between 1920 and 1950) in Taiwan married, suppressed their same-sex desires, and gained release only through public sex. They lived in traditional heteropatriarchal Chinese family settings that viewed homosexuality as a disease or sexual perversion, a form of abnormal and immoral behavior, and an unhealthy lifestyle that would bring shame on the family (Brainer 2019; Taiwan Tongzhi Hotlines 2010).

The emergence of contemporary *tongzhi* identities and cultures in Taiwan during the 1980s and 1990s was intimately connected to the rapid industrialization and urbanization process launched in the 1970s under the authoritarian political regime and was largely advanced by the postwar baby generation. It was driven, first, by feminism and broader social movements addressing the issues surrounding gender, sexuality, and labor and, second, by the literary production of homosexuality in academic texts and literary-media practices in popular culture.

The *tongzhi* movement can be seen as part of a broad sociodemocratic movement. Many radical cultural theorists of gender and sexuality in Taiwan have their roots in Marxism and have reclaimed Marxism as a critique of "the unifying link of forces between the imperial centers . . . and the semi-, ex-, or still-existing colonies" (Chen 1998, 28; see also Liu 2015). This new Marxism on Taiwanese soil has emerged not just in the narrow sense of class politics but also as a contemporary pan-leftist social movement comprising "gay and lesbian, bi- and trans-sexual, feminist, labor, farmer, environmental, aboriginal, anti-racist, and anti-war groups" who "collectively confront the global structures of heterosexism, sexism, capitalism, racism, ethicism, and statism, and super-statism" (Chen 1998, 28).

In postwar Taiwan, Lu Hsiu-lien wrote important treatises on the "new women" who inaugurated the "new feminist movement" in the 1970s. In 1982, Li Yuanzhen established the Awakening Foundation and a journal of the same name to raise women's consciousness, inspiring a number of women's organizations (Liu 2015). From the 1980s onward, the women's movement gradually morphed into state feminism, with Taiwan's leading feminists regarding women's entry into politics as the only path toward greater gender equality. Lu Hsiu-lien, for example, was elected vice president of the ROC, serving from 2000 to 2008. The rise of gender-based state feminism, however, reflects a highly political bifurcation between that feminism and sex-positive feminism, the latter of which has a history of alliance with labor movements, particularly those of ex-licensed prostitutes and migrant workers (Ho, Ning, and Ding 2005; Huang 2011; Liu 2015). Taiwan's *tongzhi* movement emerged with a strong association with labor movements and sex-positive feminism although Lin (2015) argues that later *tongzhi* activism (since the 2000s) has tended to be more in tune with state feminism.[24]

A visible and even vibrant *tongzhi* movement, centered on university students and academics, emerged in the 1990s and early 2000s. In 1990, lesbians formed Taiwan's first *tongzhi* group, Between Us. In 1992, when the Taipei Golden Horse International Film Festival translated "New Queer Cinema" as *xin tongzhi dianying*, the term *tongzhi*, which was borrowed from Hong Kong, started to gain popularity in Taiwan (Lim 2008). Queer was also translated as *guaitai* ("freak") and then *ku'er* ("cool child"), the latter term popularized among Taiwanese academics and the intelligentsia (Chao 2000). In 1993, Gay Chat became the first officially registered and recognized gay student organization; in 1995, the first gay demonstration was staged to protest the publication of Dr. Tu Xingzhe's *Homosexual Epidemiology*, state-commissioned AIDS research laden with scientific bias and homophobia, and in the same year *tongzhi* groups lobbied the legislature over the AIDS Act of 1990, which criminalized the transmission of AIDS through sex. In 1995, the Tongzhi Space Action Network was organized to contest the Taipei city government's attempt to "de-gay" Taipei New Park. In 1998, four organizations (the Gay Counselors Association, Queer & Class, the LGBT Civil Rights Alliance, and the Gay Teachers' Alliance) came together to establish Tongzhi Hotlines after a series of *tongzhi* teen suicides, and the Gender Sexuality Rights Association Taiwan was established after several members of the Awakening Foundation were fired, thereby splitting with state feminism (Ho, Ning, and Ding 2005; Huang 2011). In the same year, the police raided a gay gym called the AG Club. And in 2003, the Gin Gin Bookshop (opened in 1999) was prosecuted. The 1998 and 2003 prosecutions exemplified the stigmatization of gay sexuality and the discriminatory practices of law enforcement with respect to public obscenity and the distribution of obscene materials, prompting *tongzhi* groups to publicly protest (Ke 2016a, 2016b; Kuan 2019a).

The second major factor in the rise of Taiwan's modern *tongzhi* identity and culture was literary production in popular culture. Literature became the dominant medium for producing, circulating, and reproducing knowledge of homosexuality and functioned as a relatively liberal haven for political and sexual dissidents under the police state in the 1960s (Chi 2017). Pai Hsien-yung's (also known as Bai Xianyong) *Niezi* (Crystal boys, 1983) is seen as an iconic literary text for its representation of homosexuality in Taiwan (Martin 2003; see also Chen 2011). The novel depicts the underground world in 1970s Taipei of the first and second *tongzhi* generations, many of whom lived like orphans in Taipei New Park, with secrecy, shame, and guilt. Another notable example is the establishment of the radical leftist journal *Isle Margin* (1991–1996), which published a regular special feature on lesbian sexuality and a special issue on queer theory in 1994.[25]

Taiwan's process of identity-building in the 1990s exposed cultural elites to a complex entanglement of the appropriation and translation of Western (primarily American) gender and sexual knowledges and cultures and the Taiwanese public to Western queer theoretical discourse (Chao 2000; Chiang and Wang 2017; Martin 2003). The 1990–1997 period witnessed an explosion of *tongzhi*-themed publications, including novels, documentaries, biographies, and movies, which helped the Taiwanese public begin to understand the real-life situation of *tongzhi* through popular culture and the literary mediascape.[26] The vibrant civil rights movement, as well as cultural activism, nurtured subsequent *tongzhi* generations, who became more self-reliant and began to fight for their rights, in turn reshaping the sexual and gender laws and norms of society.

With the lifting of martial law in 1986, Taiwan gradually shifted from authoritarian rule to become a multiparty democracy in 1996. Its sociopolitical climate has also become more liberal, with the revitalization of civil society through the rise of social movements (Hsiao and Kuan 2016; Zhou and Hu 2020). Since the 2000s, Taiwan has witnessed the full blossoming of the *tongzhi* world. The pink economy has flourished, hallmarked by the establishment of an open area with numerous bars, cafes, restaurants, and shops outside Red House in the Ximending neighborhood of Taipei City; the emergence of male same-sex prostitution, based primarily in massage parlors; and the launch of circuit parties around Gay Pride and New Year, which attract gay men from across Asia and beyond. There is also increasing *tongzhi* visibility in media and culture, as evidenced by the launch of the glossy lifestyle magazine *G&L* (1996–2001); the popular TV program *Kangxi Lai Le* (2004–2016), fronted by out gay host Kevin Tsai; the launch of the Taiwan International Queer Film Festival (2014–) and the production of gay- and lesbian-themed movies;[27] and the establishment of Asia's biggest LGBT+ video streaming site GagaOOlala (2016–). Other notable phenomena have been the vibrant growth of new media, the Internet, and interuniversity networks;[28] the burgeoning of gender and sexuality studies—notably, the establishment of the Center for the Study of Sexualities at National Central University (1995–), which provides an important research- and information-based resource center and organizes an annual conference that draws scholars from

FIG. 1.3. Taiwan Pride Walk 2019 (source: Taiwan Tongzhi [LGBTQ+] Hotline Association).

FIG. 1.4. Mother of Yeh Yung-Chih (*second from left*), speaking at Kaohsiung Pride in 2010 (source: Taiwan Gender Equity Education Association).

Hong Kong and mainland China;[29] the regular participation of academics in both the political democratic movement and formal politics (serving as government officials and leaders of political parties), which has resulted in closer links between sexual politics and academic studies; and, finally, the emergence of vibrant *tongzhi* activism that culminated in Taiwan's first pride parade in 2003, which remains the largest LGBT+ pride event in Asia.

As in the case of Hong Kong, a social-materialist framework that emphasizes the interplay of the state, the market, and civil society helps us understand the present contour of *tongzhi* development in Taiwan: the pro-gay Taiwanese government, a religious backlash, and the new logic of governance inside the *tongzhi* community. The Taiwanese government's pro-gay stance is the result of a long history of lobbying and struggles with *tongzhi* activists and organizations (Kuan 2019b, 2019c). Since the 2000s, the Taiwanese government has strategically facilitated the realization of *tongzhi* rights by launching a range of antidiscrimination policies to improve the social, educational, and occupational environments for sexual minorities, including assisting in the first gay pride event in Taipei in 2003; enacting the Gender Equity Education Act in 2004, triggered by the Yeh Yung-chih incident, which obliges schools to provide a safe campus and gender-friendly environment for students, faculty, and staff of different genders, gender temperaments, gender identities, and sexual orientations;[30] enacting the 2008 Act of Gender Equality in Employment, under which gender discrimination in the workplace includes discrimination based on sexual orientation;[31] and endorsing same-sex marriage in 2019 (Kuan 2019b, 2019c). Although the endorsement of such rights is subject to legal interpretation and judicial power, it is believed that Taiwan's internationally marginalized status, owing to the One China policy, has resulted in a desire to win recognition from advanced Western countries and prove its position as part of the civilized world by adopting an open attitude toward gay rights, thus distancing itself from both its authoritarian past and "barbarian" neighbor, the PRC (Huang 2017; Patton 1998). Former Taipei mayor Ma Ying-jeou (later KMT president from 2008–2012) and Democratic Progressive Party president Chen Shui-bian (2000–2008) both gave their support to branding Taipei City a pro-gay rights international metropolis in the early 2000s despite resistance from older generations and conservatives (Chu 2003; Ho 2017).

But the development of a *tongzhi* movement has faced a religious backlash. The government's pro-gay stance, as well as the vibrancy of *tongzhi* activism, has triggered opposition from conservatives, mainly religious groups, who are "a blend of a prudish brand of Confucian teaching and an evangelical style of Christian morality" (Lee 2017, 688) that "urges a stable positioning of sexual norms and gender roles" (687). Gaining support from a transnational religious network that encompasses Singapore, South Korea, and Hong Kong, Christian groups in Taiwan have become more vocal about homosexual issues in public (Kao 2018). For example, in 2000, eight denominations, ninety churches, and 408 individuals signed a petition protesting the use of public funding for Taiwan's first gay pride event (*Taipei tongwan jie*; Tongzhi LGBT Festival), which was sponsored by the government, on the grounds that it would encourage homosexuality.[32] As argued by Huang (2017), in 2006, Christian politicians and megachurch leaders accused the government of facilitating gay marriage, which would "make Taipei City a breeding ground for AIDS" (118), and in 2009 a Presbyterian pastor led three hundred congregants in a "God's Love Surpassing Everything" (119) demonstration and claimed to "represent 90 percent of the Taiwanese population" (119) in wanting to "correct the wrong love among homosexuals" (119). Christian groups have been even more proactive since 2010. They began downplaying their Christian identity and faith and, rather than oppose gay rights, which could be condemned as discriminatory, they advocated for the positive values of protecting family institutions and caring for children. They claimed that any legal adjustment that protected gay rights would threaten the family institution, child rights, and even the morality of Taiwan, all of which would constitute reverse discrimination (a lesson learned from Hong Kong). These groups present themselves as the "gentle, silent majority" (123) that has been repressed by a "militant minority" (123) of gay-rights activists. Notable events include the large-scale protest movement initiated by the League of Taiwan Guardians of Family, which in 2013 saw three hundred thousand members participate in public demonstrations against a draft law proposed by the Taiwan Alliance to Promote Civil Partnership Rights (TAPCPR) that would allow diverse family formations, same-sex marriage, civil partnership, and multiperson families of choice. A violent confrontation in 2014 resulted in numerous injuries to both proponents and opponents of the law. An intense battle over the legalization of same-sex marriage ensued between the marriage-equality camp (led by the TAPCPR and, later, the Coalition for Marriage Equality) and anti–marriage-equality camp (led by Christian and parent groups), culminating in a ten-question referendum in 2018 (with five questions concerning LGBT+ rights and same-sex marriage) and passage of Judicial Yuan Interpretation No. 748 in 2019, which finally gave same-sex couples the legal right to register as married couples (Kuan 2019b, 2019c).

Along with this religious backlash, *tongzhi* development has been subject to a new logic of hetero/homonormativities infused with neoliberalism, cosmopolitanism, and capitalism. The *tongzhi* community itself has increased the demarcation between good and bad homosexuals, and members of the community have become increasingly concerned with being seen as good sexual citizens deemed important for political inclusion (Hung 2015). For example, the proposed theme of the Eleventh Taiwan LGBT Pride parade in 2013 was "Make LGBT Visible 2.0—The Voice of [the] Sexual Sufferer," with sexual sufferers including HIV carriers, BDSM practitioners, sex workers, and chemsex/chem-fun participants. The inclusion of these marginalized groups drew severe criticism within the *tongzhi* community, with the term *sexual sufferer* deemed overly harsh, negative, or stigmatizing. It seemed to threaten the respectability of the *tongzhi* community, particularly at a time when Taiwan was debating amendments to the civil code that sought to incorporate same-sex marriage and other citizenship rights (Kong, Lau, and Hui 2019).

This intricate interplay within the state, religion, and civil society over many decades formed a new environment for today's *tongzhi* generations. Taiwan's first *tongzhi* generation, characterized as "Crystal Boys," has been replaced by generations who have fought for full sexual citizenship by making conduct-, identity-, and relationship-based rights claims. The social outcast has been transformed into a liberal *tongzhi* subject. The post-'90s generation *tongzhi* were born in the post–martial-law era and live in a democratic society with a distinctive Taiwanese identity. Although they struggle with a stagnant economy, low salaries, and a high unemployment rate, they benefit from a well-established and resourceful *tongzhi* world with a strong, positive gay identity.

Mainland China: From Maoism to the Postreform State and from Hooligan/Mental Patient to *Suzhi* Urban *Tongzhi* Subject

In mainland China, the emergence and development of *tongzhi* identities and cultures have been shaped by the political ideology of the Communist Party, the Western biomedical model, and patriarchal family and marriage institutions. Owing to the traditional ambivalence toward homosexuality (Ruan 1991) and the state's post-1949 affiliation with Marxism-inspired atheism, religion has never played a crucial role in regulating homosexuality in mainland China. In contrast to the British colonial government in Hong

Kong and the pro-US Taiwanese government, the Chinese government has always been skeptical of the West (particularly of the United States) but has been much more receptive to capitalism since the reform era.

Following the PRC's establishment in 1949, the Mao period (1949–1976) was characterized by revolutionary passion and class struggle and guided by the organizing principles of Marxism-Leninism-Maoism and the overarching goal of socialist development (Jeffreys and Yu 2015, 151). As Tian (2019) has argued, the biological understanding of sex/sexuality was Chinese Communist Party (CCP) doctrine for three main reasons: stable heterosexual family units were required for the social production of workers and homogeneous state formation, heterosexual monogamy was associated with sexual modernity and homosexuality with premodern disorder and incivility, and sociology was banned (from 1952–1978), with sociological or critical study of sexuality replaced by the Western medical framework privileging monogamous, reproductive sex (cf. Evans 1995, 1997). Until the end of the Cultural Revolution in the late 1970s, public discussion of homosexuality was almost entirely absent, and there were no established same-sex venues. Given the nearly universal marriage rate prior to that period (Davis and Friedman 2014), the first *tongzhi* generation that was born between 1920 and 1950, like their counterparts in Hong Kong and Taiwan, were largely closeted and governed by heteropatriarchal norms. Most of them married and suppressed their same-sex desires or found release in public toilets in parks or railway stations (An 1995; Fang 1995; Li and Wang 1992).

The early phase of the post-Mao reform era (1979 to the mid-1990s) witnessed increased state attention to homosexuality as a mental disorder and, with regard to male same-sex sexuality, as potentially criminal behavior. The first version of the *Chinese Classification of Mental Disorders* (CCMD) issued in 1978 classified homosexuality as a sexual disorder (Wu 2003, 128). The first Criminal Law of the PRC promulgated in 1979 did not expressly mention homosexuality but introduced the "crime of hooliganism" (Provision 160) and an "analogy clause" (Provision 79) that made it possible for the authorities to punish anal sex between men under "other hooligan activities" (Gao 1995; Guo 2007; Kang 2012; Li 2006; Worth et al. 2019). Thus, from the official state perspective of the 1980s through the mid-1990s, homosexuals were defined primarily as male and fell somewhere between mental patients and hooligans or both. Moreover, in 1989, the Office of the National Work Group for Combating Pornography and Illegal Publications (NWGCPP) set out regulations restricting the publication of obscene and pornographic materials, including the "obscene description of homosexual behavior."[33]

Sexual culture remained profoundly conservative in the 1980s. As market reforms gathered speed in the 1990s, urban and rural society witnessed decreased state monitoring of private life and the burgeoning of social and consumer spaces for sexual and romantic interactions (Farrer 2002; Jeffreys 2006; Pan 2006; Rofel 2007). Contemporary *tongzhi* identities and communities slowly began to emerge, almost ten years later than in Hong Kong and Taiwan, partially with the help of transnational *tongzhi* activists from Hong Kong, Taiwan, and overseas who set up health organizations and national hotlines to tackle HIV/AIDS and who encouraged adoption of the Hong Kong–style gay business model, especially in South China. Beginning in Beijing, Shanghai, Guangzhou, and Shenzhen, and later spreading to other major cities, the new *tongzhi* generations (born from the 1950s to 1960s) began meeting to socialize and build a community, explore their same-sex desires and identities, and put down nascent organizational roots to identify shared needs. At the same time, however, they remained confined by the heteropatriarchal family institution, which demands filial piety—as expressed by fulfilling parental expectations to marry, bear children, and avoid bringing shame (or a loss of face) on the family—as well as by discrimination arising from the prevailing societal view of homosexuals as hooligans or mental patients (Engebretsen 2014; He and Jolly 2002; Ho 2010; Kam 2013; Kong 2011, 145–73; Rofel 2007, 85–110).

The situation began to change in the late 1990s. The new Criminal Law of 1997 deleted the crime of hooliganism and the analogy clause, implicitly decriminalizing homosexuality in legal statutes, although the police continued to arrest men suspected of engaging in sex work or group sex (female same-sex sexual behavior has never been criminalized in China) (Guo 2007; Kang 2012). The *CCMD*-III published in 2001 demedicalized homosexuality in line with international precedent following a concerted campaign by the Aizhi Action Program and its founder, Wan Yanhai, a public health advocate and gay rights activist (Kang 2012; Wu 2003, 133). The government officially recognized the existence of homosexuals in 2003, owing to the AIDS epidemic (He and Detels 2005, 826). The state retained its medical understanding of homosexuality but shifted from a pathological to national public health framework (Kong 2016; Wong 2016), thereby paving the way for homosexuality to be openly discussed and researched. These legal, medical, and public health developments successfully dissociated homosexuality from pathological and deviant connotations.

Since the 2000s, there has been ample evidence of the proliferation of *tongzhi* identities and cultures. First, the pink economy is flourishing, with the emergence of various LGBT+ consumer markets and communities, particularly in major cities such as Beijing, Shanghai, Shenzhen, and Chengdu, and the burgeoning of male brothels and massage parlors (Kong 2012b; Yau and Kong 2021). Second, there is increasing LGBT+ visibility in the mass media. Notable examples include the TV shows *I Can I BB* (*Qi Pa Shuo*, 2014–2021) and *Jin Xing Show* (2015–2017) and the mushrooming of *tongzhi* stories (also known as comrade literature) on gay websites, including *Beijing Gushi* (A story from Beijing; 1998), later adapted as the film *Lan Yu* (dir. Stanley Kwan, 2001), and *Ni ya shang yin liao* (Are you addicted; 2013), later made into a webTV drama series *Shang Yin* (*Addicted*) in 2016. Third, there has been marked expansion in social media platforms and new media outlets facilitating event promotion and organizational activities, including sites specializing in gay dating or matchmaking for gay men and lesbians seeking "contract marriage" partners to model a heterosexual marriage while maintaining same-sex relationships. Dating apps such as Blued (2012–) and ZANK (2013–2017) also provide platforms for live-streaming, e-commerce, gaming, and health services (overseas surrogacy consultation), thereby promoting *tongzhi* visibility while strategically framing its content with a for-profit orientation to avoid government censorship (S. Wang 2019b). Fourth, a number of independent queer filmmakers have emerged, including Cui Zi'en, Fan Popo, Shitou, and Mingming, who founded and run the Beijing Queer Film Festival (2001–), which screens numerous independent movies/videos on queer issues. China's only independent LGBT+ webcast, *Queer Comrades*, was also established in 2007 (Bao 2018). Fifth, LGBT+ organizations and community centers have proliferated, including the Beijing Tongzhi Zhongxin (Beijing LGBT Center), established in 2008; Kuaxingbie Zhongxin (Trans Center), established in 2016; as well as family support and counseling groups like Tongxinglian Qinyou Hui (Parents and Friends of Lesbians and Gays, or PFLAG), started in 2008; cultural festivals (Shanghai Pride, started in 2009); and the business network Tongzhi Shangwu (WorkForLGBT), started in 2013. Finally, courses on LGBT+ issues have been launched at universities, and a biannual conference and workshop on sexuality has been held at Renmin University since 2007 (organized by Pan Suiming and Huang Yingying).[34] With invited scholars and activists from Hong Kong and Taiwan, the conference/workshop showcases research on sexuality and *tongzhi* activism and encourages critical rethinking of the applicability of Western theories to the study of Chinese sexuality (Huang and Pan 2009; Huang et al. 2009). These encouraging developments have nurtured positive identity formation in the younger *tongzhi* generations.

However, in the absence of Western religion (Christianity in particular) as a major opposing force as in Hong Kong and Taiwan, such vibrant *tongzhi* developments have always been confined by the Chinese state. Nonetheless, the relationship among the state, the market, and civil society (especially between the state and NGOs) is again a significant factor in shaping the contours of *tongzhi* development. The government's general attitude toward homosexuality is "no encouraging, no discouraging, and no promoting" under the public-health paradigm. Although the expansion of *tongzhi* spaces has always been controlled by the government, under President Xi Jinping (2012–), tighter controls have been imposed, primarily through censorship and the control of NGOs. Censorship is a form of governance. As King, Pan, and Roberts (2013) argue, censorship in China is less concerned with suppressing criticism of the state or CCP than with reducing the likelihood of collective action by silencing comments that represent, reinforce, or spur social mobilization, regardless of content. Seen in this light, the censorship of homosexuality can be understood as stemming from homosexuality becoming more visible in the media and thus entering the public sphere, with the potential to spark collective action because it can easily be politicized with human rights discourse. Since the 2000s, governmental control of homosexuality has been increasingly linked to pornography and prostitution, primarily because of greater *tongzhi* visibility in the cultural industries and the burgeoning of male prostitution, with homosexual content seen by the state as pornographic, obscene, and vulgar. Since 2004, websites containing homosexual content and sexually explicit images of men have frequently been removed from the Internet, although they sometimes later emerge in another incarnation. Same-sex prostitution has been treated the same as female prostitution since 2004, when a man named Li Ning was sentenced to prison for eight years and fined sixty thousand yuan (roughly $8,879) for organizing male-male prostitution (Jeffreys 2007). In 2015, homosexuality was listed as a censored topic for television, on the grounds that it represents unnatural sexual behavior. In 2016, *Addicted*, an extremely popular Boys Love (BL)-type gay romance web series, and several other gay-themed shows streaming on major video portals, were taken offline. In 2017, eighteen live-streaming platforms, including the gay apps ZANK and Bluesky, were permanently removed for disseminating illegal content, with staff detained, male streamers arrested, and corporate representatives hunted by the police (S. Wang 2019a, 2019b).

Official suspicion of Western values and Western-influenced civil society has created an increasingly narrow space for civil-society activism. Imple-

FIG. 1.5. Recruiting members for *Zhiheshe* (a student society concerned with gender and sexuality issues) at Fudan University in 2017 (source: participant's photo).

mentation of the 2016 Charity Law and 2017 International NGO Law have intensified state regulation of NGO funding and limited NGOs' scope of operation (Spires 2011, 2019), dealing a heavy blow to LGBT+ organizations, which have historically relied on foreign funding and often collaborated with international organizations. Outward-facing programs have also been curtailed by the government crackdown on feminist activism. A notable example is the arrest of five young feminist activists (later dubbed the Feminist Five), some of them lesbians, to prevent them from launching a campaign against sexual harassment on public transportation on International Women's Day on March 6, 2015. There is an official tendency to collapse gender- and sexuality-related movements, making homosexuality an equally suspect basis for organizational mobilization. Since 2015, for example, most courses on gender and sexuality and *tongzhi* student organizations have been shut down.

In the face of such strict censorship and control, activists and NGO practitioners tend to identify themselves as *gongyi* (public interest) organizations, which is a more acceptable and less politically sensitive term, to categorize all kinds of campaigning, community organizing, social-service provision, and activism (Wu 2017). *Tongzhi* businesspeople, activists, and organizers also identity themselves as doing *gongyi* and have deployed a number of strategies. Confrontational tactics are rare, as they carry a high risk of arrest or detention, as in the case of the Feminist Five. Some have adopted guerrilla-style resistance. For example, the founders of the Beijing Queer Film Festival have organized what they call the China Queer Film Festival Tour, screening films in cities across the country in university classrooms, bars, or clubs, with screening times and venues announced at the last minute to escape government control (Bao 2018). Others collaborate with the government. The most common means of doing so is to camouflage as an HIV/AIDS organization to obtain funding and offer programs that serve *tongzhi*—that is, claiming to focus on public health rather than identity and politics, which attract government surveillance.[35] Danlan is a good example. Launched in 2000 by Geng Le, Danlan is a gay website whose content includes gay-related news, information on HIV/AIDS prevention and treatment, and gay blogging, and it thus plays the HIV/AIDS card by actively participating in government-funded HIV/AIDS programs to demonstrate its commitment to social responsibility and the CCP's core values. Geng Le also set up Blued in 2012, now the most popular gay dating app in China, claiming over forty-nine million users in 2020.[36] In contrast to other dating apps, which stress individuality, sociability, and identity, Blued claims to be "an interest-based social app that promotes positive, healthy and humanitarian living" with no direct reference to gays or *tongzhi*.[37] It is basically a gay business, but it emphasizes its *gongyi* components. In other words, its success depends on its strategic play with nationalism, homonormativity, and consumerism. Another example of collaboration with the government is PFLAG China. PFLAG was originally founded in the United States in 1974. Founded in 2008, PFLAG China is the largest *tongzhi* (and *gongyi*) group in mainland China. In contrast to Blued, which omits any homosexuality-related terms, PFLAG China (Tongxinglian Qinyou Hui) deliberately uses the term *tongxinglian* (homosexual) instead of gay or *tongzhi* to articulate its target service group. However, it changed its name to Trueself in 2021 to remove any direct connotation of homosexuality due to pressure from the authorities. Further, whereas Blued aligns HIV/AIDS prevention with nationalism, PFLAG China aligns it with Confucian values emphasizing parental love, care, and support for LGBT+ people. As Rofel (2012, 158) points out, activists in China are "creative, thoughtful, flexible and nimble in relation to where

FIG. 1.6. Closing ceremony of the eleventh PFLAG (Trueself) national conference in main-land China in 2019 (source: Trueself).

the government draws the line between what is permissible and what is not."
According to one activist, "Only by continually testing the limits imposed on
our activities can we know where these lines are" (quoted in Chase 2012,
158; see also Cao and Guo 2016; Spires 2011; Tian 2019).[38]

As in Hong Kong and Taiwan, the *tongzhi* community in mainland China
as a whole tends to embrace cosmopolitanism and nascent capitalism, which
serves less to enhance solidarity and identification than it does to demarcate
those who can fully access the urban and cosmopolitan ideal from those who
cannot, such as poor, rural, HIV-positive, and nonmonogamous *tongzhi* and
those who sell sex. Among the latter, "money boys," Chinese parlance for
men who sell sex to other men, represent a typical sexual other: low *suzhi*
(quality), immoral, and unrespectable (Fu 2012; Ho 2010; Jones 2007; Kong
2012b, 2017; Rofel 2010).

Regardless of whether *tongxinglian/tongxing'ai*, gay (or "lala" for lesbian),
tongzhi, or *ku'er* (queer) is preferred, the newly emergent sexual identity
of the younger *tongzhi* generations in mainland China, including the post-
'90s generation, has slowly dissociated itself from its earlier pathological
(mental patient) or deviant (hooligan) connotation. These generations view
homosexuality not as sickness or deviance but as a new kind of humanity
(Rofel 2007, 1) characterized by individuality, difference, sophistication,

liberation, and modernity. However, the family and the institution of marriage remain major sites of negotiation for gay men and lesbians. Across the generations, class spectrum, and urban-rural divide, men and women in mainland China face overwhelming familial and societal pressure to marry and bear children. In the early 2000s, public attention was drawn by media reports to the plight of *tongqi*, heterosexual women who had unwittingly married gay men only to later discover their husbands' sexual orientation (Zhu 2017). The younger generations are increasingly rejecting heterosexual marriage, opting either for a contract marriage with a *tongzhi* of the opposite sex or remaining single to pursue a same-sex relationship (and, in some cases, seeking to marry a same-sex partner, either ritually in mainland China or legally abroad) (Choi and Luo 2016; Engebretsen 2016; Kam 2015; S. Y. Wang 2019). Although many resort to contract marriages to appease their parents and access assisted reproductive technologies (legal access to which is restricted to heterosexual married couples in mainland China), a growing number are choosing to pursue childbearing outside marriage, often by traveling abroad to access surrogacy and egg donation (for gay men) or in-vitro fertilization and sperm donation (for lesbians) (Lin 2019; Wei 2021).

A Sociomaterialist Analysis and the *Tongzhi* Generations

Although Hong Kong, Taiwan, and mainland China broadly share social and cultural norms rooted in Confucian values and Chinese family ideals, they have undergone distinct political and economic trajectories since 1949 that have created very different possibilities and paths for the development of *tongzhi* identities, cultures, and communities. Coming out of the Cold War milieu of the 1950s–1970s, all three societies witnessed the blossoming of sexuality-based identities in the 1980s and 1990s, accompanied by the rise of *tongzhi* cultures and sexual communities, the fight for sexual rights, and organized political activism. By the late twentieth century, flows of people, ideas, concepts, and relationships were becoming increasingly salient for emerging forms of identification and modes of organization. Diverse combinations of democracy, socialism, authoritarianism, postcolonialism, neoliberalism, and developmentalism, which have formed scattered hegemonies (Grewal and Kaplan 1994), have shaped the content and direction of sexuality-based identities and the sexual rights movement in the three societies. Although their shared histories and cultures have created significant commonalities, their differing degrees of physical and societal openness and access to domestic and foreign interlocutors have produced striking differences in their political-rights claims and cultural expression of *tongzhi* identities, relationships, cultures, and communities (see table 1.1).

THE STATE, THE MARKET, AND CIVIL SOCIETY   A transnational queer sociological approach allows for a sociomaterialist analysis that demonstrates the interplay among the state, the market, and civil society as sites of governance and resistance that have formed different assemblages at different times and in turn have shaped the different but interrelated and interinfluenced trajectories of *tongzhi* identities, cultures, communities, and movements in the three locales. This section puts the previous separate discussions of that interplay into an engaged and comparative conversation. The state has clearly played a significant role in shaping gay and lesbian identities and communities in all three locales. The state is not just a bureaucratic apparatus but also a powerful site of material, symbolic, and cultural production (Cooper 2002). It comprises a contradictory set of institutions—both enabling and restricting—that shape the contours of sexual identities, practices, and cultures, as evidenced by the change in penal codes or other laws governing homosexuality and/or sexual conduct, identities, and relationships. In British-ruled Hong Kong, male homosexual acts were criminalized in 1842 and decriminalized in 1991, a change initiated by the government rather than by queer activists, unlike in Western liberal states. The HKSAR government, established in 1997, has adopted a policy of gradual accommodation and delay (rather than repression) owing to its close relationship with evangelical Christianity and profamily conservatism. There is still no law governing discrimination on the basis of sexual orientation, nor are there any legal arrangements for civil partnership or same-sex marriage. It also remains indifferent to capitalizing on the pink dollar for economic gain or emphasizing the gay index to construct Hong Kong as a creative city. Due to the guarded approach to politics of both the colonial and HKSAR governments, *tongzhi* identities and cultures are largely framed around economic development and cultural expression for the pursuit of cultural rather than political citizenship. In contrast to the colonial government in Hong Kong, the authoritarian KMT government in Taiwan (1945–2000) was more ambivalent toward homosexuality. Although homosexuality was never a criminal offense, gay men were often charged with offenses against "virtuous customs." Unlike the HKSAR government, the Taiwanese government has, since the 2000s, strategically exhibited a mostly positive stance toward homosexuality by incorporating homosexuality into nationalism, owing to its determination to gain recognition from Western countries and distance itself from mainland China. It has thereby facilitated the development of a fuller sense of sexual citizenship based on conduct-, identity-, and relationship-based rights claims. In mainland China, the state (1949–) is primarily concerned with social stability. Anything construed as threatening the government's authority will be censored, dismissed, and controlled. Homosexuality, with its mobilizing potential and affiliation with human rights, is part of such negative governance. Framed under the public health paradigm, the state's overall attitude toward homosexuality is ambivalent, and it has been both decriminalized (1997) and demedicalized (2001); yet the development of the *tongzhi* world—from entertainment venues to male brothels, the mass media, websites and dating apps, school curricula, and *tongzhi* activism—has been regulated and censored, especially under the Xi Jinping regime. The only exceptions seem to be Blued and PFLAG (Trueself), both of which work with the government and its notion of nationalism. Although the state has traditionally been seen as antihomosexuality, recent years have seen a shift in the relationship among the state, capitalism, and sexuality. Notable in this respect is Puar's (2007) notion of "homonationalism," a term she coined to describe the process by which certain queer subjects are included in the US national imagination. In this sense, Taiwan can be seen as an incorporative case of homonationalism, whereas Hong Kong represents a failed or deficient case, and China a form of pragmatic homonationalism. The relationship among the state, homosexuality, and the civic-political activism of the post-'90s generation will be further discussed in chapter 5.

Moreover, the market economy, especially its embrace of neoliberalism, has played a greater role in the formation of modern queer identities in Asia than in the West, as most governments in Asia are strongly promarket in orientation (Jackson 2003). The neoliberal political project was gradual in East Asia, as these states had long been implementing state-led developmentalism, first by Japan and later followed by South Korea, Taiwan, Hong Kong, and Singapore (the four "East Asian tigers") and then Malaysia, Thailand, China, and Vietnam ("newly industrializing" Asian countries). East Asian developmental states first began to experiment with neoliberal reforms in the 1980s. The result has been the coupling or mixture of developmentalism and neoliberalism, or "developmental neoliberalism," in the region (Hill, Park, and Saito 2012). Under neoliberalism or developmentalism, Hong Kong, in parallel with Thailand, was the first among the three societies under study to establish a gay business model that has nurtured a well-established, visible gay commercial market since the late 1980s as well as a distinctive culture of Westerner-Chinese intimate pairings. It has also provided a platform for the development of a vibrant, Westernized queer-elite subculture and has also been adopted by most gay businesses in Southern China since the early 2000s. In Taiwan, owing to martial law (1949–1987) and a slower pace of economic development, the pink economy emerged almost ten years later than in Hong Kong. Although political suppression was strong during the martial-law period, cultural expression, including the cultural production of homosexuality, was vibrant. Both Hong Kong and Taiwan are capitalist societies and thus receptive to the market economy. By contrast, mainland China took a cautious approach to the market economy from 1949 to the 1980s, as it was seen as representing an excess of capitalism and the corruption of spiritual civilization. However, since the 1990s, the Chinese state has fostered a strong market economy that encompasses both state-owned corporations and smaller privately owned businesses, resulting in a proliferation of *tongzhi* businesses, be they gay websites, dating apps, or male prostitution, although they are still under strict surveillance.[39]

And the three societies have developed distinct civil societies in which I articulate three sites of governance and resistance—namely, religion, family, and the *tongzhi* world—for discussion. Chinese religion (Buddhism or Taoism) says little about homosexuality, whereas Western religion (Christianity) is the main colonizing and opposing force to homosexuality. Transnational Christian/evangelical groups in Hong Kong, Taiwan, South Korea, and Singapore, which often make use of the traditional heteropatriarchal family discourse, are the main opposing force to the *tongzhi* movement in Hong Kong (Wong 2013) and Taiwan (Ho 2008; Huang 2017; Lee 2017), whereas in mainland China it is the government (Engebretsen and Schroeder 2015). Family remains the main institution that most *tongzhi* across the three sites struggle with, especially in coming out, although this is particularly true of mainland China, where marriage is paramount. The family carries the cultural values of Confucianism and filial ideology, which are manifested in the need to protect the family's face and family pressure to marry and bear children (Chou 2000) as well as in material conditions due to the family being closely related to the government's housing and land policies.[40] Coming out to the family usually involves a dual closet: heterosexuality versus homosexuality and the good (filial) versus the bad (unfilial) child. The complicated relationship among family, marriage, love, and *tongzhi* will be discussed in chapters 2 and 4.

The *tongzhi* world has developed, with Hong Kong and Taiwan leading the way in the 1980s, followed by mainland China in the late 1990s. There are many dimensions of the *tongzhi* world, ranging from explicitly political dimensions such as rallies, marches, and demonstrations to self-help groups and *tongzhi* organizations, *tongzhi* media and intellectual and academic endeavors, and the pink economy and *tongzhi*-identified commercial venues such as bars, clubs, saunas, and massage parlors. This world also encompasses amorphous "scenes" such as public toilets, parks, and various communities that connect with one another through sexuality, language, values, and interests and in the online virtual world.

The development of the *tongzhi* world has differed in each locale, reflecting different paths of the pursuit of sexual citizenship under the changing state–civil society relationship. Three aspects of that development are worthy of note: the development of political or cultural sexual citizenship, the style of *tongzhi* activism, and the internal logic of governance. First, political participation became vital in Taiwan after the lifting of martial law in 1986. Political participation gained momentum in Hong Kong in the 2000s before being circumscribed by the introduction of the National Security Law in 2020, and it has been strictly controlled by the state in mainland China since 1989. As a result, the *tongzhi* movement in Taiwan has had greater room to fight for legal sexual rights based on conduct-, identity-, and relationship-based rights claims (as evidenced by the legalization of same-sex marriage) than in Hong Kong or mainland China. The *tongzhi* political world manifested in rallies, marches, and demonstrations is well established in Taiwan and Hong Kong, although public space in the latter has considerably diminished since 2020 and remains scarce in mainland China. Accordingly, the strong state and weak civil society in Taiwan before 1986, and currently in Hong Kong and mainland China, have made economic and cultural participation a more important force than political participation for the development of sexual citizenship, as manifested in popular culture, the media, and the pink economy, which nurture a collective consciousness, community connections, and solidarity. That is why we have seen a vibrant arts scene and queer cultural media production, first in Taiwan and Hong Kong, with Hong Kong's scene then shaping mainland China's queer cultural production in the 1990s and Taiwan's influencing Hong Kong queer media in the mid-1990s. Such cultural and media production has flourished in mainland China since the 2000s.

Second, the state–civil society relationship also affects the style and sites of *tongzhi* activism. In mainland China, *tongzhi* groups prioritize an inward-facing community and identity-building in the face of government restrictions on outward-oriented organizing and rights promotion, whereas their counterparts in Hong Kong and Taiwan have been able to cultivate politically active, publicly visible *tongzhi* movements. Some groups focus on health and well-being (HIV/AIDS prevention or mental health), whereas others have openly pursued antidiscrimination campaigns and mobilized in support of legal rights and recognition. Academics in Taiwan have played a significant role in both the political democratic movement and formal politics, serving as government officials and leaders of political parties, which has resulted in closer links between sexual politics and academic studies. Partly owing to Hong Kong's academic conservativism and China's state control over academia, the main sites of *tongzhi* activism are popular culture and the media, often advanced by public intellectuals and/or NGO activists rather than by university campuses.[41] However, as freedom of speech is prohibited in mainland China, and increasingly in Hong Kong, cultural queer politics and *tongzhi* academic activism are struggling.

Third, the *tongzhi* communities in all three societies seem quite un-critical of nascent capitalism, with the *tongzhi* world highly stratified in terms of class, gender, body, and sexual preference. The creation of the good and bad homosexual and decent and indecent sexual citizen is thus much in evidence. Although such distinctions have been important in the fight for sexual citizenship and political inclusion in Taiwan, as well as for economic and cultural inclusion in Hong Kong and mainland China, they inevitably privilege urban, middle-class, cosmopolitan, and other neoliberal and heteronormative values. More specifically, the gay world has witnessed the domination of what I call *homonormative masculinity*. The development of the market economy and the *tongzhi* community will be dealt with in greater depth in chapter 3.

THE *TONGZHI* GENERATIONS   The differing social and material conditions of Hong Kong, Taiwan, and mainland China have produced a complex interplay between social institutions and sexuality. In all three, the first *tongzhi* generation, whose members were characterized as criminals, mental patients, or hooligans, usually lived with sadness, shame, and secrecy, slowly giving way to the postwar generation, which can be seen as the "coming-out" generation, characterized by a strong middle-class and Western/cosmopolitan sensibility. Social institutions (especially the state) played a greater role in shaping the development of *tongzhi* identities, practices, and cultures in the early phase (the being-made process), whereas there has been a more dynamic interplay between mutually constituted institutions and sexuality for later *tongzhi* generations (the self-making process). The construction of the homosexual as a criminal or social outcast has shifted to the liberal and democratic (Taiwan), cosmopolitan and consumerist (Hong Kong), or postreform, *suzhi* and urban (mainland China) *tongzhi* subject with the core values of responsibility, respectability, and middle-class sensibility. The post-'90s generation in all three sites was born in an era in which homosexuality was no longer seen as a crime or mental illness, and Hong Kong, Taiwan, and major cities in mainland China now boast a substantial queer consumer market, vibrant queer cultural productions, and burgeoning queer communities (mainly online in mainland China); and queer NGOs and activism have also emerged (in Hong Kong and Taiwan, at least). Accordingly, younger *tongzhi* have developed a strong gay identity and view homosexuality as more or less the same as heterosexuality. Let us now turn to the lives of this generation in detail.

TABLE 1.1. A brief comparison of the status of homosexuality in Hong Kong, Taiwan, and mainland China.

	Hong Kong
History	
Regime	British colonialism (1842–1997)
	Japanese occupation (1941–1945)
	HKSAR (1997–)
Major events	Criminalization of homosexual acts (1842–1990) and decriminalization (1991–)
	Removal of homosexuality as a form of mental illness (1973)
	Equalized age of consent between heterosexuals and homosexuals (2005)
	Domestic violence ordinance applied to same-sex relationships (2009)
	Victory in several legal cases pertaining to housing, migration, and inheritance (2013–)
Governance	
Government	Deficient homonationalism: ambivalence, gradual accommodation, and delay
Main opposing force	Religion (Christianity)
Family	Dual closet: homosexuality/heterosexuality and filiality/unfiliality
Civil Society	
Pink economy	Flourishing and well-established (e.g., Lan Kwai Fong)
LGBT+ community	Visibility in popular culture (e.g., HKLGFF)
Major LGBT+ events	IDAHOT (2005–), Pride Walk (2008–), Pink Dot (2014–), Gay Games (2023)

Taiwan	Mainland China
Early colonization by the Dutch and Spanish (1624–1662) Cheng Kingdom (1662–1683) Qing empire (1683–1895) Japanese occupation (1895–1945) Republic of China (1949–) Martial law (1949–1987) Representative democracy (1987–)	Republican era (1912–1949) Mao period (1949–1976) Reform China (1978–) Xi Jinping regime (2012–)
Removal of homosexuality as a form of mental illness (1973) Gender-equity acts in education (2004) and employment (2008) Legalization of same-sex marriage (2019)	Revised criminal law (1997) Removal of homosexuality as a form of mental illness (2001)
Incorporative homonationalism: strategically pro-gay	Pragmatic homonationalism: ambivalence, "no encouraging, no discouraging, and no promoting" Stricter control over civil society (2012–): media, pink economy, education, and activism
Religion (Christianity)	The state
Dual closet: homosexuality/heterosexuality and filiality/unfiliality	Dual closet: homosexuality/heterosexuality and filiality/unfiliality; marriage pressure still strong
Flourishing and well-established (e.g., Red House, circuit parties)	Pink economy in big cities (e.g., Shanghai, Shenzhen, Beijing, Chengdu), subject to sporadic police raid
Visibility in popular culture (e.g., GagaOOlala)	Community (including the Internet) heavily censored
Gay Pride (2003–)	Heavily regulated

2

Coming Out as Relational Politics

As the cornerstone of Chinese society, the family has traditionally been seen as heteronormative and the antithesis of homosexuality. It has always been considered an indispensable site for establishing one's humanness and social identity and, therefore, in Chinese societies the most powerful institution circumscribing gay and lesbian lives (Rofel 2007, 100). Indeed, it is the major site for negotiating sexual identity in China. This likely explains the overwhelming focus on coming out to the family in the Chinese literature on homosexuality. Notable examples of this literature include Kong (2011, 2020, 2021), Tang (2011), and Wong (2007) for Hong Kong; Brainer (2019), Liu and Ding (2005), and Wang, Bih, and Brennan (2009) for Taiwan; Engebretsen (2014), Kam (2013), and Li and Wang (1992) for mainland China; and Chou (2000) for all three sites. Hence, coming out is best viewed not just through the lens of identity politics, as in Western literature, but rather through that of relational politics, with gay men and lesbians embedding the self within kinship ties, family, and community.

As both an institution and as social practice, the family is itself a site of change in Hong Kong, Taiwan, and mainland China in recent times. Major changes—in family structure, function, and culture and in its relation to other social institutions such as the state—have necessarily affected young gay men's lives in the three locales. The family now nurtures neoliberal values that emphasize individual success, competition, and performance, in turn favoring the formation of neoliberal entrepreneurial masculinity. How does this neoliberal masculinity relate to young gay sexuality? Does parenting culture still focus on authority, obedience, and discipline, or has it shifted to reciprocal understanding, equality, and care? And how does such an intimate turn facilitate or hinder coming out? Are traditional filial values such as marrying and having children still compelling? Overall, how does the family regulate the moral code of practice for young gay men under patriarchy and heteronormativity, or what I call *familial heteronormativity* (Kong 2011, 98)? Using coming out as an example, this chapter offers understanding of the interplay between individual agency and family life among young gay generations in precarious, competitive, and neoliberal Chinese societies.

Coming Out and the Family in the Chinese Context

From the 1960s to 1970s, lesbian and gay studies in Euro-American societies focused overwhelmingly on issues of identity and coming out, critiquing the family as universally hostile to homosexuality. Informed by social constructionism (in particular symbolic interaction and labeling theory), "homosexual identity formation" is a process: identity confusion → comparison → tolerance → acceptance → pride → synthesis (e.g., Cass 1984; Troiden 1988). This model is the foundation of identity politics in the West: "a struggle for identity, a development of sexual communities, and the growth of political movements" (Weeks 1985, 195). Here sexuality is a core element of self-identity; the self seeks to "confess" (Foucault 1980) its sexuality first to oneself, then to one's parents and friends, and finally to the workplace and the world (Boellstorff 2005, 203). Then the self integrates that sexuality into other aspects of life. The self's authenticity thus depends on coming out as a form of self-development. The self assumes that "the individual is autonomous and indivisible with a freestanding inner self" (Yan 2016, 254). It is autonomous in the sense of having the "capacity to leave the collectivity and establish full self-sufficiency" (Schalet 2011, 82). The Euro-American notion of growing up and coming out usually entails leaving home (the natal family), which is "a place to be left behind, to be escaped in order to emerge into another, more liberatory space" (Gopinath 2005, 14).

However, this model may neglect the social and economic context of coming out and risks essentializing identity (Butler 1993, 226–30). Some critics see the conceptualization of coming out as disclosing one's sexual orientation to oneself and others as too static, assuming a one-off turning point before and after disclosure, and as too individualistic, overemphasizing queer agency without taking the role of others into account (Jhang 2018). Some further argue that the social significance of the closet has declined since the 2000s (Seidman 2002), especially among the young who do not define their lives through sexuality and see themselves as virtually normal in a postgay era (Savin-Williams 2005).

Moreover, the notion of the self, as part of individualism in sociology, has been criticized, as "relationality" remains central to late modern selves, even in Euro-American societies (Crossley 2001; Heaphy 2007; Smart 2007). This criticism of the individualized self challenges the myth that queers in Western countries find it easier to come out based on the experience of middle-class, white gay men and women in the United Kingdom and United States, neglecting racial and class differences. Accordingly, Western cultures are not homogenous. Italy and Spain both have notions of self-embedment in a collective, family-centered culture informed by Catholicism (e.g., Bertone and Franchi 2014), so queer people in Southern Europe under the "shadow of the parental household" have greater difficulty coming out than those in other Euro-American societies (Therborn 2004, 221).

Whether the Western self is individualized or relational is subject to debate, but the notion of a relational self embedded in the socially reciprocal relationship network is evident in family-centered Chinese culture informed by Confucianism. This is especially true in Chinese literature (Fei 1992; Yan 2016) and especially in coming-out literature (Brainer 2019; Chou 2000; Kong 2011; Liu and Ding 2005). The self is intimately related to the family network, and there is no leaving the natal family behind in Chinese culture; hence, coming out is best understood in the family context.

It is worth asking if coming out is part of neoliberalism-driven individualization, in which individuals are increasingly disembedded from traditional social institutions and forced to create their own biographies (e.g., Beck and Beck-Gernsheim 1995; Giddens 1991). This detraditionalization thesis overstates the move away from tradition, because ideas and practices deemed "traditional" still play a part in personal life in the West (Carter and Duncan 2018; Jackson and Ho 2020). Moreover it overlooks how individuals are reembedded in multiple networks of social relations such as the Internet, social media, and mobile apps (Rainie and Wellman 2012). This research suggests that in the Chinese context, young gay men are still struggling to create their own biographies within traditional social institutions such as the family and marriage, which embrace neoliberal values that enable and constrain the development of the entrepreneur of the self. Moreover, they simultaneously reembed themselves in the Internet, social media, and dating apps for self-creation, which will be dealt with in the next chapter.

Indeed, neoliberalism and other emergent dynamics have transformed the family and marriage in late-modern societies, and Hong Kong, Taiwan, and mainland China are no exception (Davis and Friedman 2014).[1] The most salient changes in all three locales have been those in family structure, function, and culture and its relation to other social institutions such as the state. First, changes in family size and structure include smaller families, fewer traditional family types, increasing dominance of the nuclear family, the emergence of neoconventional family types, and the rise of new marriage-like arrangements like cohabitation.[2] These changes affect family dynamics, especially the child-parent relationship. Second, the neoliberal state is shifting financial and social welfare provisions—notably, family and elderly care—to the family.[3] The family thus serves as an important source of governance over private lives and as a social institution for nurturing neoliberal values, including neoliberal masculinity. Third, traditional familism, defined as emphasizing "the primacy of family interests over those of its individual members and of loyalty to the family over allegiances to any outside social organizations" (Yan 2018, 185), has shifted to varying forms of neofamilism. Common features include a downward focus on the happiness and well-being of the young; emphasis on success, especially measured in materialist terms; intimate disclosure between generations (notably through a shift from authoritarian to reciprocal parenting); and primacy of individual over family interests (Yan 2016, 2018; see also Bedford and Yeh 2019; Leung, Lam, and Liang 2020; Yeh et al. 2013).

It is in this context that we can understand coming out in Chinese societies. The extant literature does not explicitly articulate features of the coming-out experience in the Chinese context but implicitly maps out two: the double closet and a scaffolding process.[4] First, Chinese *tongzhi* identity has always been subject to a double closet: of heterosexuality and of a traditional familial role (e.g., that of a son/daughter who fulfils his/her duty of filial piety by marrying and bearing children). Coming out to the family thus also exerts dual tension: heterosexuality versus homosexuality and the good (filial) versus bad (unfilial) child (Berry 2001; Kong 2011, 94–119, 145–73, 2020, 2021). Coming out of the first closet involves consideration of the sociopolitical environment, including the laws governing homosexuality; public discussion and societal tolerance/intolerance of homosexuality; the presence of LGBT+ subcultures, NGOs, and activism; and even access to physical (living) space. Coming out of the second closet involves a redefinition of the traditional notion of filial piety under familism: (1) unconditional respect and obedience, (2) financial support and affectual care by adult children, and (3) perpetuation of the line of descent through marriage and reproduction and the provision of ritual services to ancestors (Yan 2016).

Second, coming out can be seen as a scaffolding dynamic, an iterative and ongoing process of reconciling the discrepancy between parental expectations and children's expectations of a personal and family life (Jhang 2018). Generally speaking, parents' expectations of their children have shifted from "be normal" to "be happy" while children's expectations of themselves in relation to their parents have shifted from "please one's parents" to "be yourself." Those expectations have changed in conjunction with growing societal acceptance of homosexuality, changes in parenting culture, and a shift toward individualism among the younger Chinese generations (Brainer 2019; Wei and Yan 2021).

Traditionally parents' expectations have been that their children follow the conventional (heterosexual) life course: obtain a stable job, buy an apartment, get married, and have children.[5] Chinese parents tend to equate a lack of conformity with these expectations with unfiliality, shame, and a loss of face (*mianzi*) (cf. Jhang 2018; Shi 2021). This traditional parenting culture shifted toward a new paradigm in the 1980s and early 1990s, which emphasized expert opinions, often from the West, that focused less on children's material needs and more on their emotional and psychological needs and on understanding, communication, and quality time together. This new parenting culture is class-specific, endorsing middle-class privileges[6] even though traditional parenting practices such as corporal discipline are not uncommon.[7] Parents' expectations have slowly shifted to a be-happy discourse, where their children's happiness is fundamental to their own (i.e., what is most important is that one lives a happy life) (Engebretsen 2019).[8]

For children, the dominant expectation is to please one's parents, avoid conflict, or at least maintain a family life in which parents allow them to lead their lives as they see fit (Jhang 2018). Since the 1990s, when the shifting meaning of filial piety emerged as part of the individualization process undergone by the young generation, a "be yourself" discourse slowly emerged, privileging a more individualist quest that asserts "I am who I am" without much care about the reaction of one's parents or one's relationship with them.[9]

The Chinese literature suggests a number of closeting and coming-out strategies. Among various strategies for concealing one's identity are *pianhun* ("fraudulent marriage," such as a gay man marrying a straight woman, usually without disclosing his sexuality to her; Zhu 2017), *xinghun* ("cooperative," "fake," "pro forma," "contract," or "nominal" marriages, such as a gay man marrying a lesbian; see Choi and Luo 2016; Liu and Tan 2020), simply lying (using the "no time, no money" excuse), keeping silent (Kong 2011, 107), leaving home, and compartmentalizing one's family and gay life (Wang, Bih, and Brennan 2009). Coming out can be done with one direct verbal statement or with a two-step approach (first come out as a successful citizen in terms of education and/or career and then as a less-than-desirable son or daughter; Kam 2013, 99). Moreover, disclosure can be planned (deciding to come out at a particular moment and treating it as a big, memorable event) or unplanned (coming out after being suddenly and unexpectedly asked about one's sexual identity by family members). Tacit disclosure is also possible, such as when one implies, "I know you know" (Decena 2008), which is similar to Liu and Ding's (2005) concept of *hanxu* ("implicit," "reserved") in their discussion of the poetics of reticence.[10] One example of this is "coming home," when one brings home an intimate partner without disclosing the same-sex relationship. It is particularly common among those who have departed the family home for study or work and visit their parents only during important annual events such as the Spring Festival (Brainer 2019; Chou 2000; Lee 2018; Wong 2007). "Coming with" is an accommodating strategy. One example is that a gay man simultaneously affirms his sexual identity by implicitly or explicitly telling his parents about his sexuality while conforming to the marriage institution by marrying a lesbian (*xinghun*), thus maintaining family belonging (Huang and Brouwer 2018). More resilient strategies for handling sexuality within the family and wider kinship have emerged but have been adopted primarily by (educated) young people whose pursuit of education and employment allows internal and international migration that renders them often away and distant from home ("stretched kinship"; Wei 2020). Disclosure is not necessarily a one-off event but an ongoing process, with some having to come out repeatedly to certain family members (Grafsky 2014; Jhang 2018). It may lead to full acceptance. Most often, however, it results in a transparent closet (acknowledged with no further discussion) or family closet (hidden from one's broader kinship network, neighbors, friends, and colleagues; Svab and Kuhar 2014), with parents, mothers in particular, fearing being perceived as moral failures (Fields 2001).

No matter which strategy is adopted, gay men act within the parameters of family biopolitics (Ong 1999, 117–19), the series of family practices and ideologies that regulate economic, productive, and successful Chinese bodies. Familial heteronormativity can be seen as the deployment of family biopolitics to produce a subject's sense of moral worth. It requires children, especially sons, to comply with such parental wishes as marrying and bearing children to continue the family blood line and doing nothing to harm the family's status and reputation (Kong 2011, 98). Coming out disrupts those biopolitics, affecting the emotional and moral economies of the family's dyadic relationships. Coming out is not simply a form of identity work or identity politics, as it usually is in the literature of the United States/ United Kingdom, but rather a relational strategy (Brainer 2019), or a form of what I call *relational politics*, under the transformation of family life. The three Chinese societies under study share a Confucian tradition of patrilineal family formation but exhibit distinct socioeconomic and cultural conventions. We now examine how young gay men in the three societies negotiate relational politics under the sway of familial heteronormativity in specific family settings.

Mainland China: Marriage Pressure, Tacit Disclosure, and Not Coming Out as Protection

Over the past few decades, mainland China has witnessed many changes in the structure and functions of the family. The People's Republic of China (PRC) had dictated marital fertility through the one-child policy starting in 1979 but began allowing couples to have two children in 2016 and announced the three-child policy in 2021.[11] The average age of a first marriage in China was 25.7 in 2005 and 28.7 in 2020. The percentage of college-educated men aged twenty-five to twenty-nine who were still single was relatively low in 2005 (46.9 percent in China as a whole and 61.3 percent in Shanghai). It had increased substantially by 2020 (63.6 percent in China as a whole and 64 percent in urban areas), and virtually all college-educated men were married by their late-thirties.[12] Marriage and the pressure to marry remain the norm. Although the three-generation family is in decline, giving way to the nuclear family, and many neoconventional family types and marriage-like arrangements have emerged, the family itself still plays a significant role in China. It not only provides moral privilege and access to social and material power for men but also means that heterosexual marriage (encoded in both the 1950 and 1980 marriage laws) is part of being a filial son or daughter (Kong 2011, 145–73; Kam 2013, 59–71).

With its quest to ensure that people's ultimate loyalty was to the nation, the Chinese Communist Party (CCP) rejected filial piety, most radically during the Cultural Revolution, when it encouraged the young to rebel against their parents, dealing a heavy blow to the ethical basis for intergenerational solidarity. However, traditional filial piety seems to have been restored since the 1980s (Whyte 1997). Moreover, since the 1990s, neoliberal reforms have prompted the Chinese government to reduce its own financial burden by withdrawing from the provision of social welfare and health care. The state has declared that the elderly belong to their children and thus redirected elderly support and care to the family (Tang and Jiang 2013, 1–14; Huang and Brouwer 2018). The government has skillfully commercialized the intergenerational relationship by marketing filial piety through the Family Support Agreement, requiring children to care for their parents. First implemented in rural areas, the agreement is now finding its way to cities (Yeh et al. 2013). Such privatization also means that the family has replaced state authorities as "the chief monitor of people's private lives" and "an effective agent of social control over non-heterosexual subjects" (Kam 2013, 90). Finally, under the Xi regime, the state has reemphasized the importance of traditional family values (filial piety) for the construction of a healthy, civilized, and socialist family nation; it actively incorporates familism into patriotism (Yan 2021). Accordingly, a social-structural lens is relevant, which links state power with family power and the political economy of the family (intergenerational wealth flow, housing payment, the provision of social welfare and health care, the marketization of filial piety) into consideration.

Children of the post-'90s generation were born into this environment. They are the result of the one-child policy, live with family pressure to take care of their parents, received nine years of compulsory education, and enjoy affluence and a consumption-led lifestyle. They face serious homeownership challenges and are critical of urban-rural disparities. Rural-to-urban migration is a common experience, be it for education, work, or love.

Born in 1991 in a small town near Xi'an, Xiaofei is the only son in his family. He lived at home before moving to Shanghai in 2016 to take up a managerial position at an airline company. Xiaofei joined the CCP while studying at a university in Xi'an. His parents both work in state-owned enterprises. He was relatively thin but tall and wore glasses when we first met in 2017. He said his parents were very strict when he was young and overly concerned with his studies: "It was popular at primary school to *kao shuang bai* [obtain "two hundreds," meaning getting full marks in Chinese language and mathematics]. I remember very clearly, at one time, I got 98 and 100. When I got home, my mom used a shoe sole to beat me!"

His mother remains a dominant figure in his life while his father "doesn't govern [*guan*] anything about the family. He never scolds or beats me. His principle is that if you study well, everything is fine."

Xiaofei struggled with his sexuality when he was young. Self-acceptance occurred slowly after making *tongzhi* friends at university. Heteronormative culture, prevalent in cities like Xi'an, was hard to bear: "People think that once you have graduated, you have to get married, you have to have children, you have to buy a flat, and you have to buy a car. If you don't do these things, you have a problem, and you definitely won't be happy." Xiaofei recalled that whenever he and his parents watched television together, his mother would exhibit disgust whenever a feminine male singer appeared or there was a report about gay pride in another country and questioned how it was possible for two men to be together. His mother's disapproval of homosexuality was clear. Migration to big cities like Shanghai is a hidden way out for many *tongzhi* in China (Kong 2011, 145–73; Liu and Tan 2020), and Xiaofei followed suit. When he lived in Shanghai, he talked to his parents only by telephone and at their initiative. He described their conversations in 2017 as follows:

> She is very direct, and asks when I will get married. . . . I make my case by saying that I prefer being single and am very picky, can't really find any girl who suits me. . . . This is the excuse that I make but the pressure is getting more intense, and I am not sure how long this excuse can last. . . . One time I asked whether she would be happy only if she could have grandchildren [even if that meant I married a girl I didn't like]? She said yes! . . . My parents are very traditional. They have lived their whole lives in a *xiaoqu* [microdistrict] of Xi'an. People know people, and parents in China live through other people's eyes. . . . They care too much about whether others think you are happy. If I tell them [about my homosexuality], they will be very sad.

In 2020, Xiaofei went home for Chinese New Year and ended up staying longer than planned because of the COVID-19 outbreak. He seemed to have gained a bit of weight when we chatted over Zoom. He told me that he had had a huge fight with his mother, in which he implicitly came out to her:

> She kept chasing me about the marriage thing. . . . I got very angry and said that I had bought so many things for the family. I [told her that I] didn't buy them because I liked them, but [bought] what you like . . . even if I think it's crap. . . . This is how I treat you, [so] why can't you treat me

like this? I . . . got very emotional, and then I cried for half an hour and locked myself in my bedroom. Later, she knocked on my door, and she started to cry, and she said she knew it [that I am gay], and it's fine if you are happy. . . . The situation was better for only three months, and after that she started to ask me to get married again!

Xiaofei does not like the idea of *pianhun* (marrying a straight woman), as he considers it irresponsible, or *xinghun* (marrying a lesbian), as he doesn't have enough money to do so. He is happy, working in Shanghai on his own without a boyfriend, and having a rather distant relationship with his parents. Since obtaining a master's degree, he has had no financial exchanges with his parents: "They don't give me any money, and neither do I [give them any]. We are quite independent. I don't want them to ask anything about me, and the only way to achieve that is to be financially independent."

Xiaofei's experience is a common one among the young gay generation in China. The family actively nurtures neoliberal values in general and neoliberal masculinity in particular, which reinforces the primacy of individual success, competition, and performance, expressed in Xiaofei's case through his parents' overwhelming concern with his education. Societal understandings of homosexuality help keep such young men in this first closet. Despite the legal and official recognition of homosexuality since the late 1990s, the public discourse (as manifested in media constructions) on gay and lesbian subjects remains negative: crime victims because of their inherent weakness, violent subjects, enemies of traditional values, and a source of social instability (Chang and Ren 2017). Most mainland Chinese participants came from rural areas or remote cities with fewer resources than their urban counterparts. They experienced more difficulties coming out, as their families might not have heard of homosexuality or formed a highly negative opinion of it, and most lacked the support of *tongzhi* NGOs. Coming out of the second closet involves the redefinition of filial piety. Of the three main features of filial piety—obedience, financial support, and marriage—it is marriage that they most commonly reject. China is essentially a marriage society because procreation and social care are primarily arranged within the marriage institution. Homosexuality is not new in Chinese history; what is new is young people using their same-sex love as a justification for rejecting marriage (Shi 2021). Even after Xiaofei tacitly came out to his mother, she still wanted him to get married, but he refused. In the scaffolding process of coming out, he has also modified the other components of filial piety by offering conditional respect to his parents and remaining financially independent as a way to gain autonomy.

Xiaofei's mother wants him to marry simply because it is the norm. Here, the issue of *mianzi* also comes into play. There are two senses of face in China: *lian*, individual face, or a fundamental representation of the integrity of a person's moral character, and *mianzi*, social face, which indicates one's social prestige over and above one's *lian* (Hu 1944). *Mianzi* serves as a parameter of the closet and maintains the heteronormative terms of the moral boundary. Western societies usually view sexuality, intimacy, and marriage as private matters whereas China treats them as family and *mianzi* (social) matters (Choi and Luo 2016). Xiaofei believed that his parents lived in tune with other people's expectations and thus were overly concerned with losing face in the *mianzi* sense. Children generally want to please their parents or at least maintain a stable relationship with them. Of the various coming-out strategies discussed previously, Xiaofei relied primarily on denial (playing the "being picky and wanting to be single" card) and then tacit disclosure. Although he did not speak explicitly about his sexuality to his mother, he recognized that she intuited it and knew that he was gay, especially after their big fight.

Doudou's experience has been very different. Born in Anhui in 1990, he is the only son of a middle-class family, owing to the one-child policy. He moved to Shanghai in 2014 and worked as a freelancer in advertising. He has a medium build, wears glasses, speaks in a soft voice, and does not try to hide his flamboyant mannerisms. When we met in 2017, he told me during the interview that he had had no problem coming out, as he had never hidden his identity, even when young. Although Doudou has a very good relationship with his parents, he developed depression in high school owing to bullying and study pressures. He was prescribed an antidepressant and came out to his parents. Although his parents "felt his pain" and just wanted him to get better, once they realized that he still had strong desires for men, they were not happy. Doudou's parents are medical doctors. Although "fine" with homosexuality as it pertains to others, they were not fine with their son being gay. When his mother insisted that his sexuality "could be changed," he challenged her by asking whether that meant that she could change and be attracted to women: "She then searched [for] information from websites, made notes, talked to her relatives, and finally came to a conclusion that she already knew . . . [that] homosexuality is not a disease!"

Doudou found a job as a translator at an NGO in 2016. He then joined PFLAG, which allowed him to meet other *tongzhi* and their parents and to realize that he was not alone. He then invited his mother to join the group: "She came for a three-day meeting and cried the whole time. She felt much better after that. She later joined as a volunteer and is now responsible for counselling hotlines." His father is an introvert, he explained, and asked that his wife not to be overly harsh with their son. His main concern is that Doudou is happy. Both parents accept his sexuality: "We are now very happy. We can talk about everything, and I am very happy with it." He left Shanghai to stay with his parents during the serious phase of COVID-19 in early 2020 but subsequently moved back. When we chatted over Zoom in late 2020, he was living on his own in Shanghai but still maintained a close relationship with his parents, who help him pay his rent. He also gives them money, but they sometimes help him out financially when he struggles.

Doudou represents an emerging coming-out trend among the young gay generation in China. He experienced few problems coming out as a gay man. He did not need to come out of the first closet, as he considered homosexuality to be as normal as heterosexuality. The second closest was more difficult, however, as he struggled to justify himself as a filial son. Unlike Xiaofei, who maintains a distant relationship with his parents, Doudou enjoys the closeness of his relationship with his parents. Although his redefined conception of filial piety admits rejecting marriage, he still considers it important to provide his parents with financial and emotional support. Doudou came out to his parents after suffering from depression without worrying about his parents' reaction, and they eventually came to embrace his sexuality.

Xiaofei and Doudou represent two poles of the proposed coming-out relational framework. Xiaofei's long struggle with his sexuality contrasts with Doudou's easy acceptance of his. Xiaofei's parents adopted the traditional discourse of "being normal," whereas Doudou's embraced the "be happy" discourse. Xiaofei chose living in the closet, or tacit disclosure, as a way to protect himself and please his parents, whereas Doudou chose to be himself regardless of his parents' reaction. The young generation, particularly the urban middle class, tends to view the traditionally popular closeting strategies, be it *pianhun* or *xinghun*, as generational strategies. They overwhelmingly reject *pianhun*, as they believe it to be both unfair to the straight woman involved and contrary to their true self. Some might consider *xinghun* to be an option, constituting an attempt to "strike a balance between the desire to develop same-sex intimacy and the hope of not being rejected by their parents" (Choi and Luo 2016, 277) but often have to contend with the material difficulties of engaging in such a marriage (Liu and Tan 2020).

Hong Kong: Family Coresidence, "Monster Parents," and Self-Revelation

Hong Kong has also witnessed many changes in family structure and functions in the past few decades: a reduction in family size due to a birth-control campaign, a delay in marriage and parenthood due to increased female participation in the labor force, the increased involvement of grandparents and foreign domestic helpers in childcare, the emergence of so-called monster parents who control every aspect of their children's lives, the increase of marital disruption in families, and the emergence of new, quasi, or nontraditional family arrangements such as cohabitation, double-income no-kids (DINK) families, late-marriage families, step-families, and cross-border families (Leung and Shek 2018). The percentage of college-educated men aged twenty-five to twenty-nine who are still single has been constantly high in Hong Kong (87.7 percent in 2005 and 87.1 percent in 2016).[13]

Traditional familism gave way in postwar Hong Kong to a utilitarian familism that emphasized the norms of mutual assistance in economic exchange, family ownership of property, and economic cooperation (Lau 1982). However, such familism is not inherent in Chinese culture but the effect of state disciplining of refugee/immigrant families. Colonial governance drew skillfully on Chinese filial piety and utilitarian intentions to manage colonialism (Ho 2004; Law 1998), encouraging the people of Hong Kong to seek help from their families (or voluntary agencies or the market) rather than from the government to meet their welfare needs (Ong 1999, 117–19). The situation has changed little since 1997, with the new Hong Kong Special Administrative Region (HKSAR) government endorsing neoliberal values of privatization. The family is thus an important tool of governance over private lives. Neoliberalism prescribes self-responsibility, rendering individuals responsible for their own economic lives. The family has been privatized to the extent that parents expect to be self-reliant and self-managing and do not expect their children to take care of them in their old age (Leung, Lam, and Liang 2020). Accordingly, Hong Kong parents have fewer expectations of grandchildren than their counterparts in China. Although the family has been delinked from the economy and the religiocultural focus on patriliny has weakened, the family has not lost its function and still wields control over the young, especially when they are in their teens (Koo and Wong 2009; Lui 2007). The post-'90s generation live in a materially abundant environment and enjoy a consumption-led lifestyle, but they face a highly competitive educational and working environment and very high property prices as well as a nondemocratic political system increasingly controlled by Beijing.

Born in 2000 into a working-class family, Yoyo lives with his decorator father and cashier mother on a public housing estate. He is his parents' only son. He is six feet tall with a large, quite chubby body. He calls himself "fatfat." Yoyo is the youngest of the research participants. When I met him in 2018, he was studying for a diploma in hotel management and described his parents and their expectations as follows:

> They are monster parents. [When I was a teenager], after school, I had to learn various things requested by my parents: Latin dancing, table tennis, swimming, badminton, volleyball, Chinese painting, calligraphy, drawing, magic, mathematical Olympiad, and piano... but piano [was] the only thing that I really wanted to learn....
>
> They had already planned a life for me... a life I didn't want.... They expected me to be competent, obedient, to study [hard], know good people, etcetera.

Being a good son means being responsible to one's parents, studying hard, and finding a good job. However, once Yoyo was older, his parents began to compromise, respecting his choices and giving him the freedom to develop his own interests and career. That freedom may have stemmed from an individualization process whereby both young people and their parents aspire to be self-reliant and self-responsible, leaving room for the former to develop when they reach young adulthood.

In terms of sexuality, Yoyo realized he was gay when he was ten and has had numerous sexual and romantic experiences since the age of fourteen. He continued his story, "I don't have a private room but I ask my gay friends to come over and play video games.... One time, [my parents] checked my phone and computer and found videos [gay porn] and messages with boys in my chat history.... They then asked me if I was gay. I said, 'If you think I am, then I am.' And then we got into a fight. She [his mother] hit me, and I hit her back." After days of not speaking, his parents softened: "They reluctantly accepted that I won't have children and cannot continue the family bloodline and worry that I might get HIV/AIDS." Yoyo said that although his parents "still want me to 'be normal' and get married," they have accepted that it will never happen. They rarely discuss it these days. Since 2020, he has been working as a concierge at a club, still living with his parents, and maintaining "an okay" relationship with them.

Born in 1991, John is the only child of a middle-class family. He is quite skinny, wears glasses, and has a bookish appearance. He was my first interviewee in Hong Kong. When we talked in early 2017, he told me his coming-out story. He realized he was gay in primary school but also realized that he could be "a smart gay." Although he was quite "sissy," he said, he avoided being bullied by lending his homework to classmates. Hong Kong's highly competitive education environment imposes tremendous pressure on students, but John was always a top student. He graduated from a top university after studying at a traditional, elite secondary school. He has been teaching at a secondary school since graduation. He planned his coming-out for a long time and believed he had laid good groundwork by fulfilling his parents' expectations that he study hard and find a good job and would thus be regarded as a good son with the exception of his sexuality. When he was in Form 6 at secondary school around 1999 and was going out with a guy, he still lived at home.[14] His father would regularly check the messages on his phone. One day during their regular dinner "meetings," his father asked him why he talked to a man for hours every day and exchanged numerous messages with him: "At first, I didn't say I was; I asked[,] 'What's wrong with being gay?' ... I told them there are many gay people who are good and successful ... and then I came out." John said he had a good relationship with his parents, whom he "would never abandon." He moved out in 2016 and lived with his then boyfriend in a tiny rented apartment but visited his parents once a week. After the COVID-19 outbreak in 2020, he told me he moved back in with his parents and now has a new boyfriend. He has introduced all of his boyfriends to his parents, although his father can only remember the name of his current boyfriend, which John thinks is "a good sign." His boyfriend also seems to get along with his parents, even chatting with them on WhatsApp. I told him he should be careful, as they might share secrets about you! Although his parents expect him to be happy, his father frequently reminds him that "this is not an easy road" and is concerned about his health because being a secondary school teacher comes with considerable pressure.

Like the family in mainland China, the family in Hong Kong actively nurtures neoliberal values in general and neoliberal masculinity in particular, which reinforces the primacy of individual success, competition, and performance. Unlike in mainland China, family coresidence is very common in Hong Kong, especially for young unmarried people and the working class (Luk 2020). Although such a living arrangement is by no means new in Hong Kong, what is new is the change in parenting culture.

In the past, when large families were the norm, parents often worked such long hours and were so busy contributing to the family economy that they left their children unattended or to be taken care of by their siblings (Lui 2007). With the reduction in family size and greater societal affluence, Hong Kong parents today, especially middle-class parents, expend greater time, effort, and resources on nurturing their children to give them a head start in life, which is commonly called "winning at the starting line." As a result, they are highly involved and intervene frequently in their children's daily lives, as we saw in the case of the huge array of extracurricular activities in which Yoyo was expected to participate and in John's and his father's daily dinner "meetings." These "monster parents" (Leung and Shek 2018), through their over-parenting and over-nurturing, actively monitor their children's bodies, behaviors, and choices, making it almost impossible for the children to not come out.

The Hong Kong participants, like their mainland counterparts, struggle with two closets: heterosexuality and filial piety. In coming out of the first, young gay men still struggle to convince their parents that homosexuality is not a disease, sin, or abnormal behavior but rather a normal sexual orientation, positive life choice, and human rights issue. In contrast with young gay men in mainland China and previous generations in Hong Kong, however, they have many more resources as society is more tolerant of sexual diversity owing to LGBT+ activism, the pink economy, and the visibility of queerness in the media and public culture. Some of the Hong Kong participants have joined and even brought their parents to gay NGOs.

With respect to the second closet, the decline of parental authority, rise of youth autonomy and power, and greater financial independence have transformed the meaning of filial piety. Yoyo and John, for example, like many of the other Hong Kong participants, interpret filial piety less in terms of obedience to authority and more in terms of affection-based repayment to parents (Yeh et al. 2013). These participants work to fulfill the societal (and parental) expectation that they embrace a neoliberal entrepreneurial masculinity, measured by individual competence and material success in the realms of education and work. They actively reject the requirement to marry and may or may not financially support their parents, depending on their relationship with them and their own salaries.

At the same time, parents' expectation that their children follow a conventional, heteronormative, masculine life course and script has been challenged in Hong Kong. Parents are aware of the difficulties of getting into an elite school, finding a stable job, and buying an apartment and of the various possibilities for intimate relationships such as remaining single, cohabitating, living in a childless or stepfamily, and even same-sex coupledom. In contrast with mainland Chinese families, which tend to view study, work, and marriage as public aspects of life, there is a greater compartmentalization of expectations in Hong Kong, with education and work seen as public, while the issues of marriage and family formation remain private matters for their children. Although Yoyo's parents still adhere to the "be normal" discourse, most of the Hong Kong participants reported that their parents, like John's, tend to endorse the "be happy" discourse, a development that no doubt stems from a modern (particularly middle-class) parenting culture that stresses the well-being and rights of children.

All of the Hong Kong participants have come out to their families, either partially or fully. Their expectations oscillate between pleasing their parents and pleasing themselves, with the latter in the ascendency. John opted for a two-step coming-out process to please his parents: first establishing himself as a successful young man and then as a gay man. Yoyo adopted the straightforward method of self-revelation, caring little about how his parents reacted. Some other participants preferred tacit disclosure ("I know you know"). The closeting strategies of lying, using the "no time, no money" excuse, and keeping silent, common among previous generations (Kong 2011, 107), were rarely reported, as were the practices of *pianhun* and *xinghun* commonly seen in China, which were perceived as irresponsible and contrary to being one's true self. Hong Kong parents' reactions were less oppositional.[15] In some cases, like John's, the reaction was total acceptance. The most commonly reported reaction was silent tolerance. For example, Yoyo's parents did not want to discuss his sexuality, placing him in a transparent closet, or family closet.

Taiwan: Societal and Parental Acceptance and Active Self-Revelation

Similarly, Taiwan has experienced significant demographic changes such as a decrease in the fertility rate, an increase in life expectancy, the postponement of marriage and childbearing, a decline in the marriage rate, and an increase in the divorce rate. The number of college-educated men aged twenty-five to twenty-nine who are still single is high in Taiwan (88 percent in 2010; Davis and Freidman 2014). All of these factors have effected a change in family structures, most obviously the general decline of multigenerational households and nuclear families and the rise of single-person, single-parent, and skipped-generation households (Wang and Yang 2019). Since the 1990s, Taiwan has faced the social impacts of an aging population and low fertility rate, with elderly people living alone or even being homeless becoming increasingly pressing social issues. On the grounds of the three-generation family being the ideal family form, the Taiwanese government has shifted the responsibility for elderly care to individual families, although it has established an elderly care system (F. Wang 2014). Filial belief has changed from an "authoritarian" to "reciprocal" form, with adult children expected to offer financial support to repay parents' care and kindness in raising them (Yeh 2009). Since 2000, in response to strong advocacy for gender equality from state feminism, the Taiwanese government has initiated a series of reforms and policies to rearrange family-care responsibilities: both defamilization policies such as public childcare services and refamilization measures such as parental leave and maternity provisions (Wang and Wang 2014; Yeh, Chou, and Yang 2020). Overall, although the state has tried to redistribute family responsibilities to improve women's social status, social welfare policy in Taiwan still tends toward an "explicit familialism" that reinforces the family role (Fu 2010; S. Y. Wang 2014). The post-'90s generation live in a materially abundant environment and enjoy a consumption-led lifestyle in a fully democratic society, although they are marginalized within international politics, under pressure from mainland China, and suffer low salaries, unemployment, and rising housing prices.

Born in 1993, Hiro lives in a working-class family in Taipei. His father is a private driver for a company, and his mother works in the catering industry. He has three older sisters. He was studying for a master's degree in sociology and living in a university dormitory when I first met him in early 2017. He was quite short and a bit chubby with short hair and was wearing a white sweater. He would be labeled a *bear* in the gay community, although he rejected that term. He talked in a soft voice when he conveyed his coming-out story. Hiro realized he was gay when he was very young and had same-sex sexual experiences while in secondary school. He said he had come out around the time of the 2015 or 2016 Gay Pride event in Taiwan, which attracted considerable media attention:

> It was a few days before Gay Pride, and my mom suddenly came to my room and asked me what I thought about same-sex marriage. I said homosexuals should be able to marry, as it is their basic human right. But she said, this is not what I want to ask; I want to ask if you are homosexual

or not. I didn't reply directly. I just asked, "What if I am?" She then got quite emotional and left my room. The next day, my dad...said, "Your mom said you are a homosexual. Are you?" I thought my dad was quite a sensible person, and so I told him yes. He then said, "Oh, so you won't get married and have children, so you don't need to worship all these ancestral plaques, and you can destroy them."[16] He then cried in front of me. That was the first time and the only time I saw my dad cry. But he does not oppose or deny [me].

Since then, his father has never spoken to him about it, although his mother will occasionally ask him whether he has or wants a girlfriend. His usual reply is, "No...no target...or I don't have such thoughts." His father still presses him about pursuing a career in law, given that his first degree was in this. His mother remains traditional: "She had three daughters before she had me. My grandfather has two sons, my dad and my uncle, and my dad only has me. So the continuation of the lineage is very important for her. I am the spoilt son. She really wants me to get married and have children." When he was studying for his master's degree, he worked as a tutor and regularly gave money to his parents at his mother's request. In 2020, he had just graduated, moved back in with his family, and hoped to start working soon.

I have briefly mentioned Hao in the introduction. He is the only son in his family. His father has passed away, and he lives with his mother. He told me his coming-out story when we first met in the summer of 2017. He said he realized that he had same-sex desires as a secondary school senior when Tongzhi Hotlines came to his school to give a talk. Hao had a very good, intimate relationship with his mother: "Our relationship is not like mother and son but like friends." One day, while having a hotpot meal with his mother, he decided to come out to her as he had a boyfriend:

I really liked him and just wanted to share [my happiness] with my mom. I didn't say I liked boys; I said I liked people older than me...and I showed her a photo, and she said he looked like an indigenous person...and I said yes. And then she was basically willing to listen, and kind of accepted it, but she still said something like that I might be bi[sexual]...as I was too young at that time....After I turned eighteen, she came to realize and accept the fact that I purely like boys....She is quite into Chinese fortune telling, and a *bazhi* [a form of Chinese horoscope] teacher predicted that I would marry late and have two children, so she thinks that I might change later and marry a woman and have two children or marry an older guy and have two children through surrogacy.

Hao was never close to his father and had not come out to him before his death. When I interviewed him again in 2020, he had a new boyfriend who visited him often. His mother considers him to be "a nice guy" who will take care of Hao and so doesn't have any problems with him. His mother supports the family on her own by running a small boutique but has encountered economic difficulties since the outbreak of COVID-19. Hao asked her whether he should suspend his studies and work full time, but she insisted that he finish his master's degree. She would even like him to study for a PhD.

As in mainland China and Hong Kong, the family in Taiwan actively nurtures neoliberal values in general and neoliberal masculinity in particular, which reinforces the primacy of individual success, competition, and performance. The young gay generation in Taiwan also still struggles with the two closets: heterosexuality and filial piety. The first closet is much easier to come out of, though. Even the older generation in Taiwan has fairly good knowledge of homosexuality. Although some parents still view it as abnormal, their children have many resources, allowing them to defend homosexuality as a normal sexual orientation, positive life choice, and human rights issue. The progay government, LGBT+ activism, pink economy, and visibility of queerness in the media and public culture all play a role in shaping the coming-out discourse. Of the three locales under study, LGBT+ activism has achieved the most success in Taiwan. The enactment of the Gender Equity Education Act in 2004 was a landmark achievement, and the young generation has greatly benefited from it. Although many of the Taiwanese participants experienced bullying (primarily in primary or junior high), LGBT+ organizations such as Tongzhi Hotlines regularly give talks on sexual diversity in secondary schools.

To come out of the second closet, the young gay generation has had to redefine filial piety. Filial piety is still considered a core value in Taiwan but has shifted from an authoritarian concept stressing obedience to normative authority to a reciprocal one stressing spontaneous affection and from it fulfilled the desire for collective identification to the psychological need for mutual relatedness within the family. As a result, adult children are expected to offer financial support to their parents to repay them for their care and kindness in raising them (Yeh et al. 2013). With the decline of parental authority and the rise of youth autonomy, Hiro and Hao (and others like them) have chosen to reject marriage, to support their parents financially, and to exhibit limited obedience toward their parents in accordance with the new definition of filial piety.

The expectations of Hiro's parents still belong to the older script of normality, as seen from his father's view that being gay equates to ceasing to worship one's ancestors and his mother's continued request that he marry. His father also wanted him to keep his sexuality secret so as not to bring shame on the family. *Mianzi* remains strong for some Taiwanese families. As we saw in the case of some of the Hong Kong participants' parents, Hiro's parents have compartmentalized their concerns for their son, being more concerned about his public face, as displayed in study and work, and leaving intimacy to the private sphere, which should be covered up, thereby adhering to the transparent family and closeted family scripts. At the same time, rather than seeking to please his parents, Hiro chose self-revelation. Thereafter, both parties kept their distance and no longer discussed the matter. The expectations of Hao's mother, by contrast, hewed more closely to the new-happiness discourse, with the two maintaining an intimate relationship based on communication, understanding, and intimate disclosure. Although his mother would still like him to marry, she would be willing to accept his marriage to a man, with children borne through surrogacy, thereby displaying the rather traditional expectation of marriage and children, albeit with a queer twist. Hao, like many others, has opted to be himself, with his actively planned coming out constituting a memorable episode in his life. Among the young gay generation in Taiwan, most participants have come out to their families (fully or partially) and most chose self-revelation, most actively like Hao—who shared with his mother that he had a boyfriend—although a few did so passively, such as Hiro, when he was asked for his opinion of same-sex marriage during Gay Pride.[17]

Coming Out as Relational Politics

Changes in the family structure, function, and culture and its reconfiguration by the state have had profound impacts on the younger generations in all three societies. At the macro level, the Chinese family has a collaborative relationship with the state under neoliberalism. Through the familization of social-welfare provisions, the state has shifted its financial burden to the family, most notably by promoting filial piety as a cultural asset, and thus the Chinese family, instead of the state, has become a tool of governance and the key provider of social welfare. At the micro level, the Chinese family has shifted from traditional familism to various forms of neofamilism, radically changing the relationship between generations and the younger generations' understanding of success, happiness, and well-being. As we have seen here, the family serves as an important social institution for nurturing neoliberal values, exerting strong control over the participants' lives, and enabling and reinforcing the primacy of individual success, competition, and performance. Neoliberal family forms in the three societies thus govern young gay male bodies at a distance to produce neoliberal entrepreneurial masculinity, albeit in varying degrees. Families in mainland China tend to view study, work, and marriage as three public aspects of *mianzi* whereas Hong Kong and Taiwanese families tend to compartmentalize study and work as public *mianzi* issues while considering marriage a separate, private issue that should be respected and kept silent about.

Neoliberalism, via the family, thus nurtures an environment where these young men believe they are free and rational agents who are able to change themselves and make their own choices (e.g., coming out, getting married, finding a job) but sets the parameters that stress competition, performativity, and heteronormativity for them to follow. The participants of this study, as members of the post-'90s generation, can be seen as active negotiators of what constitutes an appropriate gender role in such a neoliberal culture. Like their heterosexual counterparts, they are under constant pressure to strive for excellence at school and in the workplace. Unlike their heterosexual counterparts, they actively embrace gay masculinity and have turned it from a subordinate masculinity into a more open, acceptable, and normal masculinity. They even challenge straight masculinity as boring, constraining, and rigid. They are creating a new script for gay masculinity within the larger heteronormative culture. They are competitive, performance-oriented, self-reliant, self-responsible, and self-enterprising (Kong 2020). However, the process of gender formation is not simply a process of individualization. These young men must make and remake themselves through a complex series of social interactions. They are not completely disembedded from traditional social institutions such as the family. They have to reconcile their same-sex desires with a heteronormative way of life and negotiate filial piety within the family institution (the double closet) and undertake a process of scaffolding that involves reconciliation between their parents' and their own expectations. Relative to previous generations, the young generation today generally chooses to come out. Nearly all of the Hong Kong and Taiwanese participants have come out to their families in full or in part, although their mainland counterparts are still struggling between coming out and living in the closet, with those living in urban areas generally finding it easier to come out than those living in rural areas. These young Chinese men, embracing the enterprising self, devise various coming-out and closeting tactics to conform to, negotiate, resist, or even challenge neoliberal family values to differing extents in the three societies, which reflect the different processes of individualization and degrees of family disembeddedness arising from the particular sociopolitical circumstances of Hong Kong (Koo and Wong 2009), Taiwan (S. Y. Wang 2014), and mainland China (Hansen and Svarverud 2010; Yan 2010).

Coming out to the family has always been difficult in most places across the globe, and there are many similarities between the Western and Chinese experiences. However, the close relationship between the self and the Chinese family suggests that coming out is best viewed not just through the lens of identity politics but rather as relational politics. The participants are not expected to leave behind the collectivity of their natal family; they maintain strong bonds of reciprocal support with their parents into adulthood. Coming out is thus a reconciliation with family relations. The Chinese individual is widely understood as a relational self within a structured, socially reciprocal, and hierarchically ranked web of interpersonal relations with specific roles, duties, and obligations (Fei 1992; Yan 2016; Wang and Liu 2010).[18] Such a conceptualization of the individual consists of the small or individual self, centered on personal desires and interests, and the great or relational self, which bears the interests of a collectivity such as the family, kin, and the state. This great or relational self in traditional China was one's ancestors, but it was replaced by the socialist nation-state in the Mao era in mainland China, by utilitarian familism in postwar Hong Kong, and by traditional familism in post-1949 Taiwan. It is mostly embodied as the perfect children of the third generation, who today carry the burden of realizing the dreams of their parents and grandparents (cf. Yan 2016). The coming-out practices of the young gay generation in the three Chinese societies thus carry such a burden, exemplified by the discrepancy between the small and great self, between the individual and relational self, and between individuality and collectivity, manifested in the tension between individual and family interests. It is in this context that coming out in the Chinese context usually involves the double closet. The family is thus the main site of relational politics in identity formation: struggling with study and work within a highly competitive education and precarious working environment in order to achieve success, and partly to fulfil parental expectations; leaving one's hometown to achieve freedom (especially in mainland China and parts of Taiwan) while maintaining an acceptable or caring relationship with parents; reconciling same-sex desires with familial and social definitions of normal sexuality; yearning for sexual freedom while negotiating familial obligations of marriage and childbearing (especially in mainland China); and pursuing individual happiness and family prosperity and continuity. What lies at the core of these tensions is the pursuit of happiness (Ahmed 2010; Wielander 2019). Happiness is part of this relational politics. It is less an individual essence or state of being than a social project that tells us stories about "becoming happy, searching for happiness, struggling with unhappiness and so on" (Engebretsen 2019, 103).

Tongzhi Commons, Community, and Collectivity

If coming to terms with one's sexuality and disclosing it to close family members such as one's parents is the first coming out, then for most *tongzhi*, there is also a second coming out: coming out to the *tongzhi* world, coming into the *tongzhi* circle, and living a *tongzhi* life. This chapter focuses on this second coming out and examines the relationship between the *tongzhi* community and *tongzhi* identity. The past decade has witnessed the emergence and consolidation of new and established queer communities in most of East and Southeast Asia (McLelland and Mackie 2015; Yue and Leung 2017), and they have not neatly followed the developmental trajectory of Western gay cities such as San Francisco, London, or New York, which is primarily based on the sexual liberation/identity model. Instead, they have followed the logic of disjunctive modernities (Appadurai 1996, 2013), mediated by neoliberalism, developmentalism, colonialism, the pink economy, and the state (Yue and Leung 2017); discrepant modernity (Rofel 1999), with development always seen as deferred from Western modernity; or compressed modernity (Chang 2010), with the development of sexual identity, community, and citizenship in these societies being compressed in both time and space compared to the West.

This chapter takes a closer look at the *tongzhi* worlds of Hong Kong, Taiwan, and mainland China in all of their facets. I argue that the *tongzhi* world features two types of community engagement—large-scale collectives and small-scale personal communities or commons—where affective/ emotional and imaginative/translocal dimensions are crucial. Moreover, the *tongzhi* world, or more specifically the gay world, is governed by a new dominant ideology, what I call *homonormative masculinity*—a combination of hegemonic masculinity (Connell 1995) and homonormativity (Duggan 2002)—under the forces of neoliberalism, developmentalism, cosmopolitanism, and nascent consumerism. Young gay men in the three societies engage in the *tongzhi* world in different ways: cross-national consumption engagement in Hong Kong, fragmentary engagement in mainland China, and diffusive engagement in Taiwan. These differential engagements illustrate the disjunctive logics whereby "legislation, economic and cultural policies, activism and social movement, and the myriad quotidian practices of queer subjects do not align neatly but rather contradict or complicate one other" (Yue and Leung 2017, 761).

Queer Asian Cultures and Communities in Disjunctive, Discrepant, and Compressed Modernities

There is a well-established body of Western literature examining the complex relationship between sexuality, community, and space. I have argued (Kong 2012a, 897) that early work sought to map visible gay and lesbian communities, connect sexual politics to the politics of space (Levine, 1979), and show how people actively produce and heterosexualize space through resistance and contestation. These studies focused on the urban lives of middle-class, white, gay men in North American cities, whereas later work extended the analysis to the production of lesbian spaces (Valentine 1993) and rural queer spaces (Kramer 1995), and to the United Kingdom (Whittle 1994) and Europe (Binnie 1995). More recently scholars have highlighted the hybrid and fluid nature of sexual identities (LGBT+), acknowledging that space is simultaneously sexed, gendered, classed, and racialized. Their investigations of the multidimensionality and intersectionality of queer lives have focused on the paradigms of ethnicity (Sinfield 1996), gentrification (Bell and Binnie 2004), creativity (Florida 2002), and metronormativity (Halberstam 2005), often in discussions of such typically gay cities as San Francisco, New York, London, Toronto, and Sydney (see also Bell and Valentine 1995; Ingram, Bouthillette, and Retter 1997; Oswin 2008).

Central to this literature is the shifting meaning of the queer community, which was traditionally understood in relation to sexual liberation, linking identity with community and sexual politics under the coming-out model

(Weeks 1985). Gay life in the Western world seems to have gone through three periods. The first, the closeted era (1940s–1950s), was characterized by concealment; isolation; feelings of shame, guilt, and fear; and the living of a double life, partly in the gay scenes of parks, public toilets, and underground bars. The second, the coming-out era (1960s–early 1990s), was typified by being open and feeling positive about one's sexuality and constructing almost exclusively gay social networks. And finally the third, the postgay era (late 1990s–), is distinguished by the increasing assimilation of gays into the mainstream and the overlapping of the gay and straight worlds alongside rapid internal diversification within the gay community (Ghaziani 2011; Holt 2011; Seidman 2002). Cities have their own histories, and their development of queer communities that provide solidarity, autonomy, and safety, especially during the AIDS crisis in the 1980s, can be seen as an example of the power of love. Nonetheless, the development of queer communities can also be seen as an example of gentrification, tourism, and cosmopolitanism, with internal splits, schisms, exclusions, and domination along the lines of class, race, gender, age, and so forth (Nash and Gorman-Murray 2014; Puar 2002). Recent discussions have turned to the idea of the queer commons, instead of queer communities, to "build broader political commonalities and establish resources that serve queer communities marginalized by mainstream LGBT politics" (Millner-Larsen and Butt 2018, 401). A queer commons indicates the existence of a range of diverse economies: alternative, ethical, and not-for-profit social enterprises (Brown 2009). Various queer energies and commons-forming attempts—from activist provision of social services to the maintenance of networks centered on queer art, protest, public sex, and bar culture—sustain queer lives otherwise marginalized by heteronormative society and mainstream LGBT+ politics (Millner-Larsen and Butt 2018). The idea of a queer commons may appear anachronistic under global capitalism, which seeks to privatize and commodify social life. Another debate has centered on the decline of traditional gay communities in the past decade and, more specifically, on the decline of gay bars and other consumption venues. Anderson and Knee (2021) give three explanations for this decline: (1) society has entered a postgay era characterized by widespread social acceptance, with queer enclaves no longer necessary; (2) postgays favor the use of technology (location- and social-based smartphone applications) to form community; and (3) queer enclaves, usually located in underdeveloped but revitalized and commercialized spaces, are now attractive to heterosexuals who see them as hip and trendy and have recolonized them. Renninger (2019) argues that Grindr (a dating app for gay and bisexual men) has not killed gay bars and that the decline of gay community should be understood in the socioeconomic and political context of urban development. The third debate is to understand how individuals are disembedded from traditional communities and organizations but reembedded in multiple networks of relationships facilitated by the Internet, social media, and mobile dating apps in what Rainie and Wellman (2012) call "networked individualism." Gay men in particular seem to have benefited from these mediated sexual communities, forming "networked intimacy" (Hobbs, Owen, and Gerber 2017), wherein they conduct "flirting, courtship and the ongoing search for love and fulfilment via dating apps and smartphones" (282; cf. Chan 2018) or "collective intimacy" (Hakim 2018), wherein they desire "an intimate mode of collectivity during an historical moment when collectivity itself is being superseded by competitive, entrepreneurial individualism" (250).

As Yue and Leung (2017) have noted, Euro-American studies of gay cities have mapped the rise of commercial gay neighborhoods by combining the history of ghettos and the postcloset geography of community villages. In doing so, they provide a dominant model of sexual minority rights, group recognition, and homonormative mainstream assimilation, which links emancipation, rights, assimilation, and equality together. If Western modernity has been shaped by the Enlightenment logic that arose from industrial capitalism, a different theoretical framework is needed to understand the rise of the queer Asian city and Asian modernities. A macro approach offers a lens for an alternative modernity—be it disjunctive, discrepant, or compressed—which is a process of understanding the modern Asian city through a range of "convergent and conflictual forces of tradition, colonialism, postcolonial developmentalism, global neoliberalism as well as the everyday practices of worlding that have produced the spaces and experiences of urbanism" (Yue and Leung 2017, 750). A micro approach is to understand how young gay men in Chinese contexts engage with social institutions. As we saw in chapter 2, they are not completely disembedded from traditional social institutions such as the family. In this chapter, we will see how they are reembedded in new sexual communities through the Internet, social media, and dating apps.

The young gay men in this study have two main types of engagement with the *tongzhi* community. The first is collective community attachment, such as attending annual gay events, joining circuit parties during festive times, or visiting gay bars on the weekend. These assemblies of bodies into groups can achieve "feeling together." But what is more common is the second type of engagement, such as daily engagement (whether online or off) with personal communities (Holt 2011). These are smaller, customized, personal, and informal networks comprising boyfriends, ex-boyfriends, and gay and straight male and female friends with whom one feels a sense of belonging, solidarity, and support. While the first form of engagement offers a sense of community, indicating a shared but rather static and homogeneous collective identity embedded largely in the visible profit-driven pink businesses that constitute the mainstream commercial gay scene, the second comes closer to the notion of "the commons," where participants are not bound together by a shared identity or culture but "related primarily by their shared interest in defending or producing a set of common resources" (Gilbert 2013, 165). This engagement indicates a range of diverse, alternative, not-for-profit economies and networks outside the mainstream commercial gay communities.

In addition, regardless of whether the engagement is with large-scale collectivities or small-scale personal communities, two dimensions are important. The first is the affective-emotional dimension—that is, what binds young gay men together. This might be their commitment to some common good (fighting for equality) or identification with being gay (I am gay or *tongzhi*) but is most often a set of shared sentiments and sensations. It is this emotional attachment that makes them feel connected to the community. An emergent culture tries to "designate a specific complex of ideas, practices, experiences and sentiments which do not necessarily cohere into a single, homogeneous world view, but which are constituted by a particular 'unit of distribution'... of meanings, sentiments, sensations and possibilities" (Gilbert 2013, 151). This affective "structure of feelings" (Williams 1977)—the meanings and values we actively live and feel—is the "unstated residue of collective life" (Berlant 2012, 77). The second dimension of engagement with the *tongzhi* community is the imaginary dimension. Gay identity "entails several ways to affirm oneself and one's imagined community...in a way that creates a feeling of belonging" (Ghaziani 2011, 103). If modern nations can be seen as "imagined communities" (Anderson 1983), then modern queer experiences can be seen as imagined queer communities, characterized by Altman (1997) as a "global gay identity" that radically dichotomizes the global and the local, with the global level representing the West as the origin of gayness. However, in "imagined geographies" (Martin 2009; cf. Said 1978) this hegemonic queer worldview, which privileges a particular white male gaze, has now shifted to transnational or inter-Asian referencing rather than global gayness, a new structure of thinking and feeling about sexuality for Asian young gay men in an era of accelerated transnational flows of information and culture. For example, Kang (2017) discusses the new process of the racialization of Asianness and reorientation of young Asian men's desire away from Caucasian partners toward East Asian ones (whom he calls "white Asians"), a process facilitated by transnational or regional flows of media and communication, the Internet and telecommunications technologies in particular, the proliferation of budget airlines, and transnational or regional alignments and politics.

Finally, apart from the form and dimension of community engagement, the *tongzhi* world, or more specifically the gay community, is exhibiting a new logic of normativity. Under neoliberalism, Euro-American mainstream societies expect a particular kind of sexual citizen: "[T]o be gender conventional, link sex to love and a marriage-like relationship, defend family values, personify economic individualism, and display national pride" (Seidman 2002, 133). This neoliberal turn in the West has prompted the queer subject to move from the policing of the self to formulating a desire for normativity and respectability (Richardson 2005, 2015). It is because of this reconstruction of the queer subject that the queer community endorses the notion of homonormativity, which endorses a privatized, depoliticized gay culture centered around domesticity and consumption (Duggan 2002). The Western construction of sexualized gay imagery presents homonormativity as the model for a good sexual citizen. It is performative and judgmental, positioning "bad" homosexuals—defined as campy, fat, skinny, old, sick with HIV/AIDS, "promiscuous," on drugs, working class or provincial, for sale, into public sex—as irresponsible, shameful, and deserving of regulation and punishment (cf. Dangerous Bedfellows 1996; Halperin and Traub 2009).

Such a neoliberal turn has also occurred in Chinese societies. In the past, gay men were controlled through criminal laws governing homosexual conduct (outright criminalization in Hong Kong, offenses against virtuous customs in Taiwan, and the crime of "hooliganism" in mainland China). Such control has been relaxed in all three societies, with gay men transformed from criminals or social outcasts into liberal, democratic (Taiwan), cosmopolitan, consumerist (Hong Kong), and postreform, *suzhi* (mainland China) subjects who embrace the core values of responsibility, respectability, and middle-class sensibility (see chapter 1). Homonormativity is now widely appropriated, mediated, and circulated outside Western societies. Embedded within the logic of cosmopolitanism and neoliberal individualism, the Chinese *tongzhi* community, the gay community in particular, has combined homonormativity and hegemonic masculinity (Connell 1995), which privileges certain men and disadvantages others under a hierarchy of masculinities, into a new culture of performativity that I call *homonormative masculinity*. Chinese gay men increasingly aspire to be straight-acting (cis-gender), young (age), and possess a defined gym body (physically fit and healthy looking); privilege a coupled relationship (monogamy) or emotionally exclusive dyadic couple intimacy; and indulge in a consumption-based, cosmopolitan lifestyle (attain middle-class status). They often also endorse a privatized, domesticated, and apolitical (nonradical, nonsubversive) life. Homonormative masculinity can thus be seen as centering the sexual field on four aspects: body and gender performance, coupled intimacy, middle-class sensibility, and political conservatism.

Hong Kong: The Pink Economy and Cross-National Consumption

In Hong Kong, neoliberal development and postcolonial developmentalism have more or less followed the capitalist logic of the pink economy, which is subject to licensing regulations and the government's high land-price policy, with *tongzhi* visibility in the queer media world but with limited political development of sexual rights in civil society. The government's high land-price policy mitigates against the formation of visible queer neighborhoods. Two-generation households remain the norm, with young people unable to afford leaving the family home and aged parents unable to afford living apart from their adult children (Yue and Leung 2017; Luk 2020). Patrolling consumption venues (bars, clubs, saunas, karaoke bars, cinemas, shopping malls) or traveling to other East and Southeast Asian societies (mainland China, Taiwan, Japan, Korea, and Thailand) have become popular for gay men and lesbians. Hong Kong *tongzhi* bodies are not private, domestic bodies but rather public, consuming, cross-national bodies (Kong 2011, 73–93; Tang 2011, 41–63). Upscale, conspicuous-consumption venues are scattered primarily around Lan Kwai Fong, Soho, Wan Chai, and Causeway Bay on Hong Kong Island, whereas working-class, inconspicuous-consumption venues are centered around Tsim Sha Tsui, Jordan, Yau Ma Tei, and Mong Kok.

The Hong Kong participants in this research learned about what it means to be gay when they were in their teens through interactions with social institutions such as school and, more importantly, the Internet. Born in 1993 as the only son of a working-class family, Wei went to Beijing to study Chinese medicine at university at the age of twenty but dropped out after one year when he discovered that the discipline required memorization alone. He has been working in the catering industry since 2000. He is one of the very

陪伴是最幸福嘅安慰

FIG. 3.1. Vibranium Hong Kong, a bar in Causeway Bay where a lot of young gay men hang out (source: Vibranium).

few among the Hong Kong participants who has not come out to his parents even though he thinks his mother knows. Of average build, Wei is witty and speaks quite fast. In 2017, when I interviewed him, his engagement with the gay community was typical of the Hong Kong participants: "[When] I was in secondary school . . . I watched pornography online, men and women and men and men . . . they were all Westerners. I particularly remember a scene [in which two men] did 10 [local parlance for anal intercourse]. . . . I realized I would like that . . . and I asked myself why . . . and then I watched a lot [laughed] and searched a lot. . . . I fell in love with a classmate and we hung out all the time . . . but he wasn't [gay]." Wei's experience with pornography led him directly to sexual communities: "In Form 6, I started using tt1069 [the most popular gay website and chatroom in Hong Kong] . . . and also joined Elements [a gay nongovernmental organization (NGO)] . . . where I met my first boyfriend...but it only lasted for three months....I met my second boyfriend on Grindr." Wei has never been to a gay bar, as he does not think he would like them. He is comfortable with having sex outside a relationship and usually goes to saunas for sex. Thus far, he has had six intimate relationships, all with men he met through *tongzhi* NGOs, saunas, or dating apps. He is now with his sixth boyfriend and enjoys being part of a couple but has little engagement with the gay community, although he once took part in a pride walk with Elements: "I was holding a banner but didn't feel anything very special."

Andy enjoys a colorful consumption-based, cross-national gay life. Born in 1992 to a middle-class family, he was educated in Canada and holds a Canadian passport. He currently works in finance in Hong Kong and lives with his boyfriend. He has a handsome face with a beard and a well-built body; he works out a lot at a gym. He is out to his parents and visits them frequently. Andy gave me a sense of his engagement with the gay community when I interviewed him in 2017. His initial exploration of the gay world was via Tinder (a straight dating app with an option for men interested in men). He met a man on Tinder, with whom he had his first sexual experience, but their relationship didn't work out. Andy then had a few affairs while on exchange programs in Guangdong, China, and in the United States. He met his current boyfriend while at university in Hong Kong. Andy described himself as an extrovert and his boyfriend as an introvert. In his free time, he enjoys playing online board games with his boyfriend and his boyfriend's friends, which he said offers "an important sense of belonging to others." However, he prefers going to gay bars with his own friends: "Just 'me' time....My friends and I...gather together and drink together, which is fine." Although he has tried saunas, he said, "It's not my thing." He often travels to attend parties in Japan, Taiwan, Korea, and Thailand, where "everyone is using drugs, and there are so many gay men coming from everywhere, and you know so many different people, and you go with your so-called sisters....It is so sweet; you take care of each other...and that sounds like a family." When I saw Andy in 2020, he had built up a lot of muscle and become quite bulky. He told me that since 2019 he has been part of a circle of seven to eight friends who are into chemfun, the local parlance for chemsex (i.e., drug consumption, often in a group context, to enhance sexual pleasure; see chapter 1, note 16, for more details). They are all "muscle bears," a slang term in gay circles that usually refers to stocky and hairy gay men. He said they meet regularly, mainly in hotels, to engage in "intense" sex and have an "intimate connection with others." He has never participated in Hong Kong Gay Pride (although has been to Gay Pride in Taiwan) but has participated in Pink Dot Hong Kong twice: "[I] just wanted to see friends, drink, and talk, and we don't really think about equality or any higher goods."

Wei and Andy represent two cases for illustration. Like many young gay men in Hong Kong, they have a rather strong gay identity. They find other gay men for love, sex, and friendship through heterosexual social institutions (school or university), traditional gay-identified communities or scenes (saunas and bars; some others report sex in public spaces such as public toilets and swimming pools), and *tongzhi* NGOs and social self-help groups (Elements) as well as through the new mediated online channels of gay websites (tt1069) and dating apps (Tinder, Grindr). These channels have increasingly become the dominant means by which young gay men in Hong Kong find emotional, romantic, and sexual liaisons.

Young gay men participate in collective community attachment or immerse themselves in personal communities or commons with affection and imagination. For example, for some of the Hong Kong participants, joining a pride walk or participating in Pink Dot helps them feel like part of the collective fighting for equality and justice, while for others, like Wei and Andy, these activities are merely ways to chill out and enjoy entertainment. For some, the consumption of recreational drugs in a chemfun setting offers a way to connect to other naked bodies intensively and intimately, allowing them to "feel together." For others, playing online video games with gay and non-gay friends or acquaintances is a way to enjoy nonproductive moments together, whereas engaging in group chats on WhatsApp or LINE; surfing, commenting on, or contributing to Hehe Secrets;[1] reading gay news on Facebook; browsing gay porn on Twitter; and following friends or admirers' posts and selfies on Instagram are all ways to learn about other gay men's life struggles (and/or to share their own) and express the anger, rage, remorse, joy, and happiness of everyday gay life. These shared (material, sexual, and affective) interests produce a set of common resources (online chat groups), a domain of creative potential (Hehe Secrets), or experimentation (chemfun) that provide a communal alternative to mainstream urban gay life (Brown 2009; Gilbert 2013). Although many Hong Kong gay men watch Western gay movies (*Call Me by Your Name*) and enjoy a queer reading of superhero tropes in Marvel movies, what they find most relevant to their lives is engagement with Asian gay culture, particularly that of Taiwan, Japan, Korea, and Thailand.[2] Owing to the relatively strong economic power of Hongkongers, traveling to other Asian countries is normalized for most Hong Kong gay men, even working-class gay men, allowing them to attend circuit experiences in Bangkok, Tokyo, Seoul, and Taipei during festive periods such as Easter, Christmas, and New Year.

Finally, encounters with homonormative masculinity are frequent for the Hong Kong participants. For example, Wei noted that the gay community "is ... divided between those who go to the gym ... and those who are sissy types," bluntly adding that gay men who are "campy, fat, old, and ugly" are highly marginalized. Almost all of the participants expressed ambivalence toward the gay community. This new homonormative masculinity is performative, emphasizing efforts to accomplish its ideal. Leonard, born in 1995 to a middle-class family, is out to his parents and lives with them on a private housing estate. After splitting up with his boyfriend in 2019, he decided to train and strengthen his body. He goes to the gym almost every day, employs three personal trainers, and engages in a hard-core training program with a strict diet and rigorous exercises. He has thus developed a lean, fit, athletic body—a standard model figure. Leonard has many followers on Instagram and is regularly photographed by amateur photographers. One of his goals for the new year of 2021 was to build up more muscle. He has never been on a pride walk and does not think participation is necessary. He buys into the whole notion of homonormative masculinity: private consumption, a middle-class lifestyle, and being politically conservative and self-enterprising. He wants to be a typical *sunshine* (similar to the US gay slang *twink*): the athletic, next-door type of key opinion leader (KOL) who educates his followers to be positive, decent good boys. For Leonard, *sunshine*, *athletic*, and *healthy* equal good while *camp*, *sissy*, and *femme* equal bad. Happy, by contrast, wants to be a bad boy. Born in 1990, he is into chemfun and barebacking. A person living with HIV, he is an erotic masseur and cyberporn star. Using steroids to build up muscle while working out every day, Happy has a sought-after, well-built, tattooed body. Although he embodies the bad-boy type, he still upholds the homonormative masculine ideal: masculine, stocky, wicked; not camp, sissy, or femme. Whether Internet celebrity or Internet porn star, Leonard and Happy are both subject to the cruel logic of homonormative masculinity. It is only very recently that some of the Hong Kong participants have challenged part of this ideal due to the divided political orientations in 2019 (see chapter 4 for details).

Mainland China: Fast-food Gays, Online Experience, and Fragmented Collectivity

Mainland China can be seen as offering another example of modernities—whether disjunctive, discrepant, or compressed—that do not follow the linear model of emancipation, rights, assimilation, and equality. The urban *tongzhi* community in mainland China has been influenced by two notable neoliberal developments. The first is rural-urban migration, with large numbers of people migrating from rural areas to major cities for work, love, and freedom or simply to experience a new world. Within this mass-scale, visible migrant flow is a hidden queer migration, with numerous young gay men moving to cities to escape the rural homophobic environment and family pressure to marry, realize their gay sexuality, and seek out romantic and sexual liaisons (Gong 2021; Kong 2011, 143–93). Some become money boys who provide sexual services to other men (Kong 2012b, 2017). The second notable development is the emergence of the gay Internet. Because physical queer spaces are regulated and frequently raided by the police, many *tongzhi* have shifted to the Internet. Cao and Lu (2014) argue that this shift has brought about two changes: the first is "to create online virtual public spaces where people can find everything necessary for a gay community" (845), and the second is "the proliferation of online queer-focused discourse among online mainstream media and straight people in recent years" (846).

In Shanghai, Wei (2015) argues that "traditional homosexual public space" (23), such as public parks, squares, gardens, bathhouses, and dance halls, has slowly been replaced by "commercialized public space" (24). Hence, the "homosexual golden triangle" (30) (i.e., the Bund, or *Waitan*, Suzhou River, and Hankou Road), featuring bars mainly tailored to and visited by homosexuals, has been replaced by a new, modern, cosmopolitan gay ghetto in the former French Concession area featuring bars, restaurants, gyms, and boutiques. This new gay ghetto contrasts sharply with the dilapidated areas north of the Suzhou River, where the La La Dancehall, a seedy dance hall catering to older married gay men, the working class, migrants, and money boys, once stood. Owing to social stigma and the state regulation of homosexuality, gay neighborhoods are not easy to form. Although political public space once existed, featuring advocacy by grassroots NGOs (primarily with respect to HIV/AIDS prevention but also focusing on reducing stigma and advocating for rights), it has been greatly diminished in recent years.

Born in Shanghai in 1997, Cody was taking a break from his university studies when I first met him in 2017 but had resumed them in 2020. He has a medium build with a very tender voice. He is still in the closet and has not come out to his parents yet. During our interview in 2017, he described his engagement with the gay community. He realized his same-sex desires while visiting porn websites around the age of ten. When he was around fifteen, he said, "I started to open up.... Dating apps started to become popular. I then used dating apps and watched forums." However, he had difficulties finding boyfriends or even friends through dating apps: "There are not many ways to know and communicate with others, so you can only use cruising as a means to connect with people." Cody has never been to a gay bar, sauna, or massage parlor, nor has he joined a parade, as he fears being arrested. But he would very much like to attend a gay pride event in Taiwan. He said, "I met a guy before coming to Shanghai, and he told me about Shanghai Pride Week. I wanted to join but then found out you needed to speak English. I just wanted to be a volunteer but their requirement was so high." A number of Shanghai Pride activities were celebrated during the course of 2020, including a pride run in June, but all activities from August onward were canceled. Even though Cody was still interested in participating to some degree, he never got the chance to do so. In 2020, when I talked to him again, he described his life as "just studying and playing video games" such as Final Fantasy FF14, World of Warcraft, and Overwatch. All of Cody's offline friends were met during online chats: "They got me into a group who played World of Warcraft, and they were all *tongzhi*. I then met with them offline once. But my feeling was that they have all known each other [for a long time]. I felt like an outsider. It was hard to get into their circle.... And I was still a student, and the talking topics were unrelated, so I quit." Now, he uses apps (Blued) primarily to find sex partners: "It's mainly for sex. They are fast-food gays. If you use apps to find friends or others, it's impossible."

Born in Anhui in 1994, Xinxin's same-sex desires were confirmed when he watched *Brokeback Mountain* on his father's phone. His parents were both school teachers. He is very hairy and skinny and would be called a *monkey* in gay circles. In 2017, he told me about his interesting engagement with the gay community: "In Anhui, the atmosphere was very conservative.... I received my whole gay education in Senior Two [grade 11 of high school] from a female classmate who was a *fujoshi* [a Japanese term referring to a female fan of Boys Love (BL) novels]." That is, his knowledge of homosexuality came from a straight girl who had learned about homosexuality through Chinese translations of Japanese manga. When he graduated from Senior Three (grade 12 of high school), Xinxin came out to his parents, who were quite accepting. He then began using dating apps: "At that time, you didn't need

FIG. 3.2. Shanghai Pride Run 2020 (source: ShanghaiPRIDE). The participants who joined this Pride Run included heterosexual and LGBT+ people. No assumption should be made about the sexual orientation of those depicted in the photo.

a VPN and could receive photos. But now you do [need a VPN]. There were very few people using Jack'd [a dating app for gay and bisexual men] in Anhui. The nearest one was 1 km [0.62 miles] away...but even just for chatting, it was the first time that I knew a real homosexual online." He did not meet any gay men in person until he moved to Shanghai to attend university. He met his first boyfriend, who was also his first sex partner, on Jack'd and continues to find boyfriends primarily through dating apps. In university, he started to explore the gay world and go to gay bars: "We went to Lucca at 10ish; there were already a lot of people there. At around 12, we were on the dancefloor, but it was so crowded that we could not stand.... I didn't like it.... I did go to darkrooms...but not saunas." His engagement with the gay community has not been through economic consumption but rather through *tongzhi gongyi* (public interest/welfare) and, more specifically, *tongzhi* activism at university. In 2014, he managed a high school *tongzhi* group and joined an independent *tongzhi* webcast, where he helped create Chinese subtitles for foreign queer movies. In 2015, he joined a queer youth-training program organized by the Beijing Tongzhi Centre, which further opened his eyes to gender and sexuality issues. With increased state control over civil society, however, Xinxin has recently encountered a number of difficulties. For example, in 2016, he helped organize the equivalent of a TED Talk. The event was then canceled the following year with no reason given, and the organizers, including Xinxin, were asked to "talk" to domestic security officers.

In contrast to their Hong Kong counterparts, young (especially middle-class) gay men in urban China engage with the gay world primarily through the Internet, as seen in the cases of both Cody, who complained of being able to find only "fast-food" gays, and Xinxin, who didn't physically meet anyone else who was gay when he lived in Anhui. They risk being caught if they cruise public spaces, which are still largely dominated by the unemployed, members of the working class, migrants, and/or money boys. In Shanghai, most gay bars and clubs (Lucca 390, Happiness 42) are located in the Changning District. They attract an international and local crowd but are subject to the occasional police raid. Moreover, most gay bars across China require patrons to reserve a table and favor pink consumption by groups rather than by singles looking for sex and/or romance. Political gay spaces flourished before 2012, but have been heavily regulated since. Online dating apps have thus become the predominant way to find others for love, sex, and friendship.

Also unlike in Hong Kong, there is hardly any collective physical community attachment in mainland China; big annual gay events are rare. Shanghai Pride Week is a cultural festival with an art exhibition, film screenings (usually held in embassies to avoid censorship), and a party but no pride walk. The event is heavily dominated by expatriates and so attracts mainly overseas queers and upper-middle-class *tongzhi*, which is why Cody, even though Shanghainese, was unable to participate even as a volunteer. In any case, Shanghai Pride Week was suspended in 2020, and it is unknown whether it will be held again in the future.[3] Big clubs in Beijing, Shanghai, Chengdu, and Shenzhen require a high level of consumption and are subject to the occasional police raid, and gay raves have largely disappeared due to the country's strict drug policy. Most *tongzhi* in China have no offline collective experience, although the younger generation is increasingly enjoying a collective experience online. Despite strict state censorship of homosexual content, they can read short-lived, gay-themed Internet novels and watch television dramas and discuss them on social media such as Weibo (the Chinese version of Twitter) and even use Twitter if they have a VPN. The most famous example of a drama discussed by the participants and the *tongzhi* community as a whole is *Addicted* on webTV, adapted from an online Boys Love (BL) novel that depicts a romantic relationship between two male high school students. It generated over ten million views when it aired in early 2016 but was then removed from all Chinese video-streaming websites by the authorities because of its explicit homosexual content. Currently popular are adaptations of gay- and BL-themed Internet novels into non-gay-themed TV dramas, with the original romance and erotic bond between two men rewritten into "socialist brotherhood" between two heterosexual men, emphasizing "bromance" and a homosocial connection (Ng and Li 2020). Frequently cited examples are *Guardian*, *The Untamed*, *Word of Honor*, and *Winter Begonia*. Collective online viewing experiences and the posting of comments on social media are crucial to helping young gay men identify with one another. Many also readily immerse themselves in personal interest–based communities that connect them with others.

It is emotional attachment that makes them feel connected to the community. Such connection is particularly important in mainland China, especially for the many rural migrants to urban areas. Life in Shanghai, for example, can be lonely, exacerbated by work and study pressures and the drive to become a cosmopolitan, *suzhi* citizen. The mainland participants were passionate about discussing the hidden romance of the socialist brotherhood depicted in television dramas (Ng and Li 2020), enthusiastic about gossiping about *wanghong* (online KOL), who make money through gift-giving on live-streaming sites and influencer marketing, and eager to condemn *mingyuan* ("socialite" or "celebrity") gay men seen as pretentious, flamboyant, and promiscuous (and probably secretly engaging in sex work). They also indulged in intimate chats and quasi-commercial exchanges with erotic *wanghuang* (Internet porn stars) (S. Wang 2019a). Moreover, the imaginary dimension of the community is also crucial, as we saw with Xinxin, who frequently uses dating apps and is eager to find other gay men. Even if all that results is a casual hello or shallow conversation, he still feels connected to a "real" person. For Cody, indulgence in online video games led to meeting other gay men offline. The imagination of gayness provides young gay men with a structure of thinking and feeling about their sexuality. Young gay men in mainland China benefit from queering the homoerotic and homosocial images, connotations, and sentiments in mainstream TV dramas, movies, and variety shows. Moreover, the imagination of gayness is transnational rather than global. The young men in mainland China also enjoy the imagined geographies that go beyond the nation in the transnational queer discourse embedded in Japanese BL, Asian gay movies (from Hong Kong, Taiwan, and increasingly from Thailand), and queer-friendly TV programs such as *Kangxi Lai Le* (2004–2016). This media constitutes an important cultural resource and source of emotional support that helps young gay men negotiate the difficulties of daily life (Martin 2009; Zhao, Yang, and Lavin 2017).

Finally, homonormative masculinity is a powerful force for the mainland participants. Xinxin explained in 2017:

> There are two types of *tongzhi* in China: one is those who are involved with the *tongzhi* movement, and the other is ordinary *tongzhi*. Ordinary *tongzhi* are those who may go to bars sometimes but mainly use dating apps to cruise and find sex or romance....They don't want to discuss anything political or serious. Dating apps cannot provide such a platform [for serious political discussions], and they are not very satisfied....Discrimination is very serious inside the circle, with the rich looking down on the poor, the manly looking down on the sissy, and the transgender...totally marginalized. Gay men despise lesbians and vice versa. And the sunshine middle class is at the top. They don't like people who are working class....Those who are into the *tongzhi* movement are better but there are a lot of schisms....Lesbians are very angry, as they have always been neglected....The movement tends to nurture and reinforce sunshine middle-class male homosexuality.

Hence, the gay world in mainland China is divided into those who engage in the *tongzhi* movement and those who participate in the pink economy. Both camps, however, adhere to the notion of homonormative masculinity, which privileges masculinity and a middle-class sensibility, emphasizes appropriate body types and mannerisms, and endorses *suzhi* sexual citizenship along the lines of class and gender.

Taiwan: Democratic Civil Society, Diffusive Engagement, and "We Have It All"

Compared with Hong Kong and mainland China, Taiwan has the most well-developed *tongzhi* world. Taiwanese civil society has witnessed the flourishing of *tongzhi* visibility in mainstream media and culture as well as on social media and dating apps; the growth of *tongzhi* self-help groups and organizations; the rapid development of the pink economy, hallmarked by the establishment of an open bar area with numerous bars, cafes, restaurants, and shops outside Red House in Ximending, the rise of male prostitution, and the flourishing of circuit parties; strong and highly visible *tongzhi* activism; and the burgeoning of academic gender and sexuality studies. Although Red House can be seen as a gay ghetto, it is not a "gayborhood," owing to family residence patterns and high property prices in Ximending. It is more of a place for tourists. Also, in Taiwan, the *tongzhi* community has been deeply influenced by gender equity education reform. In 2000, a junior high school student named Yeh Yung-chih was found dead in the school washroom (see note 30 in chapter 1). This unfortunate incident was believed to have been related to his feminine performance; it forced society and the government to face up to gender equality issues. The Gender Equity Education Act was passed in 2004, with gender identity, gender expression, and sexual orientation now incorporated into the high school curriculum. Some of the Taiwanese participants had the chance to develop a positive gay identity early in high school because of gender equity and LGBT+ education.

Born in 1990, Xiaoai grew up in Chiayi. He is among the very few of the Taiwan participants who still has not come out to his parents. He is quite short but solidly built and has dark skin. We first met in 2017, when he told me about his engagement with the gay world in Taiwan. When he was in primary school, he dated girls. He began to like boys when he was in junior high school and started watching gay porn videos. While in senior high school, he searched the Internet and found a senior high school LGBT+ club and had a few romances. He met his second boyfriend at university, and their relationship lasted four years. He has had a range of experiences in the gay world, such as a surprising encounter in a public toilet at a Taipei train station, a mutual masturbation session in the shower room of a swimming pool at the Da-an Sports Center, and endless hookups at gay bars (Funky, G-star). When he was a student, he was heavily into the *tongzhi* movement and activism. He participated in gay pride events every year, which gave him a sense of connection: "In the pride walk, we felt like we belonged to the same nation, as we shared certain values and ideologies ... but didn't want much from others." More personal, smaller communities are different, he added. There, everyone knows one another, "with twenty to thirty people going to the beach, taking photos, and posting them on Facebook." He was very proud of Taiwan's vibrant civil society: "Apart from the *tongzhi* movement, we have an anti-nuclear movement, an indigenous movement, a women's movement." During the Sunflower Movement, "I participated, I went to a sit-in. I stationed [myself] at an underground resting area, where I helped to register everyone who came there to rest and made sure the place was clean and ordered."

Xiaoai's engagement with the gay world has changed since he began working. He said: "When I was young, I did feel a sense of 'we are family' when going on the pride walk. You could see so many *tongzhi* ... it was a very collective experience; you chanted and held banners. ... But now, these past few years, when I went there with friends, it was more like a social activity, like a leisure walk ... looking for some handsome boys, that's all.

I don't really care about...the theme of this year's pride." In the past, he continued, "when you were a student, you were more passionate, and also I was studying sociology and was greatly concerned about social justice, equality, those sorts of values and ideas...and I wanted to debate with others. But now, I have found that there are many other things in life, like my job....I stopped going to saunas and gay bars. I still go to bars with friends or colleagues, but not necessarily to gay bars." When I chatted with Xiaoai on Zoom in 2020, he told me that he simply no longer has the time to socialize as much as he did in the past and now keeps in regular contact with just three to five good friends, having dinner together or playing video games, whereas when he was at university, he "met new friends all the time and participated in *tongzhi* activism."

Born in 1992 to a middle-class family, Tony still lives with his parents and younger sister. He is out to his family. He holds a master's degree and works as a civil servant. He has a well-built body and a moustache and beard, and he would likely be called a "cute bear" in gay circles even though he does not think he is cute enough. He described his engagement with the gay world during our interview in 2017. While at university, he began using a dating app but did not find anyone interesting. He later met his first boyfriend at a gym via the dating app Growlr, but it didn't work out because Tony wanted a monogamous relationship and the boyfriend did not. After they split up, Tony thought about suicide, and the trauma led him to open himself up to the online gay world. He chatted with a number of people on apps, and they all comforted him: "I decided to go one step further...I wanted to make more friends in the circle and be more active in chatting with people. I set up a Facebook account solely for this circle...and suddenly I had nine hundred Facebook friends...and would actively chat with seventy to eighty of them. I don't know why, but when I posted a photo, I would easily get a hundred 'likes.' I didn't even send out nude photos." He subsequently had numerous dating and hookup experiences. Although he frequently goes to bars, he believes parks and saunas to be for the "old generation." He attended Gay Pride once but said that what really moved him was a concert he attended in December 2016 at which many singers and celebrities expressed support for same-sex marriage. It was a collective moment at which he felt he was part of a community.

Of the three societies under study, Taiwan clearly has the most well-established *tongzhi* world. The Taiwanese participants were clearly very proud of their vibrant civil society and well-established queer world, as evidenced by their frequent pronouncement that "we have it all." For the young generation, there is less stigma attached to engagement in public sex (Xiaoai has had a variety of sexual experiences in such public places as public toilets, swimming pools, and train stations), but most (as with Tony) feel that such places are not really for the young generation. Although commercial venues such as bars, clubs, and saunas remain popular with the young crowd, social media and dating apps have become an easier way to engage in emotional and sexual liaisons. Taiwan has the largest pride walk in Asia, and most of the participants have joined it, with some, like Xiaoai, heavily involved, especially when they were students. Taiwan is the only one of the three societies to organize large-scale circuit parties, which are usually held around Gay Pride in October and at New Year, attracting large numbers of local gay men. Such a collective experience is important to them, as it is an indicator of their commitment to some common good (the fight for equality) or identification as *tongzhi*. At the same time, however, they also participate in smaller, more personal communities or commons by engaging in online group chats on LINE; reading gay news; looking for potential gay mates on Facebook, Twitter, and Instagram; playing online video games; and participating in chemsex, sex parties, and leisure activities such as hiking and swimming. For example, Xiaoai enjoys playing online video games and having dinner with his gay friends, and Tony likes chatting on Facebook with "other bears." The emotional attachment these engagements provide helps them feel connected to the community. Moreover, the inter-Asian dimension of the community is also crucial. Real and imagined transnational rather than global gayness provides a structure for feeling and thinking about sexuality. Owing to their relatively weak consumption power, traveling abroad is less common than it is for their Hong Kong counterparts. However, as Taipei has gained status as the gay capital of Asia, Taiwan's young gay men do not need to travel to meet gay Asians.

Like their counterparts in the two other locales, the Taiwanese participants are somewhat ambivalent about the gay community. On the one hand, they view it as a site for identity-building, solidarity, and support, but, on the other, they find it difficult to accomplish the norm of homonormative masculinity to which the community is subject. As Tony explained in our first interview in 2017: "The *tongzhi* circle is full of discrimination... mutual discrimination is severe. The fatties look down on the skinny. The skinny look down on the muscled. The muscled look down on the fatties.... Well, for me, if a skinny guy wanted to approach me, I would ask him to leave... I am part of it too!" And the discrimination extends beyond the body to class, taste, lifestyle, and the various forms of social and cultural capital one is expected to attain. The most privileged, he added, "look handsome, have money and good jobs and live a beautiful life and want to show you how to live, shop, and play." Tony is preparing himself to be part of the *wang-hong*: "I have been observing them silently. Those well-dressed and elegant *wanghong* . . . are my future goal, and they are my idols. Even though when I meet some of them, I think they are idiots!"

Commons, Community, and Collectivity

This chapter has pointed out that the emergence of *tongzhi* communities in Hong Kong, Taiwan, and mainland China have not neatly followed the developmental trajectory of some Western gay cities but rather are characterized more by disjunctive, discrepant, and compressed modernities. Accordingly, the lived experiences of the young gay men interviewed for this research show us that they actively engage with the *tongzhi* community, albeit in different ways and to differing degrees, owing to the sociopolitical and economic conditions of the societies in which they live. Taiwan has the most vibrant civil society, with a well-established queer world that provides the possibility of engaging in collective large-scale community attachment or smaller-scale personal communities or commons with affection and emotion as well as with global and inter-Asian imagination. Gay men in Taiwan can have a gay identity without a gay life, recalling Warner's (1999) description of the postgay identity by which one defines oneself "by 'more than sexuality,' with being critical of a 'gay ghetto' . . . and with recognizing that many gay people 'no longer see their lives solely in terms of struggle' . . . preference for 'mixed' clubs over gay or lesbian bars and clubs" (61–62). Their engagement can thus be seen as diffusive. In Hong Kong, the gay world has always been geared more toward consumption than toward *tongzhi* activism. Given that family coresidence is the norm, and given their relatively strong economic power and the popular consumption habits of tourism, most gay men in Hong Kong (even those from the working class) have the ability to travel in Asia to gain cross-national queer circuit and party experiences in Taiwan, Thailand, Japan, South Korea, and elsewhere, resulting in cross-national-consumption engagement. By contrast, in mainland China, the gay world (and civil society as a whole) is heavily regulated by the state, and young gay men's engagement is thus largely restricted to the online dating world. That is why many express eagerness to visit Hong Kong to participate in large-scale, collective, offline experiences such as Gay Pride events (although Taiwan is a less popular destination because of its stricter entry procedures).

They thus affectively engage with either online collective fan experiences or personal communities or commons and imaginative inter-Asian referencing. Their engagement can be seen as fragmentary.

Across all three sites, young gay men encounter discrepancies between the ideal gay community and the realities of gay social life. The gay community is seen as a marker of identity formation and community-building and as a site for social movements and political activism, but in reality it is stratified along class, race, gender, and age lines and, more recently, dominated by homonormative masculinity under the forces of neoliberalism, developmentalism, cosmopolitanism, and nascent consumerism. The highly performative and judgmental culture of the community results in feelings of uneasiness and ambivalence.

Rowe and Dowsett (2008) describe living a gay life as a creative and enduring struggle to belong, with gay men having to compromise between their "sexual interests, lifestyle preferences, career trajectories, personal backgrounds and histories" (336) and the imperatives of the culture in which they live in. Community can mean love, sex, friendship, and belonging, but it can also mean domination, marginalization, and discrimination. Identity and community have been delinked, and the relationship between them is imbued with a distinct sense of ambivalence (Fraser 2008; Holt 2011; Woolwine 2000). The young participants' engagement with the *tongzhi* community or the queer sense of collectivity and connectivity can be seen as a counterhegemonic practice in a political sense (*tongzhi* activism), but most often it is merely cultivation of the joy of "feeling together" (through online group chats, social media surfing, online game play, and sex, circuit, and other parties and gatherings). However, the desire for an intimate mode of collectivity and connectivity (political or otherwise) is likely to be the basis for an egalitarian, and potentially democratic, set of social relationships (Gilbert 2013), which is particularly important in the neoliberal era when performance, competition, and entrepreneurial individualism are the privileged modes of being in the world (Hakim 2018). In his discussion of "cosmopolitan sexualities," Plummer (2015) asks how to live well with human differences, such as how to connect our differences with collective values, or our uniqueness with multiple group belongings, or our sexual and gendered individualities with a broader common humanity. How do young gay men in the three societies connect with one another for love and sex? The next chapter turns to the subject of their love and sex lives to find the answer.

4

Love and Sex as Cruel Optimism

Youth is a period of ambiguity for everyone, with youth sexuality an important rite of passage characterized by sexual exploration and experimentation,
opportunities and uncertainties, successes and failures. This is particularly
the case for gay youths, who live outside the linear developmental trajectory
of the heteronormative life course. They must thus deal with various "normative cruelties" (Ringrose and Renold 2010), developmental expectations
(from an unruly childhood to controlled adulthood), and the pressures of
neoliberal masculinity, including homonormative masculinity, and work
through feelings of shame and the fear of failure (Ahmed 2004, 144–67;
Halberstam 2011).[1] The young Chinese gay men interviewed for the current
research also have love stories to tell. They all see having a relationship,
particularly a monogamous relationship, as a major component of a good
adult life, which can be seen as an example of "cruel optimism" (Berlant
2011). However, they all speak of the difficulties of finding a partner despite
the many men potentially available on dating apps. Most of them have therefore remained single, engaging in casual hookups or developing ambiguous,
loving relationships with a few men. The few who are in a relationship
tend to view monogamy as the ideal, seldom offering the political critique
of it put forward by theorists; but they find it difficult to practice in real
life. They have developed strategies to negotiate with the monogamy ideal,
venturing out—together or separately, openly or in secret, and with explicit

or implicit rules—to form various kinds of relationships. Their stories are consistent with those in previous studies conducted in Hong Kong, Taiwan, and mainland China as well as in the United Kingdom, the United States, Canada, and Australia.[2]

However, the socioeconomic and political circumstances in the three Chinese societies make their intimate stories distinctive, especially their recent histories. In Hong Kong, the love and sex lives of the young men under study are shaped by political unrest, the confinement of family co-residence patterns, and the neoliberal ethics of the self under the COVID-19 pandemic, which affected Hong Kong much more than the other two sites in 2020 and mid-2021, when the final data collection was conducted. In mainland China, young gay men live with traditional family pressure to marry, state suppression of *tongzhi* development, and the mundanity of hard work, which define their sex/love lives under desiring and enterprising China. In neoliberal Taiwan, young gay men carry the optimism of the Sunflower Movement and live in a democratic environment with freedom of speech and the legal right to engage in same-sex marriage, something the two other societies lack. This gives them a more relaxed and reflective space to think about their love and sex lives.

Monogamy as Cruel Optimism

Young gay men in Hong Kong, Taiwan, and mainland China are living under changing family, marriage, and love environments characterized by a reduction in fertility rates; the postponement of marriage; the mono-poly of monogamy as the only valid form of marriage; increasing rates of divorce, extramarital, and nonmarital affairs; and the possibility of cross-border intimacy and marriage (Davis and Friedman 2014). Sexuality for them is a rite of passage characterized by sexual exploration and experimentation. At school, many encounter the "'normative cruelties' of performing and policing 'intelligible' heteronormative masculinities and femininities" (Ringrose and Renold 2010, 573). They generally have sexual experiences when they are in their early teens, experimenting with sex or even finding their first loves and/or sexual partners among their relatives, neighbors, classmates, friends, acquaintances, or even strangers in tradi-tional social institutions (family, school, university), gay-identified spaces (bars, saunas), public spaces (public toilets, swimming pools), *tongzhi* nongovernmental organizations (NGOs), or, increasingly, via gay websites and dating apps (see chapter 3).

Most of the participants are still single, with only a few romantic episodes lasting from several weeks to several months in their lives thus far. What runs through all of their stories, like those of many young people across the world, is a desire for a romantic, loving, and committed relationship—a monogamous one. Monogamy was first criticized by Marxists and feminists for privileging "the interests of both men and capitalism, operating as it does through the mechanisms of exclusivity, possessiveness and jealousy, all filtered through the rose-tinted lens of romance" (Robinson 1997, 144). It thus signifies sexual fidelity, the institutionalization of coupledom, and the presumed ownership of another individual (Jackson and Scott 2004, 152). Sociologists later proposed various alternatives, including Giddens's (1992) notion of the "pure relationship," which is based on choice and equality and is not necessarily monogamous; Beck and Beck-Gernsheim's (1995) idea of the normal chaos of love, wherein "[l]ove is becoming a blank that the lovers must fill in themselves" (5), regardless of whether they are monogamous; Plummer's (2003) concept of "intimate citizenship," which links intimacy with the notion of citizenship and covers a wide range of citizen identities, including polyamory; and Bauman's (2003) notion of "liquid love," in which traditional ideals such as monogamy are decentered by the digital transformation of intimacy. More recently, queer scholars have criticized monogamy for being assimilationist ("queer skin, straight masks") because it bolsters heteronormative values and differentiates between legitimate and illegitimate ways of living (Ahmed 2004, 150). They thus present nonmonogamies as potentially liberating and empowering, propose more egalitarian relationships built on trust and negotiation, and critique patriarchy and heteronormativity (Barker and Landbridge 2010).

Nonetheless, in practice and almost everywhere, monogamy or nonconsensual nonmonogamy (secret affairs in an ostensibly monogamous relationship) remain the norm for a couple in a relationship (Jamieson 2004). Adultery and affairs are still regarded as major marital or relationship problems and as legitimate reasons for divorce or the breakup of a relationship, as they are seen as a breach of the marriage contract, a breach of trust between couples, and a breach of the implicit rules of erotic ethics (Kong 2011, 109–10). Hence, nonmonogamies (polyamory, swinging, an open relationship) are still considered marginal, alternative, or problematic (Barker and Landbridge 2010; Duncombe et al. 2004; Haritaworn, Lin, and Klesse 2006). The supremacy of monogamy can be seen as an example of "cruel optimism" (Berlant 2011, 1), when "something you desire is actually an obstacle to your flourishing."[3] It is optimistic because it promises the happy and sustainable relationship that most people seek, but it is cruel precisely because we believe and continue to believe that it is attainable even though we continually fail at having such a relationship. It has thus become a kind of "collectively invested form of life" wherein we imagine that normative intimacy can exist and be realized as part of the "good life" (11).

Indeed, most of the young men I spoke to cited monogamy as an ideal aspiration and also acknowledged the gap between practice and the ideal. They were torn between two sexual scripts. The first is the romantic script, commonly found in mainstream heterosexual love stories, which prescribes the ideal trajectory of a relationship through courting, dating, falling in love, lifelong commitment, and sexual exclusivity. Hence, many said that the first thing they do when they start a relationship is delete dating apps to demonstrate their fidelity. However, the romantic script runs counter to the second script, the script of sexual adventure, which emphasizes spontaneity, the explosive male sex drive, sex as fun, and pleasure without commitment, which is largely endorsed and facilitated by both the commercial gay community and online dating culture (Kong 2011, 111–17).

But they rarely expressed the political stances of theorists. Instead of revolting against monogamy, they tended to make what Berlant (2011) terms "adjustment and gestural transformation in order to stay in proximity to [it]" as one among "some aspirations that ha[ve] gotten attached to the normative good life" (249). Specifically, they tended to treat the first script—of monogamy—not as a given or as restrictive but as an active choice. The main way of following it is to form an emotionally exclusive dyadic couple in which both parties can still venture out—together or separately, openly or secretly—to have sexual adventures, ranging from casual encounters to regular partners (fuck buddies), ambiguous relationships, or even a substantial secondary relationship subject to rules, contracts, and boundaries (whether explicitly negotiated or tacitly acknowledged).[4]

Being single was the second-best option. A burgeoning body of literature on dating apps examines the multifarious aspects of men meeting men via online apps (e.g., Licoppe, Rivière, and Morel 2016; Wu 2020; Yeo and Fung 2018; see also Albury et al. 2017). The participants pointed out one cruel reality of online cruising. They described cruising on dating apps as tiring, tedious, and time-consuming, essentially hard work. Daniel, whose story will appear later in this chapter, said to me once in 2021: "You might send a 'Hi' to one hundred guys a day, but only ten reply and you can really chat with a few but no one wants to meet up. However, it eats up one hour a day!" Then when they do make a connection, finding a location for sexual and emotional intimacy is not easy. It requires a lot of calculation and planning ahead, such as deciding to meet at a certain time when one's parents will not be at home, finding a hotel, or going to a sauna together. If that works out, maintaining a relationship is difficult and, most of the time, heartbreaking. Meanwhile, digital porn is so convenient (streaming, pornhub, Tumblr, Twitter), and masturbation is an easy way to meet one's sexual needs.

The participants described another fascinating option for love: to stay between having a relationship and being single, what they called *aimei* ("to play ambiguous"). They described developing romantic and sexual feelings for men without forming any serious attachment. They may hang around with such partners frequently, with or without engaging in sex, but do not feel committed to them. They can also have more than one such relationship without being considered promiscuous. Although lighter than a committed relationship, an ambiguous relationship has more weight than a casual hookup or regular sex buddy. It thus seems to be a lighter form of Giddens's (1992) "pure relationship" or a digital example of "liquid" love (Bauman 2003), signifying the fluidity of queer youth sexuality.

Hong Kong: Family Coresidence and Political Affiliation as a Deal Breaker under COVID-19

Hong Kong has never been a welfare state. Like its colonial predecessor, the Hong Kong Special Administrative Region (HKSAR) government employs neoliberal strategies to nurture ideal citizen-subjects who are rational, self-reliant, self-responsible, self-enterprising, and self-calculating with minimal civil, political, and social rights (Ku and Pun 2004; Tsang 2006). Wong and So (2020) argue that if the old developmental politics (1997–2002) in Hong Kong emphasized the absence of nationhood, detachment from the Chinese nation, neoliberal governance, and a relatively closed political system to create atomized, depoliticized citizens with limited social and political rights, the new developmental politics (2003–2019) are substantively integrated with China, with the state driving the nationalist dimension of development and society driving the localist dimension. The result has been a shift from self-enterprising citizenship centered around private life to protest citizenship. Hong Kong society is broadly divided into the yellow-ribbon camp, crudely seen as prodemocracy, and the blue-ribbon camp, seen as progovernment, pro-police, and/or pro-Beijing. Many of the young generation belong to the yellow-ribbon camp. They openly challenge the government, particularly for its treatment of democratic development in Hong Kong as well as for Beijing's direct involvement in Hong Kong politics and the economy. Within this nearly twenty-year shift to protest citizenship and within the yellow-ribbon camp, youth politics shifted from the "peaceful, rational, nonviolent, and no foul language" (Cant., *woleifeifei*) of the 2014 Umbrella Movement to the more radical, militant, and confrontational approach of the 2019 anti–Extradition Law Amendment Bill (ELAB) protests.[5]

The government's public housing policy is closely related to its high land-price policy, a typical example of noninterventionism in which the "small" government gives way to the "big" market of housing and real estate development (Wong 2012). High housing prices remain a major obstacle to young people who want to live on their own. A person would need to save approximately HKD14,000 (approximately US$1,800) every month for six years to be able to afford the down payment on a small apartment worth HKD3 million (US$385,000), yet the median monthly income for those aged twenty-five to thirty-four is just HKD15,500 (range: HKD14,000–25,000; US$1,800–$3,200). They can't get into public housing owing to the selective nature of the welfare regime. So some young people live in tiny apartments—mini flats, mosquito-sized units, or nano flats—and most live with their parents (Luk 2020). Upward social mobility is becoming increasingly difficult, and many struggle with their precarious careers (e.g., Wong and Au-Yeung 2019). Meanwhile Hong Kong has experienced several waves of the COVID-19 pandemic since 2020, though the situation has been less serious than in Europe and North America. To mitigate the risks of transmission, the government has adopted a range of public health measures over time depending on the severity of the outbreak and has also used the slogan "protect yourself and others" to cultivate the ethics of care.[6]

The radicalism of youth politics, the family coresidence pattern, and the neoliberal ethics of the self are the three major factors shaping their love and sex lives, illustrated by the stories of Bobby and Daniel. Bobby, whose story briefly appears in the introduction, was born in 1993. He is the only son of a working-class family and lives with his parents. He studied very hard while at school and obtained a business degree, on his parents' advice, but ultimately followed his own interests to take up a job at a health NGO. He has obtained a master's degree in counseling. While he is now an officer at a health NGO, he is looking for a job as a social worker. During our interview in 2017, he conveyed the bittersweet nature of his love stories. He was bullied when he was young because of his highly feminine behavior.

Heavily influenced by Boys Love (BL) comics since he was very young (in Primary 3),[7] he strongly self-identifies as an *o zai* (Cant., bottom) and wants to find a *1 zai* (Cant., top) who can take care of him. While in Form 1, he began chatting with guys on the gay website tt1069, and he met one of them in person at a swimming pool during Form 2 when he was twelve.[8] Bobby wanted to have a romantic relationship, but the man, who said he was twenty-five years old, was interested only in sex. They ended up engaging in mutual masturbation and oral sex in a changing room. This was Bobby's first sexual experience, and he never saw the man again. Although some would view the man as a sexual predator and Bobby as the victim of sexual assault, Bobby does not view the incident in that way. At the age of thirteen, he fell in love with a sixteen-year-old who was heavily involved in the Boy Scouts. He was Bobby's dream man: "He had a lot of leg hair, very manly; oh my, I was really into him." They were together for one and a half years but eventually broke up because Bobby wanted a monogamous relationship and his boyfriend did not: "We...split up almost every day....And I cried every day....He...kept breaking his promises. One time, he had sex with a fat boy. How could I be defeated by a fat boy?! I was so pissed off....He then begged me and said 'I am sorry, I miss you, and I am so regretful, blah, blah, blah.'...It went on and on...so sometimes I would...chat with other guys (but no sex) just to show that I had value....It was a way to boost my self-esteem." Bobby finally accepted that open relationships are the norm in the gay community and began looking for sexual partners on tt1069 and later on dating apps. At around the age of sixteen, he became religious and stopped looking for sex: "I occasionally chatted with...guys, but didn't do anything. I prayed every time I masturbated." During this time, he experienced conflict between his religious beliefs and his sexuality. Nevertheless, he fell into a love triangle at church, a situation he described as similar to the plot of the Taiwanese movie *Eternal Summer*.[9] Bobby fell in love with a boy at church and developed an ambiguous, or "hehe," relationship with him and a girl who was in love with both Bobby and the other boy.[10] He eventually left the church and developed an interest in New Age spirituality. When he began studying for an associate degree at around the age of eighteen to nineteen, he became heavily engaged with the gay circle, started going to the gym regularly to build up his muscles, and entered the so-called *nanshen* (Cant., male god) circle.[11] All of the men he met were professionals. With some of them, he engaged in what is known as compensated dating,[12] or acting as a *Gong nui* (Cant., Hong girl), in that he would have dinner with them and accept gifts.[13] He also suffered depression owing to the pressure of his studies. He started taking antidepressants and gained weight, and thus fell out of the male-god circle, which made him even more depressed. Following a few unsuccessful attempts at love, Bobby is now single. He does have a regular sex partner who is much older, as well as a few ambiguous relationships with other men, one of whom is a male god. Although he has had a few intimate encounters with these men, the relationships have not developed into anything serious.

Bobby struggled for a long time with his sexuality when he was a Christian, and he came out to his parents when he began suffering depression. Since turning to New Age spirituality, he has become totally accepting of his sexuality. He has always lived with his parents on a public housing estate. He does not have his own room but shares a bunk bed with his mother, a situation that constrains his ability to find places for sexual and emotional intimacy. He said, "It requires a lot of calculation and planning; [for example,] deciding on a certain time when they [his parents] are not at home, or finding a hotel, or going to [a] sauna, or going to the guy's home." When I contacted Bobby in 2020 for an update, he told me about what has happened in the past few years, noting that politics has come into his love life. In 2019, Bobby was heavily involved in the anti-ELAB protest movement. Although he wanted to be a "brave or valiant" protester (one characterized by militancy and a confrontational approach of expression and radical action), he was frightened of the police and the blue crowd: "I was so scared as I was circled and accused by a group of 'blue' people. And the police were staring at me . . . I froze and wet my pants." He finally decided to become a peaceful protester or engage in pacifism. Political orientation is a major criterion when it comes to selecting partners. He would reject a guy if he were blue ribbon even if he were a *nanshen*. He is proud that "gay men do not just want to be pretty and go on a boat cruise; we are concerned about politics." Bobby worked to become a counselor in order to help the many young protesters who have developed post-traumatic stress disorder.

Because of COVID-19, Bobby works from home most of the time for a health NGO, mainly providing online counseling services to clients. He previously had a "complicated" relationship with his father, but the two became more intimate once they discovered they had similar political views (both were "yellow"). Sometimes he shared news about the protests with his father, and they hugged and cried together, which Bobby found "very nice." His relationship with his mother, by contrast, has worsened, as she is "blue." He loves his parents even though they still want him to get married. He worries about being able to support his family financially as his parents age. Because he lives with his parents, he takes extra precautions with respect to COVID-19. He worries that he might contract the virus and spread it to his parents. I recall one time during a follow-up interview in 2020 that he wore two masks and eye goggles and kept washing his hands with disinfecting lotion. I said, "You are a bit OCD [obsessive-compulsive disorder]," and he answered, "Yes, but there is nothing wrong with it. It only shows that you are obsessed with certain things and happy by doing it." Accordingly, he has reduced his usage of dating apps for casual hookups and rarely meets his regular sex partner. When he thinks about the future, he becomes very unhappy and feels powerless; he believes the future will be grim. Because of his social class and financial status, he is stuck in Hong Kong. He did note, however, that tarot cards indicate he will move to Australia.

Born in 1992 to a working-class family, Daniel is tall and very good-looking with a lean body. He wears glasses and looks very intellectual. He studied for his master's degree in the United Kingdom in 2015 and then came back to Hong Kong and worked as a research assistant at a university. He moved back to the United Kingdom again to start a PhD program in the fall of 2021 and holds a British National (Overseas), or BNO, passport.[14] He is out to his elder sister and his mother but not to his father. In 2020, he told me about his love stories. He was never bullied at school, but he witnessed many others being bullied and went out with girls to prove his heterosexuality. He was secretly in love with a classmate but dared not tell him; many years later he discovered that the classmate was also gay. While he was studying for an associate degree, he acquired a much more positive understanding of homosexuality and resolved the associated stigma through reading sociology. He met his first love at that time and had his first sexual encounter with him in a sauna, as both were living with their families. Daniel believed in monogamy but discovered that his boyfriend was secretly searching for chemfun partners via dating apps. He tried to help his boyfriend to quit taking drugs but only alienated him, and they eventually split up. Daniel then started to have casual sex with men he met on dating apps, but the relationships did not develop into anything serious. He later met his second boyfriend. Although he was not Daniel's ideal type, the two lived together for almost six years and had two cats. He said their life as a couple was stable but boring. His boyfriend liked to stay at home playing video games, and Daniel often went to the cinema to watch movies on his own. He had a number of secret affairs, but he later discussed them openly with his boyfriend. They decided to have an open relationship and tell each other when they had "fun" outside the relationship. They also agreed to inform their sex partners that they had a boyfriend and agreed on a set of rules such as not bringing anyone home. At first, Daniel simply engaged in casual sex but later developed ambiguous relationships with some of the men he met.

In contrast to Bobby who changed from bravery to pacifism, Daniel moved from pacifism to bravery during the anti-ELAB protest movement in 2019. Daniel said that he and that long-term boyfriend were both "deep yellow." They dated only "yellow guys" and mainly patronized yellow shops and restaurants to support the yellow economy and boycotted or buycotted blue shops that supported the Hong Kong police or red (China-owned) shops (to reduce local dependence on businesses connected to China). He is pessimistic about the chaotic political situation in Hong Kong but hopes that it will eventually bring new opportunities to Hong Kong. He also had "an episode" in a hotel with a man he met at a public protest:

> I usually went to protests with a guy I met on Tinder. In the early period of the anti-ELAB movement, lots of people rented hotel rooms near the protest area so that they would have somewhere to hide if they didn't feel safe. That time, the guy rented a hotel room, and I went there to change clothes and take a rest because we felt that the police were about to raid at any time. We were so tired, so we lay down on the bed naked after having a shower. Well...we then had sex eventually.

More recently, he began limiting his sexual contacts owing to COVID-19, as he did not want to infect his two cats. Daniel is one of the very few Hong Kong participants to have had a long-term boyfriend. He recently split up with his boyfriend though, and he is currently going out with a Taiwanese man. They want to maintain a committed relationship, even though Daniel now lives in the United Kingdom and his boyfriend is in Taiwan.

Bobby and Daniel are two typical cases of a young gay man's love story in Hong Kong. When they were young, they suffered from (or witnessed) varying degrees of bullying or normative cruelties because of the nonmasculine behavior of themselves or others. Both struggled with their sexuality (Bobby because of his Christian beliefs and Daniel because of the social stigma when they were young) but accepted it when they were older (Bobby by leaving the church and Daniel through the study of sociology). Both had their first sexual experience in their teens and have had various sexual and romantic experiences. Both believe monogamy to be the ideal form of intimate relationship, and both took a long time to realize that it is impossible to maintain in practice. Bobby eventually came to accept an open relationship as a compromise as long as it didn't go "too far," whereas Daniel has actively engaged in such a relationship. Bobby is still single but has a regular sex partner and a few ambiguous/"hehe" relationships, whereas Daniel was previously in a couple relationship with explicit rules for "adventure." He is currently in a monogamous relationship but is unsure how long it will last.

These love stories should be understood in light of the specificities of the society. In Hong Kong, the norm of family coresidence defines and constrains the possibilities for sexual and romantic intimacy, as is still the case for Bobby and was the case for Daniel when he was younger. A domesticated, coupled gay life remains a luxury in Hong Kong, especially for young gay men. Given the neoliberal ethics of care, COVID-19 further limits the possibility of sexual contact, as they do not want to infect their loved ones (Bobby's parents and Daniel's cats). The Hong Kong participants live in a nondemocratic political system but have been passionately engaged in various forms of social protest since the Umbrella Movement of 2014. Although there is a diversity of views and experiences among young men in Hong Kong, whether gay or straight, many of the participants in this study are heavily involved in what they consider the endgame in the fight for freedom in Hong Kong. They have participated, in one way or another (exhibiting bravery like Daniel or pacificism like Bobby), in what they call the "revolution of our times." The radicalism of youth politics has entered the private sphere of young gay men's lives. Political activism has become the new norm of gay masculinity, replacing political conservatism and challenging neoliberal homonormative masculinity. Political affiliation has not only become the key criterion in selecting partners but also shapes how these young men consume, live, and love. This new form of political consumption and identity economics is itself challenging neoliberal gay masculinity and defining the love lives of most young gay men in Hong Kong.

Mainland China: Precarity, Marriage Pressure, and Restless Online Cruising

Zhang and Ong (2008) describe the neoliberal reconfiguration of the capitalist market and socialist party in China since the 2000s as socialism from afar, "in which privatizing norms and practices proliferate in symbiosis with the maintenance of authoritarian rule" (4). The country's market reforms have not only nurtured the neoliberal "free market" logic but also sustained the ruling party's political legitimacy, as evidenced by its control of the administrative system, law, army, mass media, and Internet. Massive marketization with an unparalleled level of privatization, deregulation, social restratification, and labor exploitation, as well as the state's selective withdrawal from public services, has made China one of the most economically unequal societies in the world (Liu and Tan 2020). Shanghai is the largest city in China. As one of the first open coastal cities of the 1990s, it also attracted the largest amount of foreign investment. Shanghai enjoys relative autonomy in economic and administrative matters to attract foreign investment and create jobs for migrant workers and city dwellers, but its economic dynamism has greatly exacerbated social inequalities (Samara 2015). Meanwhile, neoliberalism and developmentalism have produced a desiring China that magnifies individuals' sexual, material, and affective self-interests with a wide range of aspirations, needs, and longings (Rofel 2007). It also has produced an enterprising China that emphasizes hard work, competition, and success. The result, however, is not always a desiring subject with an energetic sexual drive but sometimes a precarious labor subject suffering from fatigue. This contradictory effect is particularly significant in the lives of the young, who tend to accept precariousness as the norm. Although their lives are full of uncertainty and insecurity, they are optimistic about the future (Chong 2020), aligning with the Chinese dream promoted by the government. The desiring/enterprising China initially faced great challenges during the COVID-19 pandemic. It began in late 2019 with several suspected cases of pneumonia in Wuhan, the capital of Hubei province, and then spread to all provinces in mainland China in late January 2020, leading to a complete lockdown in the cities of Hubei and curfews in all cities. By early March 2020, the reported number of new cases had dropped to fewer than one hundred per day nationally, although sporadic local outbreaks have occurred since. Nationalist sentiment has been aroused by reports contrasting the effectiveness of the efficient Chinese state in controlling the pandemic with the inefficiency and slow response of Western bureaucratic countries that uphold human rights, privacy, and freedom of speech (de Kloet, Lin, and Chow 2020). The pandemic has had different effects on interaction in China compared to Hong Kong in 2020 (e.g., restrictions on traveling), and this has affected mainland Chinese participants in ways that differed from their Hong Kong counterparts.

Most of the mainland participants belong to the second generation of large-scale rural-to-urban migrants. Even those from middle-class families cannot afford to buy a home, and upward social mobility is becoming increasingly difficult. They received prolonged education and experienced strong family pressure to marry, as we saw in chapter 2. In terms of the COVID-19 pandemic, they reported that it has necessitated only slight adjustments to their lives.

Bei and Yifan represent two interesting cases that illustrate the complicated love lives of young gay men under labor precarity, marriage pressure, and a fragmented gay world in a desiring/enterprising China. Born in Hunan in 1998, Bei, who is short with a skinny body and a tender voice, is the only son of his two parents. However, both of his parents had children from previous marriages, so he has an elder half-brother and half-sister. His mother passed away when he was a junior in secondary (middle) school. His father is a government official who does not like Bei much because he blames him for his wife's death. He does not dare come out to his father. To escape his father's physical bullying, Bei moved to Shanghai in 2015 at the age of seventeen. He did not complete his senior secondary education. His first job was in a restaurant, where he earned a monthly salary of RMB 4,000 (roughly US$500). In a subsequent restaurant job, he had to work from 10:00 a.m. to 10:00 p.m., and there was no public transportation available to return home after work. After quitting that job, Bei was unemployed for a few months and has since had numerous part-time jobs, including a year-long stint as a waiter in a gay bar. After quitting that job, he went back to school and is currently studying finance at a postsecondary school in Shanghai. He went home for Chinese New Year in 2020, and the pandemic has kept him from returning to Shanghai since. He is currently living with the family of his elder half-brother in Guangxi. He helps out with his brother's business while studying online. Bei has come out to his half-brother and half-sister but not to his father. He always complains to me that people in Guangxi are still very homophobic compared with Shanghai: "If you don't get married by the age of twenty-five, people will gossip about you."

In 2017, Bei told me about his love life. When he first moved to Shanghai in 2015, he stayed with a friend who had a very small, shabby apartment with no toilet. They did not need to pay rent because the flat was owned by a friend of his roommate. The two had an ambiguous relationship. Bei later had a boyfriend whom he met via QQ (popular instant-messaging software in China). Then he discovered that his roommate had secretly added his boyfriend to his QQ account and flirted with him; he and his boyfriend had a huge fight and broke up. Bei then met his second boyfriend, who was from Guangzhou, via QQ. They talked every day but only saw each other in person once in half a year because of the distance between them and job precarity. Bei described his boyfriend as his "cyberpet": "Every day, I said good morning, good evening, and chatted a bit, like, 'Have you eaten?' That's all. It was actually quite boring. Love is like that. It's like a string, and it's easy to break if you have any emotional turbulence." Bei prefers having a one-to-one relationship, and he did not engage in casual sex during their long-distance relationship, although the reason he gave was that he was too busy and tired from work. When I talked to him in 2020, the two had split up, and Bei is now single. He still looks for men through social media (gay or otherwise) but does not really care whether he finds anyone. He views occasional hookups, ambiguity in love, and masturbation as good substitutes for the monogamous relationship he desires. Studying has given him renewed hope, as he believes that a good education will bring him social mobility.

Yifan's story is briefly mentioned in the introduction. He was born in 1990 in a small village in Shaanxi and is an "extra," as he has an older brother and sister. He is also one of the left-behind children. Had he been unable to attend university, he would probably have ended up becoming a rural migrant worker, like Bei, in a city. Yifan graduated from a university in Guilin. However, it is not considered a good university, and he hopes one day to repeat the public examination to get into a better one. After graduating, he took up a position in an overseas trading company in Shanghai.

Yifan is deeply closeted and uses a number of excuses to delay marriage. He once said to me in 2017 that "they [his brother and sister] do not have happy marriages. . . . I am a 'three no'—no money, no car, and no flat." He is seriously thinking about *xinghun* (marrying a lesbian) or *pianhun* (marrying a straight woman who does not know about his sexuality). When he first moved to Shanghai, he rented an apartment with a fellow (deeply closeted) recent migrant he had met in a youth hostel. His roommate, with whom Yifan had an ambiguous relationship, was also in a long-distance relationship with a man in Nanjing whom he saw twice a month. When that relationship ended, Yifan and his roommate got together. In 2020, when I spoke to him again, he said that because of the precarity of the job market, they had left Shanghai and moved to Hangzhou before finally settling down in Shenzhen. They rent a three-room apartment and maintain separate bedrooms in case family members visit. Yifan said that his elder sister stayed with him once and figured out his relationship with his boyfriend, but they did not talk about it. He and his boyfriend are still thinking about *xinghun* and having children. They enjoy being in a one-to-one relationship and very much conform to the notion of homonormative masculinity.

Monogamy remains the ideal for the young gay generation in China. Bei has almost given up on finding such a relationship, whereas Yifan is very happy to maintain one. A single gay life is usually substituted by occasional hookups, ambiguity in love, and masturbation. Unlike their Hong

Kong counterparts, the love lives of young gay men in mainland China are heavily shaped by labor precarity and the general precarity of life, family pressure to marry, and the online gay world.

Living with precarity seems to be the norm for the young generation, especially for the second generation of rural-to-urban migrants like Bei and Yifan. Migration is a desiring project—one filled with hopes, wants, and dreams—under China's quest for modernization and globalization (Pun 2005; Zhang 2001). However, living in cities can be as hard as living in rural villages. The adverse conditions of rural migrants working in Chinese cities have been well-documented. They stem in large part from the *hukou* (household registration) system as well as from other social divisions and class barriers (e.g., Guang 2003; Lee 2007; Pun 2005; Solinger 1999; Zhang 2001). Due to his social background, Bei is a precarious labor subject who moves from one job to another, from one city to another, in search of new opportunities. Living with precarity greatly affects his love life, reflected in the few temporary and short-term relationships he has had. Yifan is slightly better off as he has a university degree, but moving around the country to find jobs is also increasingly common for the university educated. He is also more fortunate in that his moves have been made with a partner; such moves more often result in a breakup.

As we saw in chapter 3, the gay world in mainland China, as opposed to those in Hong Kong and Taiwan, is largely limited to the gay Internet world (gay websites, dating apps), as political spaces (NGOs, festivals, *tongzhi* activism) are heavily suppressed, and commercial spaces (bars, clubs, saunas) are subject to frequent raids and closure by the police and are expensive for young people. Saunas are dirty and unhygienic. The online gay world is thus all that young gay men have, and even it is subject to severe censorship. Cruising on dating apps has become the only way for them to get to know one other, and it is seen by many as a tiring and time-consuming exercise. Bei, for example, cruised online intensively when he was young but now finds it exhausting and meaningless. Yifan has never really been part of the gay world and is in a monogamous relationship, which is not very common in China's gay circle. Although Bei is largely out to his siblings and to people in Shanghai, he has become much more reserved since moving to a small town in Guangxi. Yifan and his boyfriend are both deeply closeted despite living like a middle-class couple and are considering *xinghun*, as family pressure to marry remains strong in China.

What is consistent in the stories of these two young men is their optimism about the future through engagement in entrepreneurship. That is why Bei has gone back to school and Yifan is searching for better job opportunities to attain social mobility. Neoliberalism has taken a contradictory turn in China, nurturing both the desiring subject and self-enterprising subject; but it has mostly resulted in a precarious and fatigued labor subject who has either stopped desiring (for long-term couple intimacy, a good family relationship, or a better life chance) or is waiting to climb the social ladder, a wait that is generally futile for those of a migrant or working-class background.

Taiwan: "Little Assured Happiness," Imaginative Space, and Optimism

Neoliberal structural change—privatization, deregulation, industrial restructuring, and the relocation of factories to mainland China—have dealt a fatal blow to Taiwan's economy. The society has witnessed an increase in unemployment and decrease in wage levels. Upward mobility through education and hard work has become more difficult, and increasing property prices have diminished the chances of the young being able to buy their own apartments (Tseng 2014). The young generation in Taiwan has been described as a "collapsing generation" (Lin et al. 2011), a generation "confronted by economic crises, political impasse, class polarization, fertility decline, and falling wages" (Wang 2017b, 179). Neoliberalism is associated with worries about the future, with college students on the verge of entering the job market feeling ambivalent about their career prospects and life chances. Young people in Taiwan feel a sharp sense of deprivation and anxiety over Chinese competition. A few years ago, the term 22K became very popular, naming the young generation who have no means of building a prosperous future as losers.[15] They are part of the new precariat, characterized by feelings of "anger, anomie, anxiety, and alienation" (Standing 2011, 22). The 22K generation thus envisions "the future as stagnant, alienating, and precarious" (Wang 2017b, 185). However, the Sunflower Movement seems to have reversed the pessimism that prevailed among the young. The movement was grounded in antagonism along the lines of four main discourses: anti-China Taiwanese (independent) nationalism, leftist criticism of free trade, demands for democratic reforms (especially in the parliament), and a cry for generational justice (Tseng 2014). Victory in the Sunflower Movement gave the young hope and courage. It was the optimistic view that "our future is in our hands" that gave them an affective response to the uncertainties of the future induced by neoliberalism (Tseng 2014; Wang

2017b). In contrast with China's exercise of top-down control to combat the COVID-19 pandemic, Taiwan's success lies in its bottom-up process of "societalization," which demands greater accountability from the state and the health profession and nurtures civic interdependence among citizens. These dynamics in Taiwan also exemplify how democratic societies can foster social preparedness to respond to the pandemic (Lo and Hsieh 2020). Although Taiwan saw an upsurge of COVID-19 cases in 2021, the pandemic had little effect on the lives of the participants in 2020, as societalization nurtures greater self-awareness of civic interdependence among citizens.

Jay and Dajin represent two interesting cases that illustrate the intricate love lives of this collapsing generation. Jay was born in 1992. His father is from Guangdong in China, and his mother is from Taiwan. He has one elder sister and one elder brother. His first degree is in science, and he then obtained a master's degree in humanities, both from a university in Taoyuan City. During his university years, he lived with his family or in a dormitory but often went to Taipei to stay with friends on the weekends. After finishing his master's studies in 2019, he had difficulty finding a job. He eventually found a job as a web designer but was fired after just a few months. He currently works as a web designer at another company but continues to search for a job that is more meaningful and enjoyable (rather than one that simply pays more). He lives on his own in a small rented apartment in Taipei.

Jay was bullied when he was young, albeit mainly because he was fat, not because of his sexuality. He has had quite a few ambiguous relationships, most of which have not exceeded three months, as well as numerous casual sex experiences. He has also tried out recreational drugs and BDSM. Jay has had three serious relationships. The first, which was monogamous and lasted for six months, was when he was in his first year of university. His boyfriend was eight years older and had his own apartment. Jay stayed with him primarily on the weekends. However, they eventually broke up because his boyfriend found him too busy with his studies and university life and wanted them to have more of a private life as a couple. After several ambiguous relationships, Jay met his second boyfriend, who was also a student, while studying for his master's degree. After his boyfriend moved to Tainan, they maintained a long-distance relationship for a year, but their love eventually faded. Jay met his third serious boyfriend, a married man with a son, at a BDSM party in Guangdong during a trip to China. They maintained a long-distance relationship for about a year. One time, the man came to visit Jay when he was sick even though he needed to work overtime. On the day he left, Jay whispered, "My husband," and the man cried. In 2017, the man promised to come to Taipei for the Gay Pride parade but was then unable to make it. I happened to be having lunch with Jay when he found out. He was initially very excited about his boyfriend's imminent arrival, but his face turned pale when he received a message saying that he wasn't coming after all. A year later, they split up. Jay is now single, although he continues to search for love. He is involved in a number of ambiguous relationships and regularly engages in casual sex.

Jay enjoys being part of a well-established gay world and has participated in various forms of activism (volunteering at a *tongzhi* NGO). He frequently works out at a gym, regularly visits gay bars and clubs and attends parties, and uses social media and dating apps for cruising and social networking. He is very good-looking, with a moustache and beard. He would be called a wolf in Taiwan's gay circle. He speaks in a very soft voice and has participated in what he described as the circle of *mingyuan* ("socialites" or "celebrities"). However, he often feels inferior and envious, as he does not receive as many likes as the other celebrities. He also complains that he is not fit enough even though he has a sought-after body. He posted this on social media in 2021: "I'm so hungry and so want to eat. But I also want to be thinner. No one will love you if you are not thin. So, [I have] to endure." He does not suffer from an eating disorder, even though some of his comments make it sound as though he does. Jay's birthday wish for 2021 was "to reduce [his] body fat percentage to 10 percent or below, to learn how to love and be loved. . . . And no more singlehood." He did not participate in the Sunflower Movement, as he was in the army at the time. In Taiwan, men accomplish masculine identities through such "rites of passage" as *aluba* (play among schoolboys), "doing solider" (performing military service), and "flower drinking" (visiting erotic entertainment venues) (Kao and Bih 2014).[16] In contrast to most people's thinking, the army is a place of strict conformance to heteronormativity and hegemonic masculinity rather than the paradise of gay sexual fantasy. Jay, like most of the participants, had to act straight in order to avoid bullying. Finding a boyfriend or even casual hookups is not easy in the army.

Born in 1993, Dajin was twenty-four in 2017. He is tall and lean with a slight hunchback. His skin is very pale. His parents divorced, and he lived with his mother and stepfather when he was young. He studied Russian at university, during which time he lived in a shared apartment. After a one-year exchange program, he graduated, and then joined the army. Following his one-year stint, he worked in public relations for four months. Dajin is currently working as an editor and lives in a dormitory-like residence with several other men, including his current boyfriend. He has had three boyfriends thus far. He met the first while still in senior high school. They got along very well and developed the habit of eating and traveling home together. They then started engaging in more intimate acts, initially just holding hands, but later mutual masturbation and oral and anal sex in the school corridor in the early evenings. Although he did not feel very excited physically or sexually, Dajin said, he felt very emotionally connected to his first boyfriend. In retrospect, these were the happiest moments of his life, he added. However, his boyfriend was from a Christian family and was very religious, and he often prayed to God for absolution after they had sex. He often told Dajin that he planned to marry a woman when he was older. After numerous quarrels, and their acceptance by two different universities, they finally split up. Dajin was out at his university, and everyone knew he was gay. He met his second boyfriend at university. Although he was aware that the boyfriend already had a boyfriend, he was fine with it, as the boyfriend spent two nights per week with his initial boyfriend and the rest of his time with Dajin. However, he eventually felt that he was not getting enough attention, and the two broke up. He then found sex partners through dating apps. After returning from his overseas exchange, he met his current boyfriend through friends. As noted, he now lives with him and several other men. He still occasionally chats with men on dating apps and has had a few affairs during the relationship. He said he shares almost everything with his boyfriend, and he believes they have an egalitarian relationship. The boyfriend is thinking about studying for a PhD, however, and might leave Taiwan.

Dajin came out to his mother a long time ago, and she is very accepting. He regularly brings his boyfriend home, and he is now part of the family. Dajin was heavily involved with the Sunflower Movement and even skipped classes to participate. He thought of it as a chance to demonstrate against mainland China. He said he would not consider working in mainland China, especially after witnessing what happened in Hong Kong in 2019. He strongly identifies as Taiwanese.

These two cases capture the ethos of what it means to be young and gay in Taiwan. Whereas the young generation in Hong Kong feels despair and a sense of defeat while still trying to challenge the Chinese authorities, and their counterparts in China accept the reality of the highly regulated political regime and develop their own ways of living under such rule, the young generation in Taiwan enjoys a relatively democratic society, evidenced by the success of the Sunflower Movement in 2014, the legalization of same-sex marriage in 2019, and Taiwan's well-established, mature *tongzhi* community with political, economic, and cultural clout. Neoliberalism is a powerful combination of the neoliberal economy and Chinese political hegemony, and the young generation believe that the Sunflower Movement is a way to defend and safeguard the independent democratic nation-state as the last hope of escape (Wang 2017b). Although part of the "collapsing generation" (Lin et al. 2011), confronted with stagnant economic growth, growing class polarization, unemployment, falling wages, and soaring housing costs, they tend to be optimistic about the future. In a sense, they are anti-China rather than antineoliberalism. It is in this context that they have more room to be reflexive in thinking about their future in terms of work, love, and life. It is this *xiao que xin* ("little assured happiness") that they enjoy. They thus have the room to ask themselves the following questions: What do I want workwise: a job with a good salary or a career with intrinsic value? Should I work as an employee or be a small entrepreneur or the owner of a small shop? Who should I go out with? Is my current partner the right person, or should I keep searching until I meet the right person? Is monogamy the ideal relationship form, or should I practice polyamory? What is the meaning of life? What should I do to be happy? It is not that young gay men in Hong Kong and China are not reflexive or do not ask themselves these questions, but rather that the former are often too desperate and defeated to do so, whereas the latter are too occupied by their studies or work. It is the relaxed societal environment that gives Taiwanese young gay men this reflexivity, which in turn gives them the imaginative space to pause and rethink before adulthood closes in.

Love and Sex as Cruel Optimism

Youth is a period of ambiguity, a time when people feel trapped between the unruliness of childhood and adolescence and the order and predictability of adulthood. Youth sexuality is a rite of passage from childhood to adulthood, full of sexual exploration and experimentation. Like a series of snapshots, it is fragmented, incomplete, brief, and episodic. This is even more the case for queer youths, who live outside the linear developmental trajectory of the heteronormative life course, are marginal to the logic of capitalist accumulation, and dwell in "strange temporalities" (Halberstam

2005). Thus they push us to, as Torkelson (2012) puts it, "queer" the notion of "emerging adulthood" (Arnett 2004) to further understand the additional forms of queer identity instability and perspectives on adulthood.

Moreover, the young generation in all three Chinese societies live with different forms of normative cruelty: a highly competitive education system, a precarious working environment, soaring housing costs, a widening gap between classes, and stagnant social mobility. The demand to succeed is overwhelming, and many struggle in the face of either failure or the high price of success. Berlant (2011) argues that the neoliberal economy generates a good life that is characterized by "upward mobility, job security, political and social equality, and lively, durable intimacy" (3). This chapter is a testament to the struggles of Chinese young men who understand very well that the fantasies of such a good life are fraying. The young men in the three societies live different versions of transience, ambiguity, temporality, and precarity that affect their lives, including their intimate lives. They each have a distinctive, dominant love story to tell. In Hong Kong, family coresidence, political unrest, and the ethics of the self under COVID-19 are three major factors in the way the participants negotiate love and sex. Living with one's family, a common phenomenon in Hong Kong, largely constrains their negotiation of intimate relationships, and the rise of political radicalism is a significant factor in the way they structure their private, intimate lives. Political affiliation, whether yellow or blue ribbon, has become the main deal-breaker rather than fidelity or the desirable characteristics prescribed by homonormative masculinity (a nice face, a well-built body). COVID-19, manifest in the neoliberal ethics of the self, with its appeal to self-responsibility and care of the family, constrains the frequency of intimate contacts. In mainland China, it is family pressure to marry and the suppression of *tongzhi* development that have reduced the gay world to the Internet/online dating world and the mundanity of a life of hard work that restricts sex and love lives. What we see is not a desiring subject with potent sexual desires but rather a precarious, fatigued labor subject who struggles with the pressures of study and an uncertain job market, a filial subject who is torn between coming out and getting married, and a restless cruising subject who indulges in online dating without much hope. In Taiwan, the 2014 Sunflower Movement was a source of hope and optimism, and the legalization of same-sex marriage in 2019 has instilled considerable pride in being Taiwanese despite many young people seeing themselves as part of the precariat, as losers, or as members of the collapsing generation. Young gay men in Taiwan live in a well-established gay world that offers them room to explore a range of intimate possibilities. The democratic, neoliberal environment affords them both imaginative and reflective space. Intimate relationships are a major site where we can see the interplay of socioeconomic and political factors and subjectivity in the neoliberal era.

Neoliberalism and developmentalism take different shapes in the three Chinese societies, and the sociopolitical circumstances of each mark the differing contours of subject formation. Hong Kong has shifted from the self-enterprising subject to political dissident subject, whereas Taiwan has shifted from the democratic subject to neoliberal subject. However, the series of social protests since 2014 have left young people in Hong Kong feeling defeated and powerless, whereas their counterparts in Taiwan feel hopeful and optimistic. Finally, mainland China has shifted from the desiring subject with a robust sexual drive to a precarious labor subject. The next chapter leaves love and sex behind to focus on the different forms of civic-political activism that have led to the three societies' different subject formations.

Homosexuality, Homonationalism, and Homonormativity

British colonial rule in Hong Kong, martial law in Taiwan, and Maoist socialism in mainland China all privileged reproductive heteronormativity and marginalized, pathologized, or even criminalized homosexuality. However, since the 1990s or 2000s, these three Chinese societies have exhibited a relatively more tolerant and accepting stance toward gay and lesbian subjects, which has reoriented the relationship among the state, (homo)sexuality, and civil society. This chapter investigates the interplay between the state and sexuality among the young gay generations who have developed a distinctive cultural/national identity in each of the three societies. It conceptualizes each government's position on homosexuality from the perspective of homonationalism and examines—through the participants' narratives—how the post-'90s generation has developed mutually defined cultural/national identities that align with or contradict that position.

In Taiwan, the democratic, pro-*tongzhi* government's strategic inclusion of homosexuality (via the legalization of same-sex marriage) into the political and legal platform of nationalism has resulted in what I call an incorporative case of homonationalism. The young gay generation there exhibits a strong sense of Taiwanese identity, tends to endorse the state's homonationalist position, and views Taiwan as a beacon of East Asian democratization but risks overlooking the government's pinkwashing strategies. With the rise of mainland China, both the Taiwanese government and the young (gay) generation tend to draw heavily on a position of victimhood in which China (the ruling Communist Party in particular) is seen as the threatening other—a source of anxiety, ambivalence, aggression, and danger. In Hong Kong, the pro-Beijing, pro-Christian, profamily government has made no progressive advancement in terms of gender and sexuality; it labels homosexuality a controversial issue and emphasizes traditional Chinese family values as core values, a position that can be seen as a failed or deficient case of homonationalism. However, the recent political turmoil in Hong Kong has reinforced a distinctive Hong Kong identity, especially among members of the young (gay) generation, triggering protests against the government on all fronts. Most members of the young gay generation reject the government's deficient version of homonationalism and have even found a Hong Kong nationalist or homocolonialist position within a non-Hong Kong/non-China political and economic alliance, thereby complicating their civic-political activism. In mainland China, the dominant state has maintained its overriding concern for social stability but has adopted a somewhat liberal stance on homosexuality, allowing the operation of *tongzhi* nongovernmental organizations (NGOs) that pursue the goal of building a harmonious, HIV/AIDS-free society and espouse family values and patriotic responsibility while avoiding human rights discourses. The result is what I call homonationalism with Chinese characteristics, or *pragmatic homonationalism*, which aligns homosexuality with nationalism and seems to be endorsed by the young gay generation without direct confrontation. The findings also suggest the rigid polarization of the geopolitics implied by the government and by the young gay generation among the three locales to some degree.[1]

The State, Sexuality, and Homonationalism

Emerging literature on the complex relationship between the state and (homo)sexuality focuses on the state's power of regulation and governance, especially laws governing homosexual activities and other nonnormative or "deviant" sexualities (e.g., Bernstein and Schaffner 2005); it also documents queer activism against the state and the pursuit of change, especially in law—notably, the fighting for conduct-, identity- and relationship-based rights of sexual citizenship in the LGBT+ assimilation movement, hallmarked by the legalization of same-sex marriage (e.g., Bell and Binnie 2000; Richardson 2000, 2017; Seidman 2005). Besides, it examines whether the state is a unifying or heterogeneous entity that consists of many different but sometimes conflicting apparatuses such as local government, the courts, the police, and the army (Cooper 2002) and also understands the state's privileging of white, middle-class, heterosexual male subjects, evidence of its sexualized, gendered, racialized, and classed nature (e.g., Canaday 2009; Stychin 1998). In recent years, one major discussion is the notion of homonationalism that links the state with sexuality in transnational politics under global capitalism. Puar (2007, 2013) developed the concept of homonationalism in the US context to demonstrate that acceptance and tolerance for gay and lesbian subjects are barometers by which the state's legitimacy of and capacity for national sovereignty are evaluated. This was a product of her frustration at the assumption in transnational feminist and queer theories of the 1990s that queer people are inherently outlaws within a necessarily heteronormative nation-state. More specifically, Puar (2007) argues that homonationalism operates under three frames: "sexual exceptionalism," "queer as regulatory," and "the ascendency of whiteness." Sexual exceptionalism characterizes how the US state has absorbed some previously excluded LGBT+ subjects into American national life. Queer as regulatory debunks the myth about the radical meaning of queer. Queer is usually seen as an inherently transgressive category and thus a signifier of agency, autonomy, and resistance (Mendoza 2009), but it has now become regulatory and normalizing as mainstream gay and lesbians by and large endorse the notion of homonormativity (Duggan 2002) and espouse a con- servative, assimilationist politics and privatized, depoliticized gay culture centered around domesticity and consumption. The acceptance of queerness is the acceptance of such queer liberal subjects. The ascendency of whiteness describes "whiteness as a queer norm and straightness as a racial norm" (Puar 2007, xxxii), especially in contrast with Muslim sexualities, seen as patriarchal, heteronormative, and homophobic. These three frames work in tandem to produce US homonationalism, which endorses a nationally acceptable queerness—mainly white, middle-class queer liberals—and thus implicitly excludes nonwhite (queer South Asian Americans) or other queer radicals. Furthermore, Puar is not just concerned about homonationalism as a US national culture of acceptable and unacceptable modes of queer- ness but how the United States as a nation justified the War on Terror on a transnational framework. She argues that the US government positioned itself as culturally, morally, and politically advanced (tolerant of gays and lesbians) by employing orientalist myths to portray Arab/Muslim countries as culturally backward (as patriarchal and homophobic). Homonationalism thus "reiterates heterosexuality as the norm . . . fosters nationalist homosexual positionalities indebted to liberalism . . . enables a transnational discourse of U.S. sexual exceptionalism vis-à-vis perversely racialized bodies of pathologized nationalities" (Puar 2007, 51). Homonationalism can thus be seen as a historical shift in the relationship among the state, capitalism, and sexuality.

Homonationalism has been widely discussed, adapted, rearticulated, and critiqued, especially when used outside its original US context (e.g., Dhawan 2013; Kehl 2020; Langlois 2018; Rahman 2014; Schotten 2016; Sifaki, Quinan, and Loncarevic 2022; Winer and Bolzendahl 2020). For example, Schotten (2016) questions its explanatory power if it has shifted from a critique of "a racialized project of US empire" (356) to a critique of "a more generalized imperial sexual exceptionalism on the world stage" (361). Winer and Bolzendahl (2020) remind us that the concept may be overused, especially when applied outside the US context, and it might erase local complexities. Nevertheless, homonationalism is still an important analytical idea for conceptualizing the intricate relationship between the state and sexuality in the neoliberal era, and especially for teasing out the complexities of sexual politics among nations in the international political arena. More specifically, in non-US contexts, Rahman (2014) proposes homocolonialism to conceptualize the sexual politics between Western and Muslim cultures. He argues that it reifies the notion of Western/imperial exceptionalism through triangulation with homonormativity (Duggan 2002), homonationalism (Puar 2007), and the neocolonial development of the "gay international" (Massad 2007): "[T]he deployment of homonormative nationalism within a dialectic of respectability/otherness in a classic colonializing mode, directed at 'traditional' Muslim cultures as homophobic non-Western 'others' that need to be civilized or modernized but also constructing 'home' Western normative queer identities" (Rahman 2014, 279). That is, the liberation of the homosexual in the Global South from traditional, homophobic, non-Western others replicates progressive, superior, Western normative identities. Homocolonialism associates queer rights with progress and a rejection of traditionalism, which in turn means that "queer identities and rights are possible *only* in the West" (Rahman 2014, 279, emphasis in the original).

Instead of abandoning the notion of homonationalism, what we need is a multidimensional critique of neoimperialist and neocolonialist traces of homonormativity, homonationalism, and homocolonialism in Western and postcolonial societies (e.g., Dhawan 2013). In the following sections, I use the idea of homonationalism to delineate the relationship among the state, nationalism, and (homo)sexuality in Hong Kong, Taiwan, and mainland China. More specifically, I use it critically to tease out the complexities of sexual politics among the three governments in the rise of the China era. Meanwhile, I expand the notions of homonationalism, homonormativity, and homocolonialism as forms of state behavior or policy to the practices of subjects, be they organizations, groups, or individuals or whether they fall into the conservative/right or progressive/left end of the political spectrum (Schotten 2016). Following Bacchetta and Haritaworn (2011), I expand homonationalism into three levels of analysis: homonationalism as perpetuated by the state; homonationalism as understood by subjects within a nation (queer subjects); and homonationalism as circulated and produced on a transnational scale (what the authors call "homotransnationalism"). So in addition to presenting the idea of homonationalism from the state's perspective, I use the narratives of the participants to give voice to the young gay generation. I argue that the three distinctive cultural/national identities (Taiwanese, Hongkonger, and Chinese national) have given rise to three different identifications with nationalism, resulting in turn in three different forms of civic-political activism that align with or contradict the state's position on homosexuality. The result is a homotransnationalism that compares and contrasts the notion of homonationalism at both the state and individual levels on a transnational scale.

Taiwan: Incorporative Homonationalism and the Beacon of East Asian Democratization

The Taiwanese government, with its long history of being lobbied by and working with *tongzhi* organizations, has been facilitating the realization of *tongzhi* rights since the 2000s, as evidenced by its support for the first Gay Pride event in Taipei in 2003 and enactment of the Gender Equity Education Act in 2004 and the Act of Gender Equality in Employment in 2007. On May 24, 2017, the Taiwanese Constitutional Court announced Constitutional Interpretation No. 748, ruling that same-sex marriage should be seen as a human right and that the government should legalize it within two years. However, the Court did not specify whether legislation allowing same-sex marriage would require the revision of Taiwan's existing civil law or require the enactment of a new law expressly legalizing such marriage. Conservative and religious groups strongly advocated for such a law, which they thought would protect heteronormative marriage; a 2018 referendum showed widespread disapproval for the granting of *tongzhi* rights, including same-sex marriage, demonstrating the influence of those groups. However, the government responded by confirming the Court's ruling, and same-sex marriage legislation finally passed in May 2019. It was the first such legislation in Asia and was the result of a long battle between *tongzhi* organizations and activists and civil society (especially religious groups) and the state since the 1980s; but it was facilitated by more recent political events such as the electoral reform in 2008, the rise of the Sunflower Movement in 2014, and the electoral victory of the Democratic Progressive Party (DPP) in 2016 (Ho 2019b). The legislation's success should be seen as the outcome of continuous, decades-long effort by the sociodemocratic movement, of which the *tongzhi* movement is a part (see chapter 1), not simply as a liberal-facing policy of the government or a cunning government plot (Chen-Dedman 2022). Nevertheless, presidents Tsai Ing-wen (2016–), Ma Ying-jeou (2008–2016), and Chen Shui-bian (2000–2008) and a number of other Taiwanese politicians have continually and strategically used Taiwan's support for the *tongzhi* community—an internationally recognized marker of an open, globalized society—to advance their political agenda (Chu 2003; Ho 2017, iv). Such a strategic incorporation associates *tongzhi* rights with Western civilization as a discourse of progress, secularism, and modernity and a rejection of traditionalism (traditional Chinese culture, Confucianism, and evangelical Christianity). The Taiwanese government can be said to exhibit an incorporative form of homonationalism. Yet the legalization of same-sex marriage was intended to provide recognition, identity, and status only to those gay men and lesbians who fit into the model of the good citizen or *guai baobao* ("good gay"); who adhered to monogamy, the family, and the marriage institution; and who rejected polyamory or multiperson families of choice. This model also marginalized those who had called for a campaign to *huijia feihun* ("destroy the family and abolish matrimony") during the fight for same-sex marriage (Hung 2015; Lee 2017; Ning 2018). The inclusion of only the "good gay" in society thus operates in line with sexual norms (heteronormativity and homonormativity) and along the lines of class rather than race as the standard of civilization. It operates as sexual exceptionalism but also as Western exceptionalism, as the endorsement of *tongzhi* rights as human rights is also an endorsement of universal (Western) values. Moreover, such a homonationalist position affirms Taiwan as part of the global/Western civilized world. It allows Taiwan to distance itself explicitly from its authoritarian past and implicitly view mainland China as conservative and backward while remaining fully aware of the increasing military, political, and economic threats that China poses. Whereas the US version of homonationalism seeks to justify the War on Terror and conceal its imperialism, Taiwan's version seeks to increase its visibility in

FIG. 5.1. Assembly waiting for announcement of the legalization of same-sex marriage in 2019 (source: Taiwan Tongzhi [LGBTQ+] Hotline Association).

world politics and revert to a victim position with no intention of declaring a war (cf. Chi 2017, 99–100).

How does the post-'90s gay generation think about its cultural/national identity in relation to homosexuality and nationalism? Taiwan's population consists of a small number of Austronesian Taiwanese aboriginals (*yuanzhumin*; 3 percent) and the majority Han Chinese population comprising Hoklo (*fulaoren* or *minanren*; 70 percent), Hakka (*kejiaren*; 15 percent), and mainland Chinese (*waishengren*; 15 percent). In 1949, when Chiang Kai-shek retreated and relocated the Kuomintang (KMT, or Chinese Nationalist Party) to Taiwan, approximately 1.2 million mainland Chinese migrated to Taiwan from 1945 to 1960 (Lin 2018). In the KMT government's view, there was only one China—that is, both Taiwan and mainland China were part of the Republic of China. Accordingly, its ultimate goal was to liberate the mainland to achieve national unification. The KMT government thus tried to consolidate Chinese culture by both purging Japanese influences and suppressing any local Taiwanese cultural expression, whether by aboriginals, Hoklo, or Hakka. The KMT took the heavy-handed approach of martial law to facilitate the process of cultural reunification (or Sinification) during the 1949–1987 period (Chun 1996). Although the dominant identity from the 1950s to the 1970s was the pro-Han, pro-Chinese identity promoted by the KMT, the 2.28 Incident in 1947, which reflected frustration toward the KMT government and resulted in a massacre, gave birth to a broader modern Taiwanese identity framing the mainland Chinese who came to Taiwan as outsiders.[2] The end of martial law in 1987 heralded Taiwan's transformation from one-party authoritarian rule to a multiparty democracy. It was after KMT president Lee Teng-Hui (1988–2000) began reorienting Taiwan toward a Taiwanese localization movement, followed by the de-Sinification process launched by proindependence Democratic Progressive Party (DPP) president Chen Shui-bian (2000–2008), that a distinctive Taiwanese identity, in contrast to a mainland Chinese identity, was consolidated (Li and Zhang 2017), first among "seventh graders" (a term referring to those born between 1981 and 1990) and then among the post-'90s generation, the main players in the student-led Sunflower Movement in 2014. Today, neither the KMT nor DPP considers liberating the mainland to be a national goal, as Chiang Kai-shek's KMT did in the past. However, the two parties differ on the 1992 Consensus, which the KMT interprets as meaning that there is just one China, although there can be differing interpretations of what China is; while the DPP rejects that interpretation (and comfort with plural interpretations) and takes a two-China position. For its part, the People's Republic of China (PRC) interprets the 1992 Consensus as meaning that there is one China, inclusive of Taiwan, with the PRC its sole legitimate representative. These differences of interpretations have resulted in three broad positions concerning national identity in Taiwan: *Zhongguoren* (Chinese national), an identity espoused by those who identify with mainland China; *Zhonghuaminguoren* (national of the Republic of China), espoused by those who identify with the Republic of China; and *Taiwanren* (Taiwanese), espoused by those who identify with Taiwan. Although they can be distinguished analytically, they are ambiguous in terms of political stance.

Most members of the young generation call themselves Taiwanese rather than Chinese nationals or nationals of the Republic of China. Bao is no exception. Born in Tainan in 1993, he moved to Taipei to study and has lived there since 2011. He is now working as a research assistant in a university. He is very articulate and serious when he speaks. During the interview in 2017, Bao was very clear about his identity: "I've never regarded myself as a Chinese national, but I once regarded myself as a national of the Republic of China. It wasn't until 3.18 [the Sunflower Movement] that I realized that the Republic of China is not the same as Taiwan. So now I certainly call myself Taiwanese.... Chinese are foreigners, and the Chinese regime is a hostile regime. I don't hate Chinese [people], but I hate the Chinese Communist

Party and those Chinese who think that Taiwan should be unified [with mainland China]." Although most of the interviewees regard mainland China as a foreign country, they see total de-Sinification as virtually impossible because of the close ties between Taiwan and mainland China. Hao, whose story appears in the introduction and in chapter 2, expressed the difficulties this way in 2017:

> Even though my dad is a mainlander [*waishengren*]—he is from Anhui; I have never been there—I belong to Taiwan; this is our generation. Our education is not as hugely affected by Chinese nationalism as that of previous generations. We have learned the difference between Taiwan and China and realize that they are different.... [For me] China is [to Taiwan] like India is to England or France to Canada.... China is a foreign country like Japan or Korea, but it's not really like a foreign country...its "lotus roots may break but the fiber remains joined."[3]

Their distinctive Taiwanese identity but impossibility of totally cutting themselves off from China gives the young participants a strong sense of identification and pride, indeed a strong sense of nationalism, although they are critical of the DPP government and also aware of the problems of their society such as unemployment, low salaries, rising housing prices, the dominance of the PRC economy, and intervention by Beijing. They view Taiwan as a very friendly, tolerant society with a vibrant civic tradition stressing democracy and diversity, including support for gender- and sexuality-related issues such as same-sex marriage. Hao said that what makes him proud of Taiwan is that it is a pluralistic society that mixes many different cultures, including Chinese culture, Taiwanese culture, indigenous culture, and East Asian culture. He continued: "We have maintained a certain level of prosperity...and [Taiwan] is a land of freedom and equality.... Taiwan is a country...and international societies have recognized that we are a very different country [from China]." Hao cited marriage equality as a signal to the world of the great differences between the two and named the *tongzhi* movement as part of a larger democratic social movement: "We have different developments, and the difference is getting bigger and bigger.... I think at least in Taiwan the democratic movement enabled the subsequent emergence of the indigenous movement, the women's movement, and then the land movement, and then the *tongzhi* movement [and] gender movement."

A strong sense of homonationalism can be seen in the way in which Bao and other Taiwanese participants view mainland China: generally negative, with a focus on its one-party dictatorship, limits on freedom of speech, and corruption, poverty, and cultural backwardness. The Taiwanese participants also took the position that *tongzhi* activism has been suppressed in mainland China and that being gay there is very difficult, with most Chinese *tongzhi* still living in the closet and facing intense pressure to marry.

Their dislike of mainland China, mainly the Communist Party rather than the Chinese people, does not necessarily mean the rejection of romantic engagement, although those who have experienced romantic engagement have had difficulties reconciling the two different political regimes and cultures. A few participants had spent time in mainland China and/or had a mainland Chinese boyfriend. Jianggu, aged twenty-five in 2017, was born in Taichung. As a student, he went to Beijing on an exchange program and had his first romance while he was there. However, the relationship ended when the man married a woman. Jianggu subsequently studied dance in New York City before returning to Taiwan in 2020. He said in 2017, "I love China very much. The few months when I was there were the happiest of my life." He meant that he loved the Chinese people and Chinese culture, not Chinese politics or the government: "The Chinese government is disgusting. During the few months I lived there, I could feel the surveillance. It's on every single level of your life. And self-censorship is rife.... They [the Chinese people] have been brainwashed.... The government's controlling power is great." Jianggu also mentioned *lanjia* ("bluegay"; *lan* signifies the color blue of the pro-Beijing KMT, and *jia* means "the first" but rhymes with gay), insisting that he would not date gay men whose political orientation was KMT, although he recognized that such men constitute a minority in the gay community.[4] Xiaodai, aged twenty-seven in 2017, has a boyfriend from the mainland whom he met in Taiwan. Since his boyfriend's return home, they have maintained a long-distance relationship. Like Jianggu, he is very aware of being under surveillance. In a follow-up interview in 2021, he said: "I never thought our conversations on WeChat would be listened to or seen by the Chinese authorities. One day, I was talking with my boyfriend about Han Kuo-yu [a Taiwanese politician]. It was the first time that my boyfriend asked me to stop talking suddenly.... I had never felt so unsafe.... Our conversation since then has become 'Chinese' style. For example, we can't talk about the CCP [Chinese Communist Party]. In Chinese, the short name for the CPP is *Zhong Gong*. We have to type 'Zhong G,' with G implying *Gong*."

Many young Taiwanese have drawn closer to Hong Kong, which faces the same threat from mainland China. Hao explained in 2017, "I feel that Hong Kong and Taiwan share the same fate... Hong Kong and Taiwan are becoming closer and closer.... I am not sure whether China will declare war on Taiwan.... [Doing so would] involve a lot of other countries like the US, Japan, and even India.... I don't think it will happen but I am worried." At the same time, he pitied Hong Kong for its political backwardness: "But at least Taiwan seems to be a bit better than Hong Kong. At least we have more political space ... as we have undergone a full democratization process."

Taiwan can be considered an incorporative case of homonationalism at both the level of the state and the young gay generation. The state strategically legalized same-sex marriage and provided recognition for those gay men and lesbians who fit the model of the good citizen; it showcases these policies to other countries to claim a progressive national identity. For their part, the young gay generation, as represented by the participants, has a strong sense of both Taiwanese identity and nationalism and a strong desire to live in a free society without any threats. Like the state, this generation tends to applaud the Taiwanese government's positive treatment of *tongzhi* rights as a signal of a larger project of East Asian democratization and global cosmopolitanism. By aligning homosexuality with nationalism, the state and the young generation both view mainland China (mainly the CCP) as the threatening other—unfriendly and aggressive as well as backward and homophobic. Such homonationalism is incorporative in that the state integrates homosexuality into its nationalist strategy, with the young gay generation endorsing the state's incorporative homonationalism as part of its national identity formation. It is also cooperative in that the state and the young gay generation (as well as *tongzhi* organizations to some degree) work together in imagining a progressive nation that embraces homosexuality. Although the anti-Chinese/progressive West sentiment is not the main driving force of LGBT+ liberalization, such Cold War mentality or logic as the legalization of same-sex marriage = the victory of democracy = Taiwan is progressive = China is backward is often assumed and reinforced. Yet the Taiwanese version of homonationalism has its own limitations. The government tends to conceal its pinkwashing strategies and the occasions on which it has continued to discriminate against gay men and lesbians and limit their rights. Such examples include the regular police raids and crackdowns on gay establishments and events, most notably the frequent police raids of the gay sauna Aniki in 2014 and 2015, the restriction of assisted reproductive technology (ART) to heterosexual couples alone, and the denial of reproductive and adoption rights for LGBT+ (Wu 2018; Taiwan Tongzhi Hotlines 2018). The young gay men in this study also tended to overlook such concealment.

Hong Kong: Deficient Homonationalism, Homocolonialism, and Political Impasse

The Hong Kong Special Administrative Region (HKSAR) government is by and large pro-Beijing, has a close relationship with evangelical Christianity, and espouses a profamily, conservative stance. It has taken a more passive approach toward *tongzhi* rights. There is no law either banning discrimination on the basis of sexual orientation or allowing civil partnership. Although same-sex couples who married outside Hong Kong have scored a few legal victories in cases concerning spousal benefits, the government has emphasized that these cases pertain only to immigration policy and should not be seen as a challenge to the Marriage Ordinance, and Hong Kong is no closer to legislating same-sex marriage. The government is also indifferent to capitalizing on the pink dollar for economic gain or emphasizing the gay index to build Hong Kong as a creative city. Male homosexuals are still seen as a high-risk group confined to the public health domain (see chapter 1). In contrast with the Taiwanese government, the Hong Kong government does not view mainland China as a threat with respect to *tongzhi* or in general. On the contrary, like the Chinese government's ambivalent position on homosexuality (i.e., no encouraging, no discouraging, and no promoting), the Hong Kong government has itself avoided passing progressive laws pertaining to gender and sexuality by labeling such issues controversial and emphasizing traditional Chinese family values as core values in Hong Kong society. Hence, the Hong Kong government's position can be regarded as a failed or deficient case of homonationalism.

The history of national identity in Hong Kong is as complex as that of any former colony. In early colonial days (1842–1940s), Hong Kong was an integral part of South China, and there was no real Hong Kong identity as such. A Hong Kong identity slowly emerged owing to the ideological split of the Cold War that set colonial Hong Kong apart from communist China in the 1950s, rapid industrialization, and the rise of local popular cultural production (the launch of free television station TVB in 1967) in the 1960s. Then the colonial government's decolonizing project of the 1970s attempted to rebrand Hong Kong as a modern, cosmopolitan, Westernized city and to nurture an apolitical, economically driven citizenry (Law 2017; Ma 2012). The postwar baby boom generation nurtured a distinctive Hong Kong identity: Chinese plus "something more," be it affluence/cosmopolitanism/capitalism, English/colonial education/colonialism, or democracy/

human rights/the rule of law (Mathews 1997). Longitudinal studies have shown a mixed identity popular since 1997, with a Hong Kong identity first overtaking Chinese identity, an interim reversal from 2002 to 2008, and then a mixed identity and Hong Kong identity neck and neck from 2011 to 2016 (Ho 2019a, 60).

When I talked to young gay men in Hong Kong in 2017, they tended to express a complicated relationship with Chinese identity. Some embraced that identity and saw themselves as both ethnically Chinese and Chinese nationals, whereas others accepted Chinese ethnicity but not Chinese nationality. Some rejected both, emphasizing the uniqueness and exclusivity of being a Hongkonger (Kong 2019b). Other studies have reported similar findings (e.g., Ortmann 2017). By the time of follow-up interviews in 2020, however, almost all of the Hong Kong participants had shifted to identifying themselves as Hongkongers. Hong Kong identity has become a protest identity. In the wake of the 2014 Umbrella Movement, Law (2017) uses the term "right-wing localism" to describe the recent rise in Hong Kong nationalism that emphasizes the superiority of Hong Kong over mainland China, thereby radicalizing differences and the conflict between them. The movement has largely rejected the left-wing agenda of embracing cultural diversity and abandoned the *woleifeifei* (Cant., the "peaceful, rational, non-violent, and no foul language") form of resistance in favor of a more right-wing route that intensifies conflicts and tensions and employs more radical and confrontational means of expression and action. Its localism is expressed in calls for Hongkongers' right to self-determination, although there are different political stances, ranging from a desire to maintain a high degree of autonomy under the framework of one country, two systems (demanding universal suffrage) to radical calls for Hong Kong to become an independent sovereign city-state or to return to British colonial rule.

Daniel, whose story appears in chapter 4, is on the more radical end of Hong Kong nationalism. He said in 2020,

> I always call myself a Hongkonger. When I studied in the UK, I spent a lot of time explaining to people the difference between Hongkongers and Chinese.... When I was young, I found China very backward. It was very dirty, smelly, and full of cockroaches.... You could smell it when you crossed the border.... It was a scary place ... things would be stolen, you didn't know whether what you ate was safe or not, restaurants were dirty, and what pissed me off is that people didn't care about all these [things].... But my parents come from China. It's complicated. I wouldn't

say I hate mainlanders. I hate the government and its brainwashing, as a lot of people are being brainwashed.... The major difference between Hong Kong and China is the system. Hong Kong has the rule of law. China does not. Jurisdiction is not transparent.... Hong Kong inherited the British system, for example, in law, the government structure, and the election process ... [and] it is to a certain extent fair and rational.... But the most important thing that Hongkongers have is integrity. We know what to do and what should be done and what shouldn't. China does not [have that], maybe because they experienced the Cultural Revolution.... People with integrity either died or were exiled.... The rest are those who have no integrity, [who] just want to gain advantages, [or are] indifferent or ignorant. So they do things just for their own self-interest and do not care about civil society or the common good.

Despite acknowledging Hong Kong's inevitably intimate relationship with the mainland, Daniel, like many, defines "Hongkongness" (the rule of law, freedom of speech, internationalization, cosmopolitanism, cultural superiority) as the opposite of Chineseness (authoritarianism, political censorship, limited freedom of speech, cultural backwardness). It is this type of "Hong Kong nationalism" or "Hongkongism" that they are proud of.

However, the young participants feel they have been defeated—first, in the Umbrella Movement (2014); second, in the anti–Extradition Law Amendment Bill (ELAB) protests (2019); and finally, by the introduction of a Beijing-imposed national security law (2020). In their view, these changes have eroded core Hong Kong values (freedom of speech, equality and justice, the rule of law); worse, they have ended the one country, two systems regime. Daniel continued:

Hong Kong is dying, on the verge of death. During the Umbrella Movement in 2014, you had hope; you thought it would be okay if you persisted.... You camped at the protest site and thought that was resistance.... But then I changed from pacifism to bravery during the anti-ELAB protests in 2019 ... because of what I saw of how the police treated the protesters. It's integrity ... I am proud of it; I want to safeguard Hong Kong.... We protest not for any economic reasons but for justice, democracy, and freedom.

Many of the Hong Kong participants expressed admiration for (and even romanticized) Taiwan, particularly its democratic culture, much greater tolerance of gender and sexuality diversity, and alliance of various social movements. They agree with the Taiwanese participants that Taiwan is further along than Hong Kong. Daniel's view is typical:

> A few years ago, I thought Taiwan was a bit backward economically and culturally, like a mixture of Japan and China, a bit old, traditional, old-fashioned, and provincial.... But after these past few years, especially with the introduction of the national security law in Hong Kong, I think Taiwan has become much more advanced, especially politically, than Hong Kong.... Hong Kong is now undergoing white terror... something like Taiwan went through under martial law a few decades ago.... The social atmosphere in Taiwan is very positive, and there are a lot of people who support democracy and they can elect their own president.... Even though the party culture is not perfect—they mainly have two political parties—and a lot of social problems have not been resolved... at least people can choose which political party they want and also their president, which is much better than in Hong Kong.... That's how they distinguish themselves from China: they uphold human rights, democracy, big love.[5] ... Plus, they also have same-sex marriage, which I think is impossible in Hong Kong. So, at this moment, I think Taiwan is much better than Hong Kong.

Given his strong antigovernment stance, Daniel, like most of the Hong Kong participants, does not trust the Hong Kong government to pass any progressive laws, which would likely be blocked by legislators from the progovernment/pro-Beijing political parties in any case. By extension, they also do not believe that any fight for sexual rights can succeed in the near future, as they, like the Taiwanese participants, view the *tongzhi* movement as part of a larger democratic social movement. The Hong Kong participants are also skeptical about blue-ribbon Hongkongers, including blue-ribbon *tongzhi* actually fighting for *tongzhi* rights, as they emphasize social stability and order over democracy and human rights. By affirming the separation of their society into yellow- and blue-ribbon camps—and asserting that the former are real Hongkongers who are progressive and pro-*tongzhi* rights compared to the latter who are proestablishment and pro-Beijing government and thus backward, homophobic, or indifferent to *tongzhi* rights—they tend to echo homocolonialism (Rahman 2014), which demarcates Hongkongers as real or unreal, progressive or backward, and superior or inferior (see also X. Liu 2021). They want to safeguard the real Hong Kong, which is civilized and modern and embraces universal values, from a failing Hong Kong, which is governed by a puppet government manipulated by Beijing. Accordingly, they distance themselves from blue-ribbon Hongkongers (including blue-ribbon *tongzhi*) as well as from the Hong Kong and Beijing governments, while reintegrating themselves into a non-China bubble (represented by Western countries, or Taiwan, that endorse universal values) or even lingering in the colonial past, which they view as having more freedom and democracy than exist in posthandover Hong Kong. They tend to foreclose the possibility of any alliance apart from their own camp. They are not agents of Western states seeking to intervene in China's internal affairs, as the HKSAR government and CCP accuse them of being, but they are separationist, which pushes them to take a more homocolonialist position that aligns the claim of civilization, progress, openness, and universality with Western rhetoric. They are still struggling to find their own position and tend to harbor a strong desire for self-determination.

As staging any collective political movement is currently impossible, some *tongzhi* activists have separated the *tongzhi* movement from the wider democratic and political movement. Daniel complained that most of those who attended the Gay Pride gathering in 2019 were just looking for a celebration without seeking to address wider social problems. Similarly, the organizers of the 2022 (now postponed to 2023) Gay Games to be held in Hong Kong have repeatedly emphasized that the games are a cultural event that will bring together diverse groups of people to experience moments of joy through sports, arts, and culture. Their slogan is "Unity in Diversity," and they reject any discussion of human rights deemed political. We can only wait and see whether yellow-ribbon and blue-ribbon *tongzhi* will join together for this first-in-Asia LGBT+ event.

Another participant, Boris, who was born in 1994, is tall and skinny and wears a pair of glasses that gives him a bookish air. He has actively participated in social movements and the *tongzhi* movement since 2012 and admits that it is almost impossible to organize any collective movement. In a follow-up interview in 2021, he said that he has resorted to what he calls a "one-person movement":

> [The] *tongzhi* movement and democratic movement are strongly related. Under [the current] political structure, it's hard to organize a *tongzhi* movement. But I am happy that people tend to be a bit more concerned, [for example about the] sexual violence that happened during the protests. People are also concerned about sexual victims, including male [victims]...but...freedom of speech and freedom of assembly have been diminished.[6] Like in 2019, we had no Gay Pride walk but

FIG. 5.2. Hong Kong Pride Parade 2019 (source: author's photo).

a gathering.... Like Professor Ho, I would like to start a "one-person movement."[7] ... Public libraries have taken some children's books that talk about families, including gay parenting, off the shelf because they [have] received complaints [from religious groups]. I am now suing the government through a judicial review of the incident.

As part of the post-'90s generation, these young men have a strong and distinctive Hong Kong identity that challenges the legitimacy of the government on all fronts. By labeling the Hong Kong government (as well as the Beijing government and the blue-ribbon population) the enemy—and inherently conservative, homophobic, and/or indifferent to *tongzhi* rights—they strongly identify themselves as real Hongkongers who uphold progressive and universal values (e.g., equality, gay rights). Such a Hong Kong nationalist or homocolonialist position makes it difficult for the *tongzhi* movement to proceed, as it narrows the possibilities for forming alliances (say of yellow- and blue-ribbon *tongzhi*). As a result, the participants envision the *tongzhi* movement as either distancing itself from the wider social democratic movement by downplaying any forms of advocacy that could be read as political or reducing collective action to individual resistance.

Mainland China: Dominant State and
Pragmatic Homonationalism

The Chinese government's attitude toward homosexuality is ambivalent, expressed in the three nos: no encouraging, no discouraging, and no promoting. It is cautious about the *tongzhi* movement, viewing it as a potential threat to social stability, especially when it is linked to human rights issues. To maintain social stability while claiming and performing a relatively liberal stance, the Chinese government has fashioned its own version of homonationalism by aligning homosexuality with nationalism. For example, it has allowed the dating app Blued to survive because it aligns itself with the government's public health and HIV/AIDS policy and the *tongzhi* NGO PFLAG China/Trueself to operate because it emphasizes the Confucian values of parental love, care, and support rather than advocating for human rights Accordingly, Blued erases any direct references to gays or *tongzhi* while emphasizing a positive, healthy lifestyle, and PFLAG/Trueself explicitly prohibits its members from discussing political or sexual topics, soliciting hookups, or exchanging erotic texts and images. The Chinese government thus tolerates certain (mainly *suzhi*) gay men and lesbians—namely, those who espouse traditional Confucian values of parental love and care or engage in low-risk or safe sexual behavior, which aligns with its nation-building discourse stressing family values and patriotic responsibility in a harmonious and HIV/AIDS-free society. Hence, the Chinese state can be seen as displaying what I call homonationalism with Chinese characteristics or pragmatic homonationalism, which aligns homosexuality with nationalism.

Since 1949, the country's youth have been at the forefront of political and social movements through the considerable political turmoil and manmade and natural disasters. They acted as Red Guards in the Cultural Revolution (1967–1976) and played the leading role in the 1989 democratic movement that culminated in the movement's suppression at Tiananmen Square on June 4 of that year. The post-'90s generation is distinctive in the sense that its members are not actively pursuing democracy and are concerned primarily with individual pursuits, material rewards, and economic success.

All of the Shanghai participants identified as Chinese (both nationally and ethnically) but exhibited two rather contrasting views on national identity, democracy, and the *tongzhi* movement. Born in 1994 in Sichuan, Xiaoyu is the only son of a middle-class family. Both of his parents are CCP members. He is slight, wears glasses, and speaks in a confident voice. We met in 2017 after he had moved to Shanghai to study. He then went to

Australia in 2019 to study for a master's degree in anthropology but was forced to return home in 2020 owing to the COVID-19 pandemic. His plan was to go to the United States or Canada with his boyfriend to pursue a PhD in anthropology and then settle there. Unfortunately, however, all of his PhD applications were unsuccessful. He finally received an offer in a different discipline (computer science) in 2021, and he is going to accept it and move to the United States in 2022 to live with his boyfriend. In 2017, he described himself as follows.

> I am Chinese but recently I have felt quite ashamed of being Chinese. When we were young, we were educated to believe that "if the nation becomes stronger, no one is gonna bully us." ... For the post-'90s genera- tion, this has changed to "if the nation becomes stronger, no one is gonna save us." The stronger the nation becomes, especially its economy, the more its power is concentrated in the upper level [of the government], which constantly implements headstrong policies. Then you realize that the country actually doesn't care about you ... you think you have struggled to become middle class and wonder whether you could live better. You belong to a social class ... whose voices are not heard by anyone. ... There is the problem of poverty, mainly due to urban/rural disparities, and there is the problem of corruption. ... But the ultimate problem is that this is not a trustworthy government. The real problem is that there are no checks and balances on the government. Who makes policy and on what basis? We will never know.

Xiaoyu and the other Shanghai participants generally applauded China's economic success over the past few decades, and yet they recognized that the country faces a number of key problems, including increasingly stark economic inequalities, particularly between the rural and urban popula- tions, and corruption. However, what they were most ashamed of was the deprivation of political and human rights—freedom of speech in particu- lar—by the highly regulated one-party regime. That is why Xiaoyu was very sympathetic toward Hong Kong and other places affected by the One China policy. As he said in a follow-up interview in 2020: "Hong Kong is screwed and cannot go back. It's a pity. It has no future, like China. But you know what happened to Hong Kong has happened before here, like in Xinjiang, like in Inner Mongolia."

Xiaoyu's pessimistic view and critical stance toward the Chinese gov- ernment, however, contradicted the optimistic and almost patriotic stance of many of the other mainland participants who expressed the view that economic pluralism will eventually bring forth political pluralism. One of them was Yifan, whose story appears in the introduction and chapter 4 and who works in an international trading firm. He and his boyfriend are both deeply closeted but live together as a rather private middle-class couple. Yifan described his feelings about his country in 2017:

> In terms of economic achievement, it took countries like France and America a couple hundred years, but it has only taken us forty years. I think we are developing really fast. . . . I do international trading. I went to Africa and America and saw the police use guns to hit people's heads. I was shocked and [thought], "I am so lucky and happy to live in China." . . . Democracy in the mainland, I can feel it, is improving. . . . I think the government has a lot of considerations. . . . I think economic development will lead to democracy. . . .

It was clear from our follow-up interview in 2020 that his feelings about China had not changed:

> I am Chinese, and I agree with the One China policy. I don't want Hong Kong and Taiwan to be independent. I of course want unification. I can understand young people in Hong Kong. They are . . . economically disadvantaged, and that's why they use radical means. . . . I think China has become stronger and stronger. That's why the US and Europe are losing their status, and that makes them anxious. They are engaged in a kind of protectionism and in defending their own status quo.

Yifan identifies strongly with the CCP, opposes the student movements in Hong Kong and in Taiwan, and insists on the rightness of the One China principle. He believes that economic development is of paramount importance and that the principle will facilitate cross-border travel.

When asked for their views on the *tongzhi* movement, most Shanghai interviewees argued that now is not the right time to pursue it, that economic development should take precedence over any political movement, that human rights-based movements are not applicable to the context of China, or that the introduction of foreign influences would only complicate the situation. For example, Yifan said in 2020: "We need to put all our energy and resources into economic development. General economic growth should be the priority of Chinese society." Xiaofei, whose story appears in chapter 2, similarly argued in a follow-up interview in 2020 that in order to develop, the state needs to "tackle the biggest problem[s], [such as] poverty, military power, economic power, and even technological power. When everyone is not well fed and clothed, there is no one to care about the disadvantaged. It's only when the society is economically developed to a certain extent that people can pursue democracy and social equality."

Doudou (whose story appears in chapter 2) and his parents are members of PFLAG/Trueself. He supports the One China policy and does not agree with the demands for independence in Hong Kong and Taiwan. He understands and even approves of the government's preference for a *tongzhi* movement with Chinese characteristics. In a follow-up interview in 2020, he said:

> Western capitalism, policy advocacy, civil movements, raising awareness, and consciousness.... The Chinese government doesn't like ... these ideas and rhetoric. If we want to have a *tongzhi* movement, we need to develop the movement with Chinese characteristics.... I don't know how to do it. China has ... a basic structure of strong government and weak citizens.... It's difficult to copy and paste from the US [and] Europe. We need to "cross the river by feeling for the stones." ... I am just worried that the US-China relationship has worsened and that terms such as LGBT or feminism will become sensitive, and thus that the *tongzhi* issue will soon become a site of ideological battle.

Even Xiaoyu, who is highly critical of the argument that economic development should come before political pluralism, does not believe that the Western human rights-based approach is appropriate for China. He applauded PFLAG/Trueself's appeal to parental love and Confucianism in 2017 and reconfirmed this *tongzhi* strategy in 2020:

> I think bringing mothers and fathers together by emphasizing family relationships, love and care, and social tolerance of the gay movement is the right direction. They [PFLAG China] are quite smart to adopt this strategy. If you talk about the human rights of anyone, the issue will then become a sensitive topic and thus taboo.... Some feminist groups in China nowadays are very brave [he mentions the Feminist Five in particular; see the discussion in chapter 1], and I support them. However, their strategy is not smart. On the contrary, organizations like PFLAG China strategically avoid direct confrontation. Of course, I know in my heart that it's a matter of human rights ... but you can't have that kind of discourse in the mainland.... We can achieve our goal in a roundabout way.... We don't necessarily have to [be confrontational].

Hence, the Chinese state has fashioned a version of homonationalism that seems to be supported by the young gay generation. It is, the Shanghai participants argued, a form of homonationalism with Chinese characteristics that is pragmatic and nonconfrontational. The inclusion of good (*suzhi*) *tongzhi* citizens operates in conjunction with sexual norms (heteronormativity and homonormativity) and along the lines of class. Such pragmatic homonationalism is distinctive. First, it promotes sexual exceptionalism in a way that separates *tongzhi* rights from human rights and thus differs from the common-sense view of homonationalism, which usually equates the two. Second, it adheres to the Confucian values of parental love and care, which do not necessarily contradict the traditionalism that homonationalism or homocolonialism usually assumes.

Homosexuality, Homonationalism, and Homonormativity

This chapter has illustrated the intricate relationship among the state, nationalism, and (homo)sexuality in Hong Kong, Taiwan, and mainland China. Other discussions of homonationalism and homonormativity predominantly describe powerful nation-states (usually in the West) making use of nationalist claims about queerness as a weapon to demonstrate and justify their imperial dominance and superiority (the United States against the Arab world, the European Union against Eastern Europe, Israel against Palestine). As Puar (2010) argues, "To be gay friendly is to be modern, cosmopolitan, developed, first-world, global north, and, most significantly, democratic." I have shown that homonationalist claims can be made that go beyond the usual Western/Eastern, imperial/colonial, Global North/Global South binaries, evidenced in the different versions of homonationalism in the three Chinese locales under study: incorporative homonationalism in Taiwan, deficient homonationalism in Hong Kong, and pragmatic homonationalism in mainland China. More specifically, homonationalism can be advanced not just from the perspective of the powerful, as in Puar's (2007) original formulation of US-Arab relations, but also from the perspective of the marginal, as in the case of Taiwan under the political threats from China. Although some may be cautious of the risk of decontextualizing Puar's use of homonationalism in a non-US context (Chen-Dedman 2022; Winer and Bolzendahl 2020), my analysis goes beyond Puar's original usage of the term and shows that it is the marginalized (from the perspective of international politics) Taiwanese government that strategically claims to be civilized, gay friendly, and modern, thereby implicitly positioning the more powerful mainland Chinese government as barbaric, homophobic, and uncivilized. In other words, homonationalism is not just a weapon of domination wielded by the powerful; it can also be a weapon for those who assume victimhood.

Moreover, this chapter also exposes the limits of homonationalism, which can be seen as a concealed form of pinkwashing in which the state uses queer rights to perpetrate imperialist violence. Consider, for example, the Israeli state's appropriation of an image of modernity signified by Israeli gay life to conceal violations of Palestinians' human rights (Ritchie 2015). What we find in this research are other forms of pinkwashing that different governments have tried to conceal. For example, the Taiwanese government may not be as gay friendly as it purports to be, as we can see from the frequent police raids of gay establishments, denial of certain reproductive and adoption rights to *tongzhi*, and the long history of *tongzhi* activists and organizations battling with the government for full citizenship in terms of conduct-based, identity-based, and relationship-based rights claims. Further, the Chinese state's "three nos" attitude toward homosexuality ("no encouraging, no discouraging, and no promoting") is not particularly ambivalent or tolerant, as we can see from its increasing censorship and strict surveillance of *tongzhi* rights, activities, and NGOs. The Hong Kong government's deficient homonationalism, needless to say, shows no indication of any real change in the heteronormative nature of its policies despite the victories that have been achieved in a few legal cases.

The notion of homonationalism is usually employed by the state and criticized by queer activists, and thus the relationship among the state, nationalism, and (homo)sexuality is usually analyzed at the state and NGO levels. This chapter does not analyze *tongzhi* activists' views on homonationalism; it instead offers views at the individual level (i.e., the views of the post-'90s gay generation in Hong Kong, Taiwan, and mainland China) through the participants' narratives. Their differing takes on the relationship among the state, nationalism, and homosexuality reflect three distinct but interrelated cultural identities (Hongkonger, Taiwanese, and Chinese national). The Taiwanese participants, most with a distinctive Taiwanese identity and strong sense of nationalism, ally themselves with the government's strategic homonationalist claims that mainland China is the threatening other but risk overlooking the tensions between the government and homosexuality, acting as if the government were totally gay friendly. In contrast, the Hong Kong participants, with a distinctive Hong Kong identity but considerable distrust of both the Hong Kong and Chinese governments, position both governments as the evil other and have struggled with a more or less separationist approach that means either fashioning a Hong Kong nationalist position by reintegrating into the non-China bubble (making homonationalist claims like Taiwan or the United States) or lingering in the colonial British past (making homocolonialist claims). In both cases, they acknowledge the inevitable and largely inseparable relationship with mainland China. Although some have an emotional attachment to China (to Chinese culture and the Chinese people), most expressed fear of the political threats from mainland China as well as anti-China subjectivity (which they sometimes conflated with anti-CCP or even anti–mainland Chinese sentiment). The Shanghai participants, most of whom have a rather patriotic orientation, align themselves with their state's pragmatic homonationalism without direct confrontation under the increasing censorship of *tongzhi* NGOs and activities. They try to redefine the meaning of rights (*tongzhi* rights are not human rights) and argue that traditionalism can be progressive. Whereas the Taiwanese and Hong Kong participants to a greater or lesser extent utilize the Western notion of modernity and progress for national and cultural identification as well as for making *tongzhi* claims (typically sexual exceptionalism in homonationalist claims), the Shanghai participants argue for a cultural exceptionalism that makes use of traditional Chinese values (Confucianism) to put forward homonationalist and *tongzhi* claims.

It is true that in all three societies under study, the *tongzhi* subject has gone from being pathologized and criminalized to being a marker of sexual enlightenment and liberation (cf. Dhawan 2013). However, the combination of homosexuality with nationalism has usually resulted in the association of the good homosexual with nationalism and the social inclusion/exclusion of any gay man revolving around the normative (sexual) ideal and along the lines of class.

My analysis departs from the original US-centric notion of homonationalism and goes beyond the single-bounded state model to challenge such binaries as China/West and liberal/repressive. It does not present Taiwan as more open or liberal and Hong Kong or mainland China as more closed or backward. Rather, it illustrates how the three governments make use of homosexuality as a way to advance nationalism in the context of current geopolitics and exposes the limits of homonationalism as a pinkwashing strategy, especially in the case of Taiwan. This state-level analysis serves as a backdrop for examining empirically, not normatively or ideologically, through the participants' narratives how the post-'90s generation exhibits mutually defined cultural/national identities and has developed different forms of civic-political activism that align with or contradict their respective governments' positions on homosexuality. The pro-Taiwan and anti-China binary has been reinforced by the state and the participants in Taiwan, whereas the dominant One-China-marginalized Hong Kong/Taiwan binary has also been reinforced by the state and the participants in mainland China. However, in Hong Kong, the pro–Hong Kong/anti-China binary has been disabled and enabled by the government and the participants, respectively. What is needed is a way to go beyond these rigid polarizations and binaries that is sensitive to both the concrete sociomaterial conditions that shape the subjectivities of each locale and the increasingly tense geopolitics of all three locales against the backdrop of the latest global order (Berberoglu 2021; Therborn 2011)—or what Dai (2018) calls the "post-post–Cold War era"—which is characterized by the rise of China's global power (Arase 2016; Chan, Lee, and Chan 2011; Choi 2018; Fong, Wu, and Nathan 2021; see also Liu and Zhang 2022). It is from this analysis of the two levels of homonationalism and transnational analysis of the three locales that we can move beyond the static statist theory of homonationalism to take into account both the narratives of individuals and transnational, regional, and geographical politics (Puar 2022). The result is Bacchetta and Haritaworn's (2011) proposed third definition of homonationalism, what they call "homo-transnationalism," which seems best positioned to capture the complexity of state-sexuality relationships on a transnational scale.

Conclusion

I started writing this book in early 2020 and finished it at the end of 2021, at a time when COVID-19 was still affecting daily routines worldwide, with new variants emerging and spreading and people becoming used to the new normal of a masked, vaccinated, and socially distanced life. The Chinese Communist Party (CCP) celebrated its one hundredth anniversary in 2021, with President Xi Jinping warning the world in his anniversary address that China will not be oppressed. China's rise, especially its shift from "soft power" to "sharp power," has effected a change in its status from the world's factory to a major global player in every domain (political, economic, financial, military, cultural, technological), influencing or even reshaping the social, political, economic, and cultural world order, most notably through its global trading network, the Belt and Road Initiative, and by silencing the discussion of human rights issues using its economic and political clout. Relations between mainland China and most Western countries (the United States in particular) have worsened in recent years, with the CCP facing criticism over alleged human rights abuses in Xinjiang province and direct political involvement in Hong Kong, particularly since the imposition of a new national security law in the latter. Using sharp power (Wu 2021), mainland China has been influencing Hong Kong, Taiwan, and beyond in many areas (Fong, Wu, and Nathan 2021; Ho 2019a). The CCP is becoming increasingly vocal about the inviolability of its One China policy, which has heightened tensions between mainland China and Taiwan:

Taiwan sees itself as an independent state whereas the CCP sees it as an integral part of China.

This book has thus been written during these strangest of times. Using a transnational, queer, sociological approach, the book explores the stories of ninety young gay men living in Hong Kong, Taiwan, and mainland China against the backdrop of these various geopolitical tensions and the rise of China at this particular historical juncture. It offers a socio-historical and material analysis in which social institutions and sexuality are mutually constituted. More specifically, it provides a political economy of sexuality by articulating how the state, the market economy, and civil society are sites of both governance and resistance wherein the post-'90s gay generation is both being made and self-making as sexual subjects. The various chapters underscore the increasingly striking differences among the three locales resulting from the socioeconomic and political transformations of recent years but also emphasize the shared histories that create significant similarities among them.

Postreform China has not only normalized the neoliberal "free market," triggering mass-scale rural-to-urban migration, privatization and deregulation, social restratification, and labor exploitation in the process but also cemented the CCP's political legitimacy at all levels (Liu and Tan 2020; Zhang and Ong 2008). The net result seems to be the production of a desiring and enterprising China that fosters nascent consumerism, competition, and entrepreneurship, especially among the burgeoning middle class, albeit within the confines of a highly regulated and surveilled society and one-party political regime. Homosexuality is a case in point. The Chinese government's ambivalent attitude toward homosexuality has left some room for development but only under strict state control. Homosexuality has been decriminalized (1997) and demedicalized (2001), and a *tongzhi* world ranging from the pink economy to the mass media and popular culture, websites, dating apps, school curricula, and *tongzhi* activism has developed and flourished, although it has been heavily censored since 2021. A model that I call *homonationalism with Chinese characteristics* or *pragmatic homonationalism* has allowed a small remnant to survive, such as the dating app Blued, which aligns nationalism with public health (especially in terms of HIV/AIDS prevention), and the *tongzhi* organization PFLAG (which recently changed its name to Trueself to remove any connotation of homosexuality), which aligns nationalism with Confucianism and emphasizes parental love and social tolerance. The result is the toleration of certain gay men—namely, those who espouse a *suzhi*, middle-class, cosmopolitan identity and embody the ideal of homonormative masculinity.

As part of the post-'90s generation, the mainland Chinese participants were born into and have grown up in this relatively liberal but controlled environment. They do not actively pursue democracy, as did their counterparts in Taiwan during the Sunflower Movement in 2014 and those in Hong Kong during the Umbrella Movement and Extradition Law Amendment Bill (ELAB) protests in 2014 and 2019, respectively, nor do they seek to topple the system, as occurred during the Arab Spring in the early 2010s, or publicly fight against corruption, as did their predecessors on the mainland in 1989. They also differ from the post-'80s generation, which sought the meaning of life outside China by looking toward the West in particular. Given little control over their formal education, family, or the state, these young men are simply in search of "small interventions, piecemeal changes, occasional resistance and locally specific alternative subjectivities" (de Kloet and Fung 2017, 21). The recent *Sang* (loss) culture, *foxi* (Buddhist) style, and *tang ping* (lying flat) philosophy constitute an emerging ethos embraced by the young generation in protest against the culture of work, the reproductive imperative (under the three-child policy implemented in 2021), conspicuous consumption, skyrocketing housing prices, and intense state censorship. Characterized as defeatism and loss (*Sang* culture; Tan and Cheng 2020); a cool, laissez-faire life attitude (Buddhist style; Yuan 2020); or doing the bare minimum (lying flat), a structure of "loser" feelings, nonintervention strategies, or passive-aggressiveness, seems to be a powerful tactic of protest, even if only symbolically, against a desiring, enterprising, over-productive China. Unlike their Hong Kong and Taiwanese counterparts, the mainland participants still have to struggle between coming out and living in the closet, as China basically remains a marriage society. To deal with that struggle, they have developed a range of strategies, including, among others, *pianhun* (marrying straight women who do not know about their sexuality), *xinghun* (marrying a lesbian), coming home, coming with, and tacit disclosure. Their engagement with the gay world is fragmentary, since the *tongzhi* world, as part of civil society, is heavily controlled and regulated and reduced primarily to the online dating world. These structural constraints block any large-scale, collective, physical experiences and thus there is a preference for engaging in personal communities, largely online. Influences of Western (predominantly US) culture are significant, but imaginative inter-Asia referencing is a more important, and even crucial, cultural resource and source of emotional comfort to escape from the difficulties of daily life.

Although neoliberalism and developmentalism have produced a desiring and enterprising China, the result has not always been a desiring subject with abundant sexual desires or an enterprising, successful self but rather a fatigued and precarious labor subject, a filial subject struggling between sexuality and family, and an aimless, relentless (online) cruising subject. The mainland participants either give up desiring an intimate relationship or wait till they become successful, with success again constrained and limited by their class and/or migrant position. Although some members of the young gay generation are quite critical of the government, most tend to believe that economic pluralism will eventually lead to political pluralism. They tend to separate the *tongzhi* movement from the democratic movement and thus separate the fight for sexual rights from the fight for human rights and endorse the state's form of homonationalism with Chinese characteristics, which is pragmatic and nonconfrontational. When asked about their future plans, some of the participants, including Xiaofei, Doudou, Bei, and Yifan, indicated that they still fantasize about having a highly normative life by, for instance, settling down in Shanghai (or another city in China), buying an apartment, and securing a stable job and a lasting intimate relationship. Some are thinking of migrating to North America, Europe, or Japan. Xiaoyu is particularly eager to leave China. He is moving to the United States next year to study with his boyfriend and is determined to settle there. Others such as Xinxin, however, have started to question such "cruel optimism" concerning the good life (Berlant 2011) and cling to the *tang ping* (lying flat) philosophy, as wishful fantasies of the good life are increasingly at odds with the precarity of their lives amid family/marriage pressure and the demands of an enterprising and desiring society.

British colonial rule in Hong Kong ended in 1997, when Hong Kong became a special administrative region of China. Hong Kong not only successfully transformed itself from an industrial colonial city into an international financial center after 1949 but also played a key role in helping to grow China's economy from the 1980s. Since the handover, Hong Kong has increasingly become subject to direct influence from Beijing politically, economically, and culturally (Fong 2021; Ho 2019a; Wu 2021), which has slowly changed law-abiding, apolitical, self-enterprising citizenship into protest citizenship, triggered by the Umbrella Movement in 2014 and consolidated in the ELAB protests in 2019, with the major political cleavage now between the blue-ribbon and yellow-ribbon camps. In terms of sexuality, homosexuality was decriminalized in Hong Kong in 1991, and the age of consent for heterosexual and homosexual acts was equalized in 2005. The pro-Beijing, pro-Christianity government, however, exhibits a homonationalism that can be seen as deficient, as it is indifferent to any progressive advancement in terms of gender and sexuality issues, and it views homosexuality as controversial and posing a threat to traditional Chinese family values (e.g., reproductive heteronormativity). The Hong Kong citizen is not a full citizen owing to the lack of universal suffrage (equipped with the right to vote but not the right to select candidates for election). Hong Kong *tongzhi* are lesser citizens still, as there is no sexual-orientation discrimination ordinance and no recognition of same-sex marriage. Since the 1980s, when it was still under colonial rule, Hong Kong has had a well-developed pink economy. Civil society is also fairly robust, with a well-established *tongzhi* world featuring large-scale annual *tongzhi* events (e.g., International Day against Homophobia, Biphobia and Transphobia [IDAHOT], Pride Walk, and PinkDot), abundant *tongzhi* rights-based groups and self-help and lifestyle-oriented social groups, visible *tongzhi* media and arts, sought-after studies in academia, and popular dating apps and websites.

As part of the post-'90s generation, the Hong Kong participants in this study have developed a distinctive Hong Kong identity, characterized by a strong sense of cosmopolitanism and a firm belief in the rule of law as a legacy of British colonial rule. They live in a relatively affluent environment and are exposed to and enjoy a cosmopolitan, consumption-led lifestyle; but they also face a highly competitive education system; struggle to establish careers under the force of the neoliberal logic of success, competition, and performance; and are often forced to live with their families because of largely unaffordable housing costs. Most have chosen to come out and reject the idea of engaging in a fake marriage (to either a straight woman or a lesbian), an option often pursued by previous generations and their mainland counterparts alike. They largely enjoy the well-established gay world in Hong Kong, but owing to their limited physical space (most live with their families), they often turn to consumption (e.g., in shopping malls, cinemas, bars, and saunas) and cross-national tourism (in Tokyo, Taipei, Bangkok, and Seoul). Hong Kong gay bodies are not private, domestic bodies; they are in large part public, consumption and cross-national bodies. Their protest identity is best illustrated through their love lives. Political affiliation, especially the yellow/blue divide, has become the prominent deal breaker in a relationship rather than fidelity or other desirable attributes of homonormative masculinity. However, the political reality has rendered them powerless, defeated, and despairing. They have no hope of any fight for human rights (and by extension sexual rights) succeeding in the foreseeable future. In contrast to the government's deficient homonationalism, they have fashioned a notion of Hong Kong nationalism by which they either reintegrate themselves into a new non-China bubble or romanticize the colonial past (a kind of homocolonialism), both of which carry a strong sense of separatism, leading to a demarcation between real Hongkongers, whom they believe to be civilized and modern and to embrace universal values such as equality, justice, and democracy, and unreal Hongkongers who are blue ribbon (including blue-ribbon *tongzhi*), progovernment, and pro-China and therefore backward, homophobic, and indifferent to human (including sexual) rights. In such a political situation, they engage less in cruel optimism than in a kind of pessimism that is not too hopeless, which could be called merciful pessimism. When asked about their future plans, most Hong Kong participants expressed confusion and despair and the feeling that they are stuck in Hong Kong (e.g., Bobby, Wei, Boris). Some have migrated to the United Kingdom (Daniel), and others have concrete plans to migrate (e.g., John to Taiwan). Others simply engage in self-improvement such as pursuing further studies or finding a better job (e.g., Yoyo).

Taiwan has also undergone considerable transformation since 1949. Following thirty-eight years of martial law under authoritarian KMT rule, it became a representative democracy in 1996. Martial law/politically suppressed citizenship has slowly transformed into democratic and neoliberal citizenship. Like Hong Kong, Taiwan's political relationship with Beijing has had a direct impact on its own economy. Over the years, Taiwan has actively participated in turning China into an economic superpower. However, Taiwan has been influenced by mainland China in many respects such as in presidential elections, media control, tourism, religious exchange, and its growing clout in the entertainment industry (Fong 2021; Wu 2021). Taiwan was fortunate to have completed the transition to democracy before the rise of China, but the paradox it faces now is that the more complete cross-strait economic integration becomes, the greater the threat of political and cultural assimilation with mainland China (Ho 2019a, 69–70). The Taiwanese government could be seen as pro-*tongzhi* as a result of the long history of lobbying by *tongzhi* activists and organizations, exemplified by the Gender Equity Education Act (2004), Act of Gender Equality in Employment (2008), and legalization of same-sex marriage (2019). The government's strategic position on homosexuality exhibits an incorporative form of homonationalism, even though the toleration of gay men and lesbians perhaps fits more closely into the *guai baobao* ("good gay") model and on occasion conceals the government's pinkwashing strategies. As part of its vibrant civil society, Taiwan has the most well-developed *tongzhi* world, including a strong *tongzhi* presence in mainstream media and culture as well as on social media and dating apps; the mushrooming of *tongzhi* self-help groups and organizations; a well-established pink economy, hallmarked by the gay ghetto in Ximending and the organization of circuit parties; strong *tongzhi* activism; and the burgeoning of gender and sexuality studies in academia.

As part of the post-'90s generation, or what is sometimes referred to as the "collapsing generation" (Lin et al. 2011), the Taiwanese participants in this study live in a society with low fertility, prolonged education, and postponed marriage. They suffer from growing unemployment and low wages despite relatively high levels of education, not to mention soaring housing prices. Under China's constant political and economic domination, they seem to have developed a strong sense of nationalism but are reflexive, optimistic, and hopeful. They are proud to live in a democratic society that allows them to resist China, as they did in the Sunflower Movement, and embrace the universal values of democracy, pluralism, and diversity, exemplified by the legalization of same-sex marriage.

The Taiwanese participants have a very clear and positive gay identity. Even if they do not live with their families (which is generally true of those whose families are not from Taipei), most have willingly come out to them. They benefit from a fully developed *tongzhi* world, and their diffusive engagement with that world means that they are able to engage with as many aspects of it as they wish. The gay world in Taiwan provides the possibility of engaging in collective large-scale community attachment or smaller-scale personal communities or commons with affection and emotion and global and inter-Asian imagination. These young men live in an environment that gives them imaginative and reflective space to suspend, to pause, and to rethink love, work, life, and the future. They exhibit a strong Taiwanese identity and a strong sense of nationalism, applaud the *tongzhi*-friendly government's homonationalism, and are proud of living in the first society in Asia to legalize same-sex marriage, although they sometimes risk overlooking the tension between homosexuality and nationalism. They have attained full sexual citizenship: conduct-based, identity-based, and relationship-based. When asked about their future plans, most of the participants had few concrete ideas but were optimistic about the future despite low salaries, the inability to afford to buy an apartment, the lack of a stable relationship (for many), and even the fear that China might start a war with Taiwan. They either continue with their studies (e.g., Hao, Bao) or work (e.g., Hiro, Dajin, Tony, Xiaoai, Xiaodai), while others keep changing jobs (e.g., Jay, Jianggu). Very few have any migration plans. They can thus be said to engage in a form of cruel optimism, as they enjoy "little assured happiness" of the "minute things in life" (Wang 2017b, 186).

The many differences outlined above are intercategorical differences among the locales rather than intracategorical differences within each locale, but these differences have shaped the self-formation of the young men. By the same token, there are also striking similarities among the three societies that have shaped their subjectivities (see table C.1). First of all, neoliberalism and developmentalism have led to an emphasis on success, performance, and competition becoming prevalent in modernizing Asian societies. The result has been the production of "high-quality" modern subjects (Ku and Pun 2004; Lin and Mac an Ghaill 2017)—more specifically, the neoliberal entrepreneur of identity formation in Chinese societies. Across the sites, the participants are working hard to achieve neoliberal entrepreneurial masculinity, particularly reflected in the pressures of education and work in their lives.

Second, the neoliberal Chinese family has several common features across the three sites. On the one hand, it collaborates with the state to become a tool of governance and the key provider of social welfare and, on the other hand, it is an important social institution for nurturing the neoliberal values of success, competition, and performance. The gay subject has turned itself into an economic agent within the structure of the family. The family manifests "homonormative economic familism" (Lizada 2021), meaning it is subject to a homonormativity that emphasizes domesticity, private consumption, and economic security as well as familism, which structures the ethics of sonhood within the family institution in the neoliberal era.[1] That is why coming out should best be understood not simply as identity politics but as relational politics. The family is the main site wherein the embeddedness of the relational self plays out.

Third, embedded within the logic of cosmopolitanism and neoliberal individualism, the gay communities in the three societies have shown a more or less uniformed culture of new normativity—what I call *homonormative masculinity*, which can be seen as a structuration of the sexual field that centers around four aspects: body and gender performance, coupled intimacy, middle-class sensibility, and political conservatism. Homonormative masculinity is performative and judgmental and differentiates between the good and bad homosexual, positioning the latter as irresponsible, shameful, and deserving of regulation and punishment.

Fourth, what is common among these young gay men is their constant search for romantic love but difficulty finding it. For most, the ideal form of intimate relationship is still monogamy, an example of the cruel optimism of their imagination of a good life (Berlant 2011). As a result, most have remained single and engage in casual hookups or develop ambiguous loving relationships with a few men. Even those who are in a relationship have developed various strategies for negotiating the monogamy ideal: venturing out—either together or separately, openly or in secret, with explicit or implicit rules—to form different kinds of relationships.

Finally, most participants across the sites have a clear and positive gay (rather than nonbinary or queer) identity and are cisgender. They have even turned gay masculinity from a subordinate masculinity into a more open, acceptable, and normal masculinity, and they even challenge straight masculinity as boring, constraining, and rigid. So what is queer about their lives? As stated in the introduction, *queer* is used in this book less as a sexual identity marker and more as a verb, an adjective, an attitude, and an enduring practice to challenge normativity and embrace potentialities (Ahmed 2016; Butler 1990; Somerville 2014; Moussawi and Vidal-Ortiz 2020). More specifically, as Judith Butler explained in an interview, queer is less an identity than "something of the uncapturable or unpredictable trajectory of a sexual life" (Ahmed 2016, 489). The undetermined part, or the queerness, can be seen in various aspects of their lives, such as their various ways of coming out, including tacit discourse such as the coming-home strategy that decenters the notion of the closet, thus refuting the developmental or teleological path of coming out; their queer reading of popular culture (TV dramas and movies) and celebrities who can be read as outright heterosexual, ambiguous, or gay but are camouflaged as straight ("socialist brotherhood" in mainland China, "hehe" in Hong Kong); sharing in the queer pleasure of "reading against the grain" in social media to celebrate polymorphous points of identification and the misidentification of sexual and gender fluidity; and their play with ambiguity in loving relationships to implicitly challenge (or to queer) the hegemonic monogamous model and cross the boundary of lover/friend.

Youth is an ambiguous period of time, when one is trapped between unruly adolescence and orderly adulthood. These young men's lives are full of exploration and experimentalism, success and failure, despair and hope under the different forms of "normative cruelties" (Ringrose and Renold 2010), "cosmopolitan sexualities" (Plummer 2015), or "cruel optimism" (Berlant 2011).

TABLE C.1. A brief comparison of the post-'90s gay generation's negotiation with sexuality in Hong Kong, Taiwan, and mainland China

	Hong Kong	Taiwan	Mainland China
Subject formation	Cosmopolitan and neoliberalism but defeated and politically dissident subject	Cosmopolitan and neoliberalism but "collapsing" generation with optimism	Desiring and enterprising but precarious subject of fatigue
Family	Mostly out (passively and actively)	Mostly out (actively)	Struggling in and out (e.g., *pianhun, xinghun*, ARTs)
Community engagement	Cross-national consumption, on/offline engagement	Diffusive, on/offline engagement	Fragmentary, mainly online engagement
Homonormative masculinity	Class, body, and decency	Class, body, and decency	Class (*suzhi* discourse), body, and migrant status
Love and sex	Struggling with family coresidence and political affiliation as a deal breaker	Enjoying "little assured happiness" of imagined love life resulting from newly legalized same-sex marriage	Struggling with marriage and indulging in online dating with little hope
Political activism	At odds with government's deficient homonationalism, development of non-China bubble or homocolonialism	Alignment with the government's incorporative homonationalism	Alignment with the government's homonationalism with Chinese characteristics

Critiquing Globalization and Debunking
the Essentializing Myth of Chineseness

By adopting the perspective of transnational queer sociology, this book challenges the teleological trajectory of the sexual emancipation model that links sexual identity (coming out), group solidarity (community building), and sexual minority-rights claims (sexual citizenship formation) in a linear development. Rather than forcing the three societies into this model and ranking them as more closed to more open and equating openness with progressiveness, it instead emphasizes their similarities and differences. It recognizes the shared histories that have produced significant commonalities (neoliberal entrepreneurial masculinity, neofamilism, homonormative masculinity, the monogamous ideal) while emphasizing their notable differences (coming out politics, community engagement, cultural/national identity formation, civic-political activism).

The complexity of the results thus offers a critique of the globalization thesis, going beyond the usual binary and essentialist ways of framing research and analysis (global-local, West-East) to produce descriptions of mutually referenced, commonly shared, and translocally influenced queer experiences among and within different locales. My critique thus draws less on reference to the West and more on reference to other Asian cultures. This book has demonstrated that Western culture, rhetoric, and processes have impinged upon these societies, although they experience the West in different ways since Western culture, like Chinese culture, is not homogeneous and has diverse meanings at different times. Owing to its history of British colonialism, people in Hong Kong have always been receptive to the West (drawing primarily on British experiences), which has been idealized as representing modernity, sophistication, and progress, particularly during the colonial period. Postwar Taiwanese society too has been receptive to the West, manifested in signs of cultural Americanization. In contrast to capitalist Hong Kong and Taiwan, mainland China was a socialist state from 1949 to the 1980s and has thus always been more ambivalent toward the West, exercising caution over the corrupt and decadent capitalist West and viewing its own socialist society as culturally and politically superior. Since the 1990s, however, mainland China has turned into a late-socialist or state-capitalist society, with strong state involvement in capitalist practices. Moreover, Marxism, as both Western critical intellectual thought and a political force, somewhat ironically materialized not in China or colonial Hong Kong but in Taiwan. Marxism-Leninism-Maoism combined with structural functionalism (with its uncritical stance toward the state and obsession with modernization) to rebuild the "new China" (Kong, 2016), whereas Hong Kong, existing between China and Taiwan under British colonialism, remained politically ambivalent. Nevertheless, the West is seen as an authority on knowledge in all three locales. Nowadays, the West, which predominantly signifies Euro-American experiences, is the source of globalized hegemonic discourses that manifest as rhetoric on universal values such as human rights, democracy, equality, and social justice (Amnesty International, Greenpeace, anti–World Trade Organization) and in the reception of popular culture and aesthetics (Hollywood blockbusters, especially Marvel movies, HBO, Netflix) in Asia. With respect to homosexuality, that meant it was first construed as a mental illness or form of social deviance under Western medical and scientific discourse (the creation of the "modern problem") and later as a normal sexual orientation, a matter of public health, a cosmopolitan lifestyle, or a human rights issue.

A new cultural geography of East Asia has been formed (Otmazgin 2016), which can be seen in export-oriented industrialization, led first by Japan and then followed by South Korea, Taiwan, Hong Kong, Singapore, and other East and Southeast Asian countries/territories; urban and regional planning that involves Asian referencing, modeling, appropriation, and competition (Bangalore from Singapore, Singapore from Hong Kong, Hyderabad from Shanghai); and the emergence of an Asian global pop market (Chua 2015; Chong, Chow and de Kloet 2019; Yue 2011).[2]

Ong's (2011) notion of *worlding Asian cities* identifies three styles— modeling, inter-referencing, and new solidarities—in Asia's metropolitan transformation of being global. Applying her idea to the gender and sexual landscapes in Hong Kong, Taiwan, and mainland China, three styles of transformation are found in those sites as well. First, they can be seen in the gay business model in Hong Kong that has also been adopted in the southern Chinese cities of Shenzhen and Guangzhou and in the public health model in Hong Kong and Taiwan that served as a model for China in the early 1990s. Since the 2000s, Taiwan's circuit parties are modeled on those of Bangkok and mutually modeled with Tokyo and Seoul and Hong Kong's Pink Dot on Singapore. There are many examples of inter-Asia referencing. The notable example is the queer appropriation of the term *tongzhi* in Hong Kong, which then spread to Taiwan and later to mainland China in the 1990s. Although there are other more specific terms for gays and lesbians, and some members of the LGBT+ community may not use (or resist using) it for self-identification, *tongzhi* has replaced *tongxinglian* (same-sex love) as the dominant term for nonnormative Chinese genders and sexualities. The term's popularity may be due to its erasure of any sexual connotation and to its affirmation of a "positive" rather than "negative" identity, as is the case with the term *queer* (whose original meaning was *freak*) used in the Western context.[3] As the term means both political subjectivity (*tongzhi* as comrade) and sexual subjectivity (*tongzhi* as queer), it carries an elaborate pun and serious connotation in mainland China. Another example of inter-Asia referencing is the transnational Chinese Tongzhi Conference (1996, 1997, 1998), which offered the first critique of the Western model of homosexuality and even proposed the reification of an authentic Chinese homosexuality by essentializing Western (individual, confrontational) and Chinese (family, nonconfrontational, harmony) cultures (Kong 2011, 52–54; Wong 2004). Moreover, Hong Kong played a significant role in shaping the *tongzhi* cultures of mainland China in the 1990s, whereas Taiwan's *tongzhi* cultural production had a strong impact on the Hong Kong media in the mid-1990s. Later intellectual exchanges among the three sites have further intensified inter-Asia referencing, notably through the annual conference organized by the Center for the Study of Sexualities in Taiwan and the biannual conference on sexuality organized by Renmin University in mainland China, which invite scholars from the three locales and beyond to rethink the complexity of genders and sexualities in Chinese societies and elsewhere. The last example of inter-Asia referencing is the circulation of queer popular culture in magazines (Taiwan's *G&L Magazine*), TV programs (Taiwan's *Kangxi Lai Le*), videos on demand (GagaOOlala), movies (China's Internet novel *Beijing Story*, which was adapted into the Hong Kong film *Lan Yu*), and queer film festivals (the Hong Kong Lesbian and Gay Film Festival, the Taiwan International Queer Film Festival) across the three sites and beyond (Japanese manga such as Boys Love [BL] novels and BL-style TV dramas in Thailand, sexualized male K-pop and boy bands). Finally, new solidarities and alliances in terms of genders and sexualities in Asia can be seen in both the transnational religious alliance among Hong Kong, Taiwan, Singapore, and South Korea that has acted as a strong opposing force to *tongzhi* activism in Hong Kong and Taiwan and the synergies of *tongzhi* activism in fighting for human rights, equality, and democracy in the two societies.

The stories shared in this book speak for themselves. The young gay men I have interviewed selectively incorporate, revise, and reject Western ways of being gay. These closely interlinked societies are undergoing enormous political, social, and economic transformations that have transformed the lives of those who live there and their horizons of possibility, sense of identity, and life trajectories. And these transformations, in turn, can push us to think more globally about how queer transformations have intersecting and ramifying significance. For example, the Western coming-out model is just one of the many ways, and not even the dominant way, that young Chinese gay men handle their sexuality in respect of the family. Western men, once seen as offering the most desirable, even ideal, model of gay masculinity and intimate relationships, have been replaced by Chinese men or East Asian men (or what Kang [2017] calls "white Asians") as objects of desire. In engaging with the queer world, as well as with activism, the participants have fashioned Western rhetoric, rigors, and styles less than inter-Asia modeling, imagination, inter-referencing, and solidarities. They seek a form of civic-political activism that is sensitive to local specificities within global parameters (e.g., homocolonialism in Hong Kong, incorporative homonationalism in Taiwan, homonationalism with Chinese characteristics in mainland China).

The transnational queer sociology also results in a critical reflection of the rise of China discourse. Although mainland China has become a major player in the new social, political, economic, and cultural world order with its enforcement of the One China policy and the rise of Chinese nationalism, the discourse of its rise has obscured the heterogeneous transformations in interlinked locations such as Hong Kong and Taiwan. Bringing them into view to grapple with the question of their interrelationships is vital: Are they transnational or seminational or something else? Once gaining insights from Sinophone studies (Shih 2013) and queer Sinophone studies (Chiang and Heinrich 2014), one must be mindful of the politics of the Chinese-speaking worlds inside and outside China. The monolithic English term *Chinese* has many counterparts in the Chinese language: *Zhongguoren* (which historically refers to mainland Chinese), *huaqiao* (which usually refers to diasporic ethnic Chinese outside mainland China and Taiwan), and *hanren* (which refers to the ethnically Han Chinese). Although the participants are all Han Chinese, they view themselves differently in terms of cultural/national identification. For example, most of the mainland participants call themselves *Zhongguoren* (Chinese national), whereas the Hong Kong participants call themselves Hongkongers (as an ethnic identity), and the Taiwan participants call themselves Taiwanese (as both an ethnic and national identity). The identities of Hongkonger and Taiwanese are in tension with the ethnic Chinese and Chinese national identity. What is interesting is that, in the eyes of the Hong Kong and Taiwanese participants, both *Hongkonger* and *Taiwanese* represent tolerance, diversity, and cosmopolitanism in contrast to the mainland Chinese identity and sometimes conflate mainland Chinese people with the CCP, which represents poverty and cultural backwardness as well as communism and one-party dictatorship. The mainland Chinese participants also display diverse positions on nationalism and patriotism and define themselves relationally with Hong Kong and Taiwan. Hence "Chineseness" is central to the imagination and construction of Hong Kong, Taiwan, and mainland Chinese identities, although for the former two it also represents the other: a source of anxiety, ambivalence, and threat. Such rigid polarizations or binaries have formed the dominant geopolitical relationships among the young gay generations across the three sites, which tend to obscure alternative understanding and reinforce the Cold War mentality, and thus should be unpacked and deconstructed. Nevertheless, the findings expose the myth of Chineseness, as if being Chinese were something essential, fixed, or universal. Instead, the term takes on differential meanings across and within the Sinophone world. Chineseness is "conceptualized as multiple, contradictory, and fragmented: not the expression of a timeless national essence but instead the product of disjunctive regimes of cultural regulation across the multiple transnational contexts where claims to various forms of Chineseness are made" (Martin 2015, 35). Chineseness and queerness are "always already" transnational, and both should be thought of outside national boundaries and Western imagination (Leung 2008). It is this cultural logic of repositioning, which maps out the complicated "social process of discrepant transcultural practices" (Rofel 2007, 94), that gives us more insights into the intertranslatability of the ethnicity and nationality of Chineseness and queerness.

Decolonizing Sexualities

Using proposed transnational queer sociology, this book breaks, or at least blurs, the boundaries of binary conceptualizations to illustrate the hybridity of the "glocal" queer flows that are neither globalized nor localized and to demonstrate the complex meaning of Chinese young gay male sexualities, which should be understood in specific sociohistorical, economic, and political circumstances. It addresses the many gaps in the study of globalization and sexuality by articulating the nuances of the mutually referenced and influenced experiences among three main Chinese locales. It also balances material analysis of sociostructural configurations with discursive textual analysis of media and cultural representations. It thus engages sociology with queer theory by sharing concepts (queer commons, cruel optimism, and homonationalism) and methods (case studies) between the humanities and the social sciences.

Using Hong Kong, Taiwan, and mainland China as case studies, this book provincializes sociological knowledge by pointing out that sociology and queer theory are indeed part of a Eurocentric narrative of modernity. It forces sociology to rethink modernity outside the discipline's Marx-Weber-Durkheim foundation myth and challenges it to analyze gender and sexuality outside the confines of the Marx-Foucault-Butler hegemony. The coloniality of the modern gender system (Lugones 2007) and sexuality (in, e.g., queer theory; Kao 2021) should be taken seriously or seen as the mainstream in the sociology of gender and sexuality (cf., Connell 2014; Kong 2022). This book is thus part of the emerging decolonizing sexualities program (e.g., Bakshi, Jivraj, and Posocco 2016). Moreover, transnational queer sociology shares many ideas with recent decolonial work on the pluriverse (e.g., Reiter 2018), especially in Latin American studies (Escobar 2020). We both seek ways to understand the world that go beyond borders and struggles to think in the plural, the local, and the world. We are both frustrated with unduly narrow, biased, and Eurocentric knowledge that claims to cover and explain the whole world. Finally, we both aim to decenter the West and to challenge its claims of universality by provincializing it and demonstrating the coexistence of many cultures, many worlds, and many universes. In a sense, this book is a kind of ethnographic proposal and a search for a political ontology in comospolitics. I am thus talking about the pluriversal worlds found in Hong Kong, Taiwan, and mainland China in multiple Asias.

Situated within the mobilities paradigm, I call for a transnational turn in the sociology of homosexuality, joining the growing body of work attempting to decenter the Western form of "universal" knowledge in social science in general (Alatas 2003) and sociology in particular (Bhambra 2014; Connell 2014; Go 2016), with a focus on sexuality. Critical dialogue is difficult when globally connected academic lives are so unequal. As Alatas (2003) argues, "If in the colonial past, academic imperialism was maintained via colonial power, today academic neo-colonialism is maintained via the condition of academic dependency" (602). Submissions from the periphery usually use Western theory to frame non-Western data, which in the long run reinforces Western hegemony. That is why Connell (2015) calls for a new model of theory building, or "solidarity-based epistemology," which urges us to respect different formations of knowledge and to enter into educational relations with one another.[4] Transnational queer sociology constitutes one such attempt. If it is important to acknowledge "connected sociologies"

(Bhambra 2014) to link the histories of various non-Western locales with the West and to reconstruct modernity's past(s) in order to fully grasp the reality of globalization, then it is equally important to acknowledge "disconnected sociologies" to understand that globalization in its current state (global capitalism, neoliberalism) is not a universal, unified phenomenon but rather a heterogeneous and interconnected practice.[5] Such a unified worldview or empire asserted by the Euro-American metropoles needs to be undone by "difference." As a form of "postcolonial postnationalist queer studies" (Rofel 2011), this book is an attempt to undo the Western sexual knowledge of homosexuality through "difference" using the distinctive histories and cultures, and unequal positionings, of three Chinese locales through the voices of young gay men.

I miss my participants very much, especially those living in Taiwan and mainland China. It will be difficult to see them in the near future owing to the COVID-19 travel restrictions currently in place and the political tensions between mainland China and Taiwan, but I think about them a lot. If there were a chance for them to meet for a focus group discussion, I would like to put Doudou, John, and Hao from mainland China, Hong Kong, and Taiwan, respectively, into conversation, as all three are out to their families and have maintained a very good relationship with their parents. What would they learn from one another in telling their coming-out stories? I would also like to bring Bei, Bobby, and Jay from their respective locales together, as they all long for a romantic relationship but have thus far had difficulty finding one. What stories would they share? Another interesting conversation would be among Cody, Andy, and Xiaoai, as Cody lives in a solely online gay world in mainland China, whereas Andy regularly travels from Hong Kong to other Asian and even Western societies for sex, love, fun, and drugs, and Xiaoai enjoys the well-established gay world in Taipei without needing to travel abroad. I would also be curious to see whether Yifan, who displays a strong sense of patriotism toward mainland China, would engage in debate about the democratic or *tongzhi* movement with Daniel and Hao, who espouse strong Hongkonger and Taiwanese identities, respectively, and are extremely distrustful of the Chinese government. Stories breed stories, and the connected stories of commonality, connectivity, and community told in this book intertwine with disconnected stories of displacement, dislocation, and difference.

The romanization of Chinese characters follows the *pinyin* system except where marked as Cantonese romanization (Cant.). The direct literal translations of Chinese terms are given for quick reference. Readers are advised to refer to the main text for a fuller explanation of the terms.

aimei	ambiguous	曖昧
Gong nui (Cant.)	(Kong) Hong girl	港女
gongyi	public interest	公益
guai baobao	good gay	乖寶寶
hanren	ethnic Han Chinese	漢人
hanxu	implicit, reserved	含蓄
huaqiao	diasporic ethnic Chinese	華僑
huijia feihun	destroy family, abolish matrimony	毀家廢婚
hukou	household registration	戶口
jiulinghou	post-'90s generation	九零後
Kangxi Lai Le	Kangsi Coming (TV program in Taiwan)	康熙來了

lian	(individual) face	臉
liumangzui	hooliganism	流氓罪
mianzi	(social) face	面子
mingyuan	socialite, or celebrity	名媛
nanshen (Cant.)	male god	男神
pi	obsession or addiction	癖
pianhun	fraudulent marriage	騙婚
Shang Yin	*Addicted* (TV program in mainland China)	上癮
shangliang fengsu	virtuous customs	善良風俗
suzhi	quality	素質
Taiwanren	Taiwanese	台灣人
tongqi	homosexual wife	同妻
tongxing'ai	homosexual love	同性愛
tongxinglian	homosexuality	同性戀
tongzhi	"common will" or comrade	同志
wanghong	Internet celebrity	網紅
wanghuang	Internet porn star	網黃
woleifeifei (Cant.)	peaceful, rational, nonviolent, and no foul language	和理非非
waishengren	people from outside (in the Taiwanese context, referring mainly to mainland Chinese)	外省人
xiao que xin	little assured happiness	小確幸
xinghun	pro forma marriage	形婚
Zhongguoren	Chinese national	中國人
Zhonghuaminguoren	National of the Republic of China	中華民國人

Introduction

Earlier versions of the section "Transnational Queer Sociology" appeared as "Transnational Queer Sociological Analysis of Sexual Identity and Civic-Political Activism in Hong Kong, Taiwan and Mainland China," *British Journal of Sociology* 70, no. 5 (2019): 1904–25, https://doi.org/10.1111/1468-4446.12697; and "Toward a Transnational Queer Sociology: Historical Formation of Tongzhi Identities and Cultures in Hong Kong and Taiwan (1980s–1990s) and China (Late 1990s–Early 2000s)," *Journal of Homosexuality* 69, no. 3 (2022): 474–98.

1   In this book, I adopt a transnational queer sociological approach to understand the dynamics of the three Chinese locales (Hong Kong, Taiwan, and mainland China), as they are deeply marked by their distinct political histories, local cultures, civic traditions, and social structures. However, I do not intend to make any claim about the political independence of Hong Kong or Taiwan. Moreover, the word *state* is sometimes used interchangeably with the word *government* (the agent of the state) to refer to the distinct political administration of Hong Kong, Taiwan, and mainland China.

2   Hong Kong's Umbrella Movement was sparked on August 31, 2014, by a National People's Congress Standing Committee decision in China about the proposed reform of the Hong Kong electoral system. More specifically, the decision prescribed the prescreening of candidates for election as the chief executive of the HKSAR government (Ho 2019a).

3 "President Tsai Interviewed by BBC," News and Activities, Office of the President, Republic of China (Taiwan), January 18, 2020, https://english.president.gov.tw/News/5962.

4 *Postsocialism* is a term commonly used to refer to the current political economy of mainland China, but it may not be the correct usage for two reasons. First, mainland China is not postsocialist in the way that parts of the ex-Soviet bloc can be thought of as postsocialist. Second, mainland China remains a single-party state under the control of the CCP; for it to be a postsocialist state, the CCP would need to relinquish some political control to other parties, which has not yet happened. I prefer to refer to "postreform China," which can be characterized as "late socialist" because it reflects a certain degree of economic market reform and/or features state capitalism, although we have to be mindful that capitalism in mainland China is heavily controlled by the CCP rather than by the market economy as commonly understood in most Euro-American societies.

5 I use LGBT+ to refer to lesbian, gay, bisexual, transgender, and other related nonnormative identities and sexualities (intersex, asexual, pansexual, questioning, etc.), which are usually subsumed under the umbrella term *queer*. As the book uses the word *queer* less as a sexual-identity marker and more as a verb, an attitude, or an enduring practice to challenge normativity, I use LGBT+ instead of LGBTQ.

6 For Hong Kong and mainland China, see Ho et al. (2018); Kong (2011); for mainland China, see Rofel (2007); for Taiwan, see Martin (2003).

7 For Hong Kong, see Kong 2011, 48–51; for mainland China, see Kong (2016); for Taiwan, see Damm (2017).

8 For example, aversion therapy (turning gays straight) is still practiced in Hong Kong (IRCT 2020) and mainland China (IRCT 2020; Bao 2018, 93–118), although not in Taiwan since 2018. See Noah Buchan, "Rainbow Crossing: Conversion Therapy by Another Name?," *Taipei Times*, December 19, 2019, http://www.taipeitimes.com/News/feat/archives/2019/12/19/2003727797.

9 These annual parties may not be organized every year, as they are subject to various factors such as the state of pink businesses, government intervention, and health conditions (e.g., the COVID-19 pandemic).

10 For example, sexual stigma (Plummer 1975) is understood in symbolic interactionism and labeling theory.

11 Some examples of sociohistorical conditions are the emergence of gay subcultures (McIntosh 1968), professionalization of medicine (Weeks 1981), and the rise of industrial capitalism (D'Emilio 1983).

12 As I argued elsewhere (Kong 2011, 21), early Western studies of non-Western sexual cultures were mainly based on reports from missionaries, traders, and seamen. Western anthropologists have long used such reports and their own ethnographic research to understand "other" sexual cultures. Consider,

for example, Malinowski's (1922) and Mead's (1952) understanding of gender and sexuality in Melanesia; Herdt's (1981) idea of ritualized homosexuality, in which a "semen transaction" between boys and young men is a common practice supported by the whole social order in Papua New Guinea; Lancaster's (1988) notion of Nicaraguan *machistas* who have sex with other men but do not consider themselves homosexual; and the "third" gender—Thai *kathoey*, Filipino *bakla*, Indonesian *waria*, Polynesian *fa'afafine*, and Indian *hijra*—commonly found in traditional Asian and Pacific societies (Johnson, Jackson, and Herdt 2000). This body of work shows the sex/gender systems in non-Western countries to be quite different from those in the West. The binaries of male/female, masculine/feminine, and heterosexual/homosexual are more modern inventions heavily influenced by Western biological and medical discourses (Weston 1993).

13 Altman's (1997) notion of a "global gay identity" alludes to a universal gay prototype that is implicitly based on Western gay identity, characterized by such phenomena as openly expressing one's sexual identity, contesting sexual rather than gender norms, replacing the idea of male homosexuals as would-be women with new self-concepts, preferring primary homosexual relationships as opposed to marrying and engaging in "homosex" on the side, and developing various commercial venues based on sexuality and communities with a gay political consciousness. His formulation of a "global gay identity" that conflates such an identity with a white, gay male identity under the globalization of queer identities has been criticized (Manalansan 2003, 5; Rofel 2007, 89–94).

He was later critical of this formulation, writing that "western assumptions about homosexuality as the basis for identity are spreading rapidly, often in ways that displace or further marginalise more traditional assumptions about gender and sexuality. While theorists may see this as the imposition of western values … increasing numbers of people in the majority world assert 'LGBT' identities, self-consciously using terms taken from the west. … When I started to write about new gay and lesbian assertion in South East Asia at the end of the 1990s, my conclusions were based on the visibility of new groups that used western (usually American) terminology and literature to make sense of their desire to assert identities that they could relate to in their contemporary urban societies" (Altman 2013, 181).

Massad (2002) uses the term "Gay International" to refer to international rights organizations dominated by white Western males such as the International Lesbian and Gay Association (ILGA) and the International Gay and Lesbian Human Rights Commission (IGLHRC) whose mission is to defend the rights of gays and lesbians all over the world based on the Western gay emancipation model.

14 Please see the special issues "What's Queer about Queer Studies Now?" (Eng, Halberstam, and Munoz 2005) and "Left of Queer" (Eng and Puar 2020) in *Social Text*.

15　See, for example, Yau (2010) on mainland China and Hong Kong; Liu and Rofel (2010) and Liu (2015) on mainland China and Taiwan; and Chiang and Heinrich (2014) on queer Sinophone cultures.

16　This orientation to a power-resistance paradigm based on a politics of difference is derived from my earlier work. For details, please see Kong (2011, 28–32).

17　I share in the critique of a unified notion of identity offered by symbolic interactionism (e.g., Plummer 1975), deconstruction (e.g., Derrida 1976), queer theory (e.g., Butler 1990; Fuss 1989; Jagose 1996), and Black feminist thought on intersectionality (e.g., Collins 1990; Crenshaw 1991).

18　I agree with Warner, Kurtis, and Adya (2020) that scholars who use assemblage theory do not intend to replace intersectionality but rather to reenvision intersectionality as assemblage. Assemblage theory is thus partly a critique of a popular (mis)interpretation of intersectionality as representing essentialized ideas of identity.

19　Please also see Meghji (2021), who suggests in his conclusion seven strategies for decolonizing sociology: (1) situate the development of sociology in the field of colonial-imperial relations, (2) deuniversalize any cannon, (3) look for links even if you were not taught them yourself, (4) value the Global South regardless of northern valuation schemes, (5) do not "neoliberalize" decolonial work, (6) encourage students and scholars to be multilingual, (7) and accept that decolonizing sociology does not have an end point.

20　Ten participants in mainland China were first interviewed by my coinvestigator, Lin Chwen-der, but were followed up by me in subsequent interviews.

21　A brief profile of the participants (including their age, place of origin, level of education, occupation, and whether they live with their natal families) is given here. All of the information provided was obtained during the first interview. The Hong Kong participants were born between 1990 and 2000 and had an average age of twenty-four. They were all born in Hong Kong, with the exception of two who were born in South China and one who was born in Macau and moved to Hong Kong when they were children. Ten percent were secondary school students or had only a secondary level of education; more than one-third (40 percent) had completed or were currently in postsecondary education (e.g., diploma, higher diploma, associate degree); and a similar proportion (36.7 percent) were studying for or had obtained a bachelor's degree. Slightly more than ten percent (13.3) were studying for or had obtained a master's degree. Just under one-third (26.7 percent) were students, and a few (6.6 percent) were unemployed at the time of the first interview. The remainder were employed in a variety of occupations in education, finance and business, IT, medicine, catering, sales and service, and the government and nongovernment sectors. Two-thirds of the Hong Kong participants (66.7 percent) still lived with their natal families.

　　　The Taiwan participants were born between 1990 and 1999 and had an average age of 24.4. Half of them (50 percent) were born in Taipei or New

Taipei, and the rest were from middle (e.g., Taichung), southern (e.g., Tainan), or eastern (e.g., Hualien) Taiwan. Only one had not advanced beyond secondary school. More than half (60 percent) were studying for or had obtained a bachelor's degree, and more than one-third (36.7 percent) were studying for or had obtained a master's degree. The relatively large percentage of Taiwan participants with a high level of education reflects education policy in Taiwan, where most young people have an opportunity to pursue higher education, as well as the fact that there are very few diploma or associate degree programs, as most of the educational institutions that previously offered such programs have reorganized themselves as degree-bearing universities of technology or science and technology. Thirteen percent of the participants were unemployed, and more than half (60 percent) were students. The rest were employed in a variety of occupations in education, IT, management, finance, engineering, medicine, catering, sales and service, the military, and the government. Less than one-third (23 percent) still lived with their natal families, as the families of half the participants did not live in Taipei.

The mainland Chinese participants were born between 1990 and 1998 and had an average age of 23.9. Just under one-third (30 percent) were born in Shanghai; the rest were born in various regions of mainland China, including the southwest (e.g., Yunnan, Sichuan), midwest (e.g., Hunan, Jiangxi), and northeast (e.g., Liaoning). Ten percent were students in or had completed secondary (junior) education, and twenty percent had completed or were in postsecondary education (i.e., vocational or junior college education in the mainland Chinese context). More than half (56.7 percent) were studying for or had obtained a bachelor's degree, and slightly more than ten percent (13.3) were studying for or had obtained a master's degree. Roughly one-third (30 percent) were students at the time of the interview, and the rest worked in a variety of occupations in education, finance, trading, medicine, engineering, catering, sales and service, fashion, media, IT, and the government and nongovernment sectors. Less than one-third of the mainland participants (26.7 percent) still lived with their natal families, as two-thirds were migrants whose families did not live in Shanghai.

As a whole, the participants constitute a diverse although fairly educated sample.

22 There are three methodological problems that I would like to reflect upon: the problem of representation, the problem of legitimization, and the problem of ethics. The first problem consists of two separate but related questions: the question of the subjects being studied (i.e., Who is the other?) and the question of the author's place in a text or field (i.e., Who can speak for the other, from what position and on what basis?) (Denzin and Lincoln 1994, 577–78). Study of the "homosexual" in Euro-American societies can be categorized into three waves (Kong, Plummer, and Mahoney 2002). "Traditional homosexual research" was dominated by sexology, medicine, and psychiatry. Presumably, heterosexual scientists relied on a form of positivism that

drew a sharp distinction between researcher and researched and conducted standardized interviews to obtain objective accounts of the nature of homosexuality. They interviewed "abnormal" homosexuals in search of a pathological diagnosis. This positivistic and clinical approach was gradually replaced by a more hermeneutic and interpretive approach ("modernizing homosexual research") from the 1970s onward, collapsing the dichotomy between subject/researcher and object/researched and emphasizing self-awareness, reflexivity, and shared meanings. Some researchers even came out during the research process. The arrival of queer theory in the 1990s, signifying "postmodern or queer research," further complicated the issue of representation, pointing out that the gay and lesbian experiences represented are usually a reproduction of the experiences of white, middle-class, Western gay men and lesbians and neglects other marginal and queer voices. Queer theorists urged the reconciliation of our multiple fragmented selves and discursively constituted subjectivities, intersected significantly by gender, race, sexuality, and class, among the diverse social positions that mediate everyday life and the research process. Situating myself in the third research paradigm, I am mindful of my dual role as insider/outsider and my authorial voice in producing, not just describing, the participants' voices in the production of knowledge about young Chinese gay men in analyzing the stories in this book.

The second problem, that of legitimization, is traditionally seen as a problem of validity, which concerns the technical issues of finding valid answers to such questions as how to avoid lying, deception, and the display of "demand characteristics" and problems of memory and accounting for the past (Plummer 1983). The problem is partially resolved through triangulation of my various field trips, repeated interviews, and discussions with my coinvestigators, research assistants, and referred NGOs to testify to the validity of the participants' narratives. The problem cannot be totally overcome, however—claiming that the truth can be revealed risks falling into the trap of positivism. The task is to subvert the unified notion of gay identity and to paint a picture of multiple and conflicting sexual/gendered experiences. I chose life stories to highlight the tension between objectivity and subjectivity by showing participants' tendency to produce consistency in their biographies when they recast the past while also seeking out ambiguity, contradiction, flux, and diversity in their narratives to illustrate the fullness of their lived experiences.

The third problem, that of ethics, is a matter not simply of dealing with such technical issues as consent, confidentiality, anonymity, and risk/harm reduction but also of finding a way to develop an ethical strategy that is reflexive and empathic and learning the art of the boundaries and limitations of relationships or friendships formed in the field. I am fortunate to have developed beautiful friendships with my participants, who shared with me their wonderful and bittersweet stories.

23 The Sunflower Movement of 2014 in Taiwan was launched by students and civic groups in protest over the legislature's passage of the KMT's proposed Cross-Strait Service Trade Agreement without a clause-by-clause review. The protestors believed that a trade pact with the PRC would harm Taiwan's economy and leave it vulnerable to PRC political pressure (Tseng 2014).

Chapter 1. Queering Hong Kong, Taiwan, and Mainland China

This chapter is derived and modified from Travis S. K. Kong, Hsiao-Wei Kuan, Sky H. L. Lau, and Sara L. Friedman, "LGBT Movements in Taiwan, Hong Kong, and China," in *Oxford Encyclopedia of LGBT Politics and Policy*, ed. D. Haider-Markel (Oxford: Oxford University Press, 2021), https://doi.org/10.1093 /acrefore/9780190228637.013.1275; and Travis S. K. Kong, "Toward a Transnational Queer Sociology: Historical Formation of Tongzhi Identities and Cultures in Hong Kong and Taiwan (1980s–1990s) and China (Late 1990s–early 2000s)," *Journal of Homosexuality* 69, no. 3 (2022): 474–98. Owing to space limitations, this chapter focuses primarily on the development of gay (and to a lesser extent lesbian) identities. It should be noted that other nonnormative sexual identities (e.g., transgender, intersex) have different histories but cannot be fully captured in this chapter.

1 The Qing legal code of the Qing dynasty (1644–1911) introduced a substatute against male-male rape (forcible sodomy) in 1679, which was superseded by a similar substatute in 1734 that remained in force until the end of the Qing dynasty (Sommer 1997).

2 See Chiang (2010, 634–47) for the debate between Zhang Jingsheng and Pan Guangdan; see Kang (2009, 43–49) for that between Hu Qiuyuan and Yang Youtian.

3 The theory's dominant status was established after Pan Guangdan, a US-trained sociologist, translated Ellis's book into Chinese. He started his translation in 1939 and took three years to complete, but it did not go to press until 1946. In his translation, Pan provided rich annotations concerning Chinese sexual culture alongside Ellis's text and included an appendix documenting textual evidence of traditional Chinese same-sex practices (Guo 2016; see also Pan 1986, 1–7).

4 See Kong (2016) for this early development of Chinese homosexuality.

5 For examples of *tongxinglian* subcultures that seemed to flourish in the post– Second World War period, see Kong (2014, 2019a) for Hong Kong; see Chiang and Wang (2017), Huang (2011), and Taiwan Tongzhi Hotlines (2010) for Taiwan; and see Chiang (2012) and Li and Wang (1992) for mainland China.

6 Hong Kong Yearbook, *Religion and Custom*, accessed July 11, 2022, https:// www.yearbook.gov.hk/2020/en/pdf/E21.pdf.

7 There were, of course, men who had same-sex desires before the 1920s, but I refer to this generation (1920s–1950s) as the first *tongzhi* generation for

comparative purposes: some members of the generation are still alive, and they, particularly those who experienced the Second World War, had very different lived experiences with respect to (homo)sexuality in their formative years than subsequent generations.

8 The antidecriminalization alliance mainly refers to the Joint Committee on Homosexual Law led by an evangelical medical doctor and made up of thirty-one pressure groups consisting of social workers, teachers, and church leaders, while the prodecriminalization alliance was advanced by academics, journalists, the Hong Kong Human Rights Commission, and a few gay men (Ho 1997).

9 *Memba* is a local parlance used exclusively by Hong Kong gay men for self-identification. It is a Cantonese derivative of the English term *member*. Strictly speaking, it is not Cantonese Romanization. TB means tomboy, and TBG means tomboy's girl.

10 For Hong Kong, see Leung (2008); for Taiwan, see Chao (2000); for mainland China, see Bao (2018); for the three sites, see Kong, Lau, and Hui (2019).

11 In the Chinese-speaking world, queer is translated as *tongzhi*, *ku'er*, and *guaitai*, but the third translation is rarely used nowadays. Although *tongzhi* is sometimes used interchangeably with *ku'er*, the two terms bear different connotations, with *tongzhi* being associated more with LGBT+ identity politics and *ku'er* approximating the radical and deconstructive stance of queer. That is why queer theory is usually translated as *ku'er lilun* rather than *tongzhi lilun*. For a discussion of the uses of *tongzhi* and queer, please see Bao (2018, 65–91), Chao (2000), and Leung (2008, 1–7).

12 *Tongzhi* social groups include the Hong Kong Ten Percent Club (1992 [1986]), Horizons (1991), Satsanga (1993), the Buddhist group Isvara (1994), and the Blessed Minority Christian Fellowship (1995).

13 Examples could be seen in movies (e.g., *Yang ± Yin: Gender in Chinese Cinema*, dir. Stanley Kwan, 1996; *A Queer Story*, dir. Shukei, 1997; *Happy Together*, dir. Wong Kar-wai, 1997), theater plays (e.g., *How to Love a Man Who Doesn't Love Me*, dir. Edward Lam, 1989), and many works produced by queer/*tongzhi* writers and artists such as Jimmy Ngai, Julian Lee, Stanley Kwan, Maike, Yau Ching, Anson Mak, and Ellen Pau (Kong 2011, 65–66).

14 IDAHO later changed its name to International Day against Homophobia, Transphobia and Biphobia (IDAHOT).

15 For example, Rainbow of Hong Kong (1998), Rainbow Action (1998), Civil Rights for Sexual Diversities (1999), F'Union (1999), Tongzhi Community Joint Meeting (1999), Women's Coalition of HKSAR (2003), Nutong Xueshe (2005), Midnight Blue (2005), For My Colours (2008), and Gay Harmony (2009).

16 Chemsex (or chemfun in the Hong Kong context) refers to the consumption of drugs (crystal meth, poppers, ecstasy, ketamine, GBH, mephedrone) to en-

hance sexual pleasure, often in a group context, particularly among gay men or men who have sex with other men (MSM).

17 For pink venues such as bars, saunas, massage parlors, bookshops, fitness centers, and beauty salons, see "Dim Sum (DS) Magazine," Travelgay, accessed July 15, 2022, https://www.travelgay.com/venue/ds/.

18 This Hong Kong–mainland coupling echoes the earlier colonial-era interracial pairings between Westerners and Chinese.

19 Media and culture examples include films such as *Butterfly* (2004), directed by Yan Yan Mak; director Cheng Wan Cheung's (a.k.a. Scud's) trilogy *City without Baseball* (2008), *Permanent Residence* (2009), and *Amphetamine* (2010); and *Suk Suk* (2019), directed by Ray Yeung. Plays include *Queer Show* (2004, 2006, and 2008), directed by Wong Chi-lung and Leung Cho-yiu. Novels include Julian Lee's *The Map of Burning Desire* (2001) and Yip Chi Wai's *Suddenly Single* (2003) and *Almost Perfect* (2004).

20 For example, the Society of Truth and Light (1997), Hong Kong Sex Culture Society (2001), Hong Kong Alliance for Family (2003), New Creation Alliance (2003), and Family Value Foundation of Hong Kong Limited (2007).

21 In *W v. Registrar of Marriages* [2013] HKCFA 39, FACV 4/2012, the Court of Final Appeal ruled in favor of a transgender woman's (known as W) right to marry, recognizing postoperative gender rather than biological sex at birth as the basis for marriage. In *QT v. Director of Immigration* [2018] HKCFA 28, FACV 1/2018, the director of immigration began permitting same-sex spouses to live as dependents in Hong Kong after a lesbian expat, QT, charged the government with unlawful discrimination for denying her a spousal visa on the basis of marital status. In *Leung Chun Kwong v. the Secretary for the Civil Service and Commissioner of Inland Revenue* [2019] HKCFA 19, FACV 8/2018, the Court of Final Appeal ruled in favor of a gay civil servant Leung applying for spousal benefits and tax assessment for his husband after they married in New Zealand.

22 There were rumors that they might be disqualified, arrested, and charged back the salaries and subsidies they received if they did not resign before taking the oath.

23 The first reported case of HIV was in 1984. The first local infection case was in 1986.

24 One major incident of the *tongzhi* movement that occurred in the 1980s should be noted. In 1986, Chi Jia-wei became Taiwan's first out gay man after holding a press conference to openly declare that he was gay and to urge society to better understand homosexuals and protect their rights. In the same year, he requested that he be allowed to marry his same-sex partner, a request that was rejected by the District Court of Taipei. As martial law was still in force at the time, his request was seen as political, and he was jailed for 162 days, reduced from an original sentence of five years (Ke 2021).

25 The Isle Margin project can be seen as a "complex 'articulation' of Western theory with local history; of New Leftist discourses with new oppositional movements; and of context, text, and post-text that tries to reconfigure political imagination from the margin, as represented by women, queers, sex workers, and migrants" (Wang 2017a, 748; see also Chen 2011).

26 Examples of tongzhi-themed novels include Chu Tien-wen's *Notes of a Desolate Man* (1994), Chi Ta-Wei's *Membranes* (1996), and Qiu Miaojin's *Notes of a Crocodile* (1994), and movies include *Wedding Banquet* (dir. Ang Lee, 1993) and *River* (dir. Tsai Ming-Liang, 1997).

27 Examples of gay- and lesbian-themed movies include *Blue Gate Crossing* (2002), directed by Yee Chin-yen; *Eternal Summer* (2006), directed by Leste Chen; *Girlfriend, Boyfriend* (2012), directed by Yang Ya-che; and *Thanatos, Drunk* (2015), directed by Chang Tso-chi.

28 This growth of cyber networks has created opportunities for bulletin-board system chat sites, online *tongzhi* discussion forums, and dating apps targeting and supported by gays and lesbians, initiating an unrestrictive, diffusive, powerful, and consciousness-provoking cyber mobilization (Berry and Martin 2003).

29 See the Center for the Study of Sexualities, "Home," National Central University, accessed July 15, 2022, http://sex.ncu.edu.tw/english/index.html.

30 A junior–high school boy named Yeh Yung-chih had been bullied by his classmates because of his feminine behavior for years. He did not dare to go to the toilet after class, as his classmates bullied him and joked that he was not really a boy. On the morning of April 20, 2000, Yeh left the classroom early as usual to go to the bathroom. He was subsequently found severely injured in the bathroom and later died in the hospital. Even though the cause of his death is unknown (i.e., whether he was attacked or whether his injuries were self-inflicted or an accident), it is widely believed that he died because of the prolonged bullying due to his gender-nonconforming behavior. Yeh's death triggered a wider discussion of gender and sexual diversity in education, leading to the enactment of the Gender Equity Education Act in 2004, which obliges schools to provide a safe campus and gender-friendly environment for students.

31 This was previously the 2002 Act of Equality between Men and Women.

32 "Taiwan Gay Movement Scene: 2000 Anti-Gay Religious Forces Assembled for the First Time," Age of Queer, accessed July 15, 2022, http://ageofqueer .com/archives/12522.

33 "Urgent Notice on Inspecting and Rectifying the Book Market," China Reform Information Database, accessed July 15, 2022, http://www.reformdata .org/1989/0711/17292.shtml.

34 Examples include a graduate seminar course called Homosexual Health Social Science, organized by Gao Yanning in 2003, and Introduction to Gay

and Lesbian Studies, organized by Sun Zhongxin in 2005, both at Fudan University in Shanghai. These courses no longer exist.

35 Ironically, the comparative lack of funding has allowed lesbian groups to address a wider range of issues, including societal discrimination, human rights, and same-sex marriage (Hildebrandt 2011, 1330, n95).

36 "Securities and Exchange Commission Form F-1 Registration Statement under the Securities Act of 1933," Securities and Exchange Commission, accessed July 15, 2022, https://www.sec.gov/Archives/edgar/data/1791278 /000119312520169977/d831427df1.htm.

37 The company also employs a large number of full-time staff to monitor content, especially "homosexual content" that could be deemed pornographic, obscene, or vulgar. Blued thus works smoothly with the government's strict control, owing to its affiliation with the official stance on homosexuality as a public-health issue, its downplaying of any notion of gay identity, which has the potential to become political, its emphasis on social recognition and harmony, and its tendency toward gay consumerism (S. Wang 2019b; see also Miao and Chan [2020]).

38 Tian (2019) discusses various tactics activists in mainland China adopted, which range from "full invisibility," "dislocated visibility," "targeted visibility," "collective visibility," to "celebratory visibility."

39 The closure of ZANK, a popular dating app, is believed to have resulted from the government's desire to distance itself from the promotion of identity politics (S. Wang 2019b).

40 For Hong Kong, see Kong (2011, 94–119); for Taiwan, see Chao (2002); for mainland China, see Kong (2011, 145–73).

41 In Hong Kong, there has been a split between local sexual politics and academic scholarship owing to social taboos and universities' drive toward internationalization, which has meant that publication in English—and on mainstream issues—is weighted more heavily than other factors in promotion and tenure decisions (Leung 2007, 6).

Chapter 2. Coming Out as Relational Politics

1 For Hong Kong, see Ho and Tsang (2012). For Taiwan, see Brainer (2019) and Lan (2014). For mainland China, see Jeffreys and Yu (2015), Rofel (2007), and Yan (2003). For the three sites, see Davis and Friedman (2014).

2 For Hong Kong, see Leung and Shek (2018). For Taiwan, see Wang and Yang (2019). For mainland China, see Tang and Jiang (2013, 1–14).

3 For Hong Kong, see Fung (2017) and Leung, Lam, and Liang (2020). For Taiwan, see Wang (2011). For mainland China, see Tang and Jiang (2013).

4 For Hong Kong, see Kong (2011), Tang (2011), and Wong (2007). For Taiwan, see Brainer (2019), Liu and Ding (2005), and Wang, Bih, and Brennan (2009).

For mainland China, see Engebretsen (2014), Kam (2013), and Li and Wang (1992). For the three sites, see Chou (2000).

5 Chinese parents, like their Euro-American counterparts, frame this expectation in terms of both child-oriented concerns (a gay child will be lonely and unhappy in old age without offspring, suffer prejudice and rejection, contract a sexually transmitted disease, be harassed or arrested, lose his/her religious belief) and parent-oriented concerns (discontinuation of the family, feelings of failure, distance from the child and larger family and community, and conflict between love for one's child and one's moral and religious beliefs) (Ben-Ari 1995; see also Lee 2018).

6 For Hong Kong, see Leung and Shek (2018). For Taiwan, see Lan (2014). For mainland China, see Fong (2004), Sun (2011), Wei (2015, 167–98), and Wei and Yan (2021).

7 This new parenting culture seems to be most prominent in Taiwan, where there have been concerted state efforts at parental education (Lan 2014). It has also been picked up in mainland China (Wei 2015, 167–98) and Hong Kong (Leung and Shek 2018), even though traditional parenting practices such as corporal discipline are not uncommon in these two locales. For Hong Kong, see Jackson and Ho (2020). For mainland China, see Qiao and Xie (2017).

8 The effect of this new parenting has been double-edged: although the new relationship enables parents to form emotional bonds with their children, it intensifies the mental and physical demands of parental labor (Lan 2014). The new emphasis on intimate disclosure is also double-edged: it can mean that children get love and understanding based on parental attentiveness and affectual bonds but can also serve as a thinly veiled mechanism of parental surveillance and control, as parents demand greater access to their children's inner world (Brainer 2019).

9 For Hong Kong, see Kong (2011, 94–119). For Taiwan, see Brainer (2019). For mainland China, see Kong (2011, 145–73).

10 Decena (2008) introduces the idea of "tacit subjects" in his analysis of Dominican gay and bisexual migrant men who live in New York. In Spanish grammar, *sujeto tácito* ("tacit subject") is "the subject that is not spoken but can be ascertained through the conjugation of the verb used in a sentence" (340). The tacit subject suggests that coming out is redundant: "[C]oming out can be a verbal declaration of something that is already understood or assumed—tacit—in an exchange. What is tacit is neither secret nor silent" (340).

11 The PRC relaxed its one-child policy in 2016 to allow couples to have two children. It then announced the three-child policy in 2021 to deal with the country's low birth rate and aging society. The impacts of these policy changes are, however, outside the scope of this book.

12 For the 2005 data, see Davis and Friedman (2014, 6–10). For the 2020 data, see National Bureau of Statistics of China (2022).

13 For the 2005 data, see Davis and Friedman (2014, 7). For the 2016 data, see the feature article "Marriage and Divorce Trends in Hong Kong, 1991 to 2016," *Hong Kong Monthly Digest of Statistics*, accessed September 7, 2022, https://www.statistics.gov.hk/pub/B71801FB2018XXXXB0100.pdf.

14 Form 6 in the Hong Kong education system is equivalent to grade 12 and year 13 in the US and UK education systems, respectively. American School Hong Kong, "Age Checker," accessed September 1, 2022, https://resources.finalsite .net/images/v1543200561/ashkhk/lh7w4rzxmk02sgevermx/AgeChecker2018 -19.pdf.

15 Apart for one exceptional case in which a participant reported that his father informed him that he would "beat" his boyfriend if he ever saw him.

16 Hiro's father assumes that being gay means having no descendants. Because Hiro is the only son in the family, his father believes that the family bloodline will end with him. He has thus asked Hiro to destroy the family's ancestral plaques, as they are no longer needed for worship.

17 There are a handful of cases who still choose not to come out for various reasons (e.g., a bad relationship with parents, do not think it is necessary, to avoid conflict). Most participants chose active self-revelation. Reasons other than Hao's include sharing the pain of break-ups with their mothers or coming out when they moved to Taipei from elsewhere in Taiwan. Passive self-revelation is rare. Apart from Hiro, another case did it when his erotic messages to fellow gay netizens were discovered by his family.

18 Fei Xiao-tung's (1992) conceptualization of the Chinese self is the most influential. He argues that the foundation of Chinese social structures or relations consists of concentric circles emanating as ripples (like throwing pebbles into a lake), with the self at the center. The social significance of the circles (i.e., social relations) decreases according to their distance from the center (the self), and the networks begin to form as ripples, from different centers overlapping and interfering with one another, thus linking the self with the family, kinship, community, and even the nation. There is a burgeoning body of literature on the Chinese notion of the self, which is usually contrasted with the Western notion of the self and centers on the individualism/ collectivism debate (see Herrmann-Pillath 2016; Wang and Liu 2010; Yan 2017).

Chapter 3. *Tongzhi* Commons, Community, and Collectivity

1 Created in 2015, Hehe Secrets is a popular Facebook page with more than fifteen thousand followers that allows contributors to share personal gay stories anonymously or post comments on others' stories (https://www.facebook .com/hehesecrets/). The Facebook page was closed in 2021, but Hehe Secrets continues to appear on Twitter (https://twitter.com/hehe_secrets?s=11&t =JiFtva3DnKB5CEZbcGGSVg). See chapter 4, note 10, for the meaning of "hehe."

2 For example, the Taiwanese TV program *Kangxi Lai Le* (2004–2016) and the online video-on-demand subscription service GagaOOlala, Japanese BL novels, Korean K-pop, and Thai BL-style TV dramas.

3 See, for example, Steven Jiang, "'End of the Rainbow': Shanghai Pride Shuts Down amid Shrinking Space for China's LGBTQ Community," CNN, August 16, 2020, https://edition.cnn.com/2020/08/14/asia/shanghai-pride-shutdown-intl-hnk/index.html; and Bruce Shen, "More Info on ShanghaiPRIDE Shutdown: Team Members Asked to 'Have Tea,'" SupChina, August 17, 2020, https://supchina.com/2020/08/17/more-info-on-shanghaipride-shutdown-team-members-asked-to-have-tea/.

Chapter 4. Love and Sex as Cruel Optimism

1 I extend Ringrose and Renold's (2010) notion of "normative cruelties" to include the performing and policing of intelligible heteronormative masculinities and femininities not just in the school setting but also in other social institutions such as the family, work, religion, and the like. See also the discussion of this idea in trans youth (Roen 2019).

2 For Hong Kong, see Kong (2011, 111–17). For Taiwan, see Shieh, Chen, and Tseng (2017) and Shieh and Tseng (2015). For mainland China, see Wu (2020). For the United Kingdom, see Heaphy, Donovan, and Weeks (2004) and Yip (1997). For the United States, see van Eeden-Moorefield, Malloy, and Benson (2016). For Canada, see Adam (2006). For Australia, see Duncan, Prestage, and Grierson (2015a, 2015b) and Philpot et al. (2017).

3 The idea of cruel optimism has also been applied to masculinity (Allan 2018), love among poor urban youths in Chile (Risor and Perez 2018), and digital dating among rural migrant workers in China (Liu, Wang, and Lin 2021).

4 See similar findings in Adam (2006); Barker and Langdridge (2010); Duncan, Prestage, and Grierson (2015a, 2015b); Mutchler (2000); Heaphy, Donovan, and Weeks (2004); Philpot et al. (2017); van Eeden-Moorefield, Malloy, and Benson (2016); and Wu (2020).

5 The term *woleifeifei* was created by netizens and combined the first Chinese word of each of the four terms *woping* (Cant., peaceful), *leising* (Cant., rational), *fei boulik* (Cant., nonviolent), and *fei couhau* (Cant., no foul language) (Lee and Chan 2018, 57).

6 During 2020–21, such measures included compulsory mask wearing in public, social-distancing measures, and limits on gatherings (a maximum of two to four people), compulsory hotel quarantine for people returning from abroad, work-from-home arrangements, the lockdown of nonessential services (sports, entertainment, and leisure venues such as swimming pools, gyms, bars, beauty salons, and massage parlors), and limited access to restaurants. The measures changed from time to time to respond to the seriousness of the pandemic.

7 Primary 3 in the Hong Kong education system is equivalent to grade 3 and year 4 in the US and UK education systems, respectively. American School Hong Kong, "Age Checker," accessed September 1, 2022, https://resources .finalsite.net/images/v1543200561/ashkhk/lh7w4rzxmk02sgevermx /AgeChecker2018-19.pdf.

8 Form 1 and Form 2 in the Hong Kong education system refer to grade 7 and 8 or year 8 and 9 in the US and UK education systems, respectively. American School Hong Kong, "Age Checker," accessed September 1, 2022, https:// resources.finalsite.net/images/v1543200561/ashkhk/lh7w4rzxmk02sgevermx /AgeChecker2018-19.pdf.

9 The film tells the bittersweet story of a closeted gay boy who is in love with his straight best friend. The friend, meanwhile, is in love with a girl who is in love with the gay protagonist.

10 "Hehe" is Cantonese slang used to jokingly refer to two male friends who are very close regardless of whether they are gay or not. The term is now used in young gay circles to refer to being gay.

11 *Nanshen* (Cant., male god) is Cantonese slang for a man who is good-looking and possesses a nice (usually athletic) body with strong sexual appeal.

12 Originating from the Japanese *enjo-kōsai*, compensated dating refers to the practice of women and girls (usually housewives and schoolgirls) going on dates with older men in exchange for money or gifts. Sexual activities may or may not be part of the arrangement. In the Hong Kong context, compensated dating usually involves a sexual exchange, although it is not regarded as prostitution by the participants.

13 *Gong nui* (Cant., Hong girl) literally means "Hong Kong girl," but it acquired a negative connotation in the 2000s to refer to a Hong Kong girl who is materialistic, superficial, self-centered, and bad tempered—essentially a gold digger with a princess complex.

14 The British National (Overseas) passport, commonly known as the BNO passport, is a British passport created in 1987 for persons with British National (Overseas) citizenship. Eligible candidates are permanent residents of Hong Kong who were born before June 30, 1997. Owing to fears of a tide of migration from Hong Kong in the face of Hong Kong's return to China, however, BNO passport holders do not have the right of abode in the United Kingdom. It was the most popular travel document for Hongkongers from 1997 until around 2015, when the less-expensive Hong Kong SAR passport, which grants visa-free access to more than 150 countries and territories, outnumbered the visa-free access granted by the BNO passport. In 2021, in response to the introduction of the national security law in Hong Kong, BNO holders can apply for limited leave to remain to work or study in the United Kingdom for up to five years and then become eligible for permanent residency.

15 Referring to NTD22,000 (approximately US$700), which was the average starting salary of a fresh university graduate.

16 The Taiwanese military service system has undergone a series of changes since 1990. In 1990, adult men had to do mandatory service for two years. In 2000, mandatory service was reduced to one year. Since 2018, military service has been voluntary. Men who were born before 1993 still have to do one year of military service, whereas those born after 1993 have to do only four months of military training. The Taiwanese participants, all of whom were born between 1990 and 2000, have done or will have to do military service or training for either four months or one year.

Chapter 5. Homosexuality, Homonationalism, and Homonormativity

An earlier version of this chapter appeared as "Transnational Queer Sociological Analysis of Sexual Identity and Civic-Political Activism in Hong Kong, Taiwan and Mainland China," *British Journal of Sociology* 70, no. 5 (2019): 1904–25, https://doi.org/10.1111/1468-4446.12697.

1 This chapter expands on my earlier work on homonationalism (Kong 2019b). Most notably, I have modified positive homonationalism in the case of Taiwan to incorporative homonationalism to show more accurately how the Taiwanese government strategically incorporates homosexuality into nationalism as well as how such an affirmative strategic case of homonationalism is also endorsed by the young gay generation. Although there are different factions and alliances within the LGBT+ communities and differences in their liberalization efforts in relation to the government (especially in the case of Taiwan, Chen-Dedman 2022), this chapter aims to start a dialogue at a higher level that compares and contrasts the relationship between the state and (homo)sexuality across the three sites. More specifically, it allows more elaborate, extensive analysis showing the nuances and complexities of how the three governments and queer subjects draw on homonationalism for their own use in the current geopolitical environment, even though both the government and queer subjects might be caught up with the Cold War mentality that reinforces the binary of progressive West (US)/repressive China or victim Taiwan/bully China confined under the US/China dyad. This complexity is also emphasized in Liu and Zhang's (2022) conceptualization of homonationalism/homotransnationalism in Taiwan, Hong Kong, and mainland China from a queer sinophone perspective (see also W. Liu 2021).

2 The 2.28 incident refers to an incident that began on February 27, 1947, when agents of the State Monopoly Bureau arrested a street peddler selling contraband cigarettes in downtown Taipei, wounding several bystanders, one of whom died the following day (hence 2.28). The incident triggered widespread resistance against the new Chinese rulers of the KMT regime. Protests were

brutally suppressed, which resulted in numerous civilians being arrested, imprisoned, killed, or going missing and the beginning of thirty-eight years of martial law. The 2.28 incident is seen as playing a pivotal role in the struggle for Taiwanese independence and the birth of a distinctive Taiwanese identity (Fleischauer 2007).

3 An old Chinese idiom meaning that even lovers who are apart still long for each other.

4 Even though the political affiliation of this minority of gay men is pro-KMT, and they regularly criticize the DPP government, they are also critical of mainland China.

5 Since the establishment of a *tongzhi* group called the BigLove Alliance in Hong Kong in 2013, Hongkongers, queer or otherwise, have tended to use "big love" to signify LGBT love or the diversity and equality of love.

6 On August 5, 2019, police arrested a female protestor. When she was being held at the Tin Shui Wai police station, her clothing was lifted up and her underwear dislodged, exposing her private parts. The incident was widely discussed in the media, which triggered more arrests the next day when a group of feminists tried to protest the event at the police station. A #MeToo rally was held later that month (on August 28) to demand that the police answer accusations of sexual violence against female and male protesters. The organizers reported that thirty thousand people attended the rally.

7 Boris is referring to Ho Sik Ying, a professor at the University of Hong Kong who has discussed the idea of a one-woman movement as a form of social protest. See Ho (2011).

Conclusion

1 The term "homonormative economic familism" is used by Lizada (2021), who argues in his discussion of movies in Hong Kong, Thailand, and the Philippines that the gay subject has been turned into an economic agent within the structure of the family.

2 The Asian global pop market includes Super Girl reality television singing idol shows in mainland China, the Bollywood industry in India, K-pop stars and boy bands in South Korea, and the Ten Years movie project, which was first set in Hong Kong and then in Thailand, Taiwan, and Japan.

3 *Tongzhi* is sometimes used strategically by LGBT+ collectivities, activists, and academics as an umbrella term, especially when communicating with the general public. In this sense, *tongzhi* is a conceptualization of the term *queer* itself and a tactic of "strategic essentialism" (Kong, Lau, and Hui 2019). *Tongzhi*'s popularity may be due to the following reasons: "[P]ositive cultural references, gender neutrality, de-sexualizing of the stigma of homosexuality,

its politics beyond the homo-hetero binarism, and its indigenous cultural identity for integrating the sexual into the social" (Chou 2001, 28).

4 Connell (2015) proposes three possible ways of building theory: the "pyramidal model," whereby Southern experiences are fit (or even forced) into a Northern framework; "mosaic epistemology," whereby separate knowledge systems (North and South) sit beside each other like tiles in a mosaic, with each based on a specific culture or historical experience and having its own claims to validity; and "solidarity-based epistemology," whereby different formations of knowledge are respected but enter into educational relations with each other. Transnational queer sociology takes the third way.

5 Thanks to my PhD student John Andrew Evangelista for suggesting the importance of acknowledging "disconnected sociologies."

Adam, Barry D. 2006. "Relationship Innovation in Male Couples." *Sexualities* 9 (1): 5–26.

Ahmed, Sara. 2004. *The Cultural Politics of Emotion*. London: Routledge.

Ahmed, Sara. 2010. *The Promise of Happiness*. Durham, NC: Duke University Press.

Ahmed, Sara. 2016. "Interview with Judith Butler." *Sexualities* 19 (4): 482–92.

Alatas, Syed Farid. 2003. "Academic Dependency and the Global Division of Labour in the Social Sciences." *Current Sociology* 51 (6): 599–613.

Albury, Kath, Jean Burgess, Ben Light, Kane Race, and Rowan Wilk. 2017. "Data Cultures of Mobile Dating and Hook-up Apps: Emerging Issues for Critical Social Science Research." *Big Data and Society* 4 (2). https://doi.org.10.1177 /2053951717720950.

Alexander, M. Jacqui, and Chandra Talpade Mohanty, eds. 1997. *Feminist Genealogies, Colonial Legacies, Democratic Futures*. New York: Routledge.

Allan, Jonathan A. 2018. "Masculinity as Cruel Optimism." *Norma: International Journal for Masculinity Studies* 13 (3–4): 175–90.

Alldred, Pam, and Nick J. Fox. 2015. "The Sexuality-Assemblages of Young Men: A New Materialist Analysis." *Sexualities* 18 (8): 905–20.

Altman, Dennis. 1997. "Global Gaze/Global Gays." *GLQ: A Journal of Lesbian and Gay Studies* 3 (4): 417–36.

Altman, Dennis. 2013. *The End of the Homosexual?* St. Lucia: University of Queensland Press.

An, Keqiang 安克強. 1995.《紅太陽下的黑靈魂：大陸同性戀現場報導》[Black souls under the Red Sun: An on-site report of mainland Chinese homosexuals]. 台北：時報出版 [Taipei: China Times Publishing].

Anderson, Austin R., and Eric Knee. 2021. "Queer Isolation or Queering Isolation? Reflecting upon the Ramifications of COVID-19 on the Future of Queer Leisure Spaces." *Leisure Sciences* 13 (1–2): 118–24. https://doi.org.10.1080/01490400.2020.1773992.

Anderson, Benedict. 1983. *Imagined Communities: Reflections on the Origin and Spread of Nationalism*. London: Verso.

Appadurai, Arjun. 1996. *Modernity at Large: Cultural Dimensions of Globalization*. Minneapolis: University of Minnesota Press.

Appadurai, Arjun. 2013. *The Future as Cultural Facts: Essays on the Global Condition*. London: Verso.

Arase, David, ed. 2016. *China's Rise and the Changing Order in East Asia*. London: Palgrave Macmillan.

Arnett, Jeffrey Jensen. 2004. *Emerging Adulthood: The Winding Road from the Late Teens through the Twenties*. New York: Oxford University Press.

Bacchetta, Paola, and Jin Haritaworn. 2011. "There Are Many Transatlantics: Homonationalism, Homotransnationalism and Feminist–Queer–Trans of Colour Theories and Practices." In *Transatlantic Conversations: Feminism as Travelling Theory*, edited by Mary Evans, 127–43. Farndam, UK: Ashgate.

Bakshi, Sandeep, Suhraiya Jivraj, and Silvia Posocco, eds. 2016. *Decolonizing Sexualities: Transnational Perspectives, Critical Interventions*. Oxford: Counterpress.

Bao, Hongwei. 2018. *Queer Comrades: Gay Identity and Tongzhi Activism in Postsocialist China*. Copenhagen: NIAS Press.

Bao, Hongwei. 2020. *Queer China: Lesbian and Gay Literature and Visual Culture under Postsocialism*. New York: Routledge.

Barker, Meg, and Darren Landbridge. 2010. "Whatever Happened to Non-monogamies? Critical Reflections on Recent Research and Theory." *Sexualities* 13 (6): 748–72.

Bauman, Zygmunt. 2003. *Liquid Love: On the Frailty of Human Bonds*. Cambridge: Polity Press.

Beck, Ulrich, and Elisabeth Beck-Gernsheim. 1995. *The Normal Chaos of Love*. Translated by Mark Ritter and Jane Wiebel. Cambridge: Polity Press.

Bedford, Olwen, and Kuang-Hui Yeh. 2019. "The History and the Future of the Psychology of Filial Piety: Chinese Norms to Contextualized Personality Construct." *Frontiers in Psychology* 10:100. https://doi.org.10.3389/fpsyg.2019.00100.

Bell, David, and Jon Binnie. 2000. *The Sexual Citizen: Queer Politics and Beyond*. Cambridge: Polity.

Bell, David, and Job Binnie. 2004. "Authenticating Queer Space: Citizenship, Urbanism and Governance." *Urban Studies* 41 (9): 1807–20.

Bell, David, and Gill Valentine. 1995. *Mapping Desire: Geographies of Sexualities*. London: Routledge.

Ben-Ari, Adital. 1995. "The Discovery That an Offspring Is Gay: Parents', Gay Men's, and Lesbians' Perspectives." *Journal of Homosexuality* 30 (1): 89–112.

Bernstein, Elizabeth, and Laurie Schaffner, eds. 2005. *Regulating Sex: The Politics of Intimacy and Identity*. London: Routledge.

Berberoglu, Berch. 2021. *The Global Rise of Authoritarianism in the 21st Century: Crisis of Neoliberal Globalization and the Nationalist Response*. London: Routledge.

Berlant, Lauren. 2011. *Cruel Optimism*. Durham, NC: Duke University Press.

Berlant, Lauren. 2012. "Affect in the End Times: A Conversation with Lauren Berlant." *Qui Parle* 20 (2): 71–90.

Berry, Chris. 2001. "Asian Values, Family Values: Film, Video, and Lesbian and Gay Identities." *Journal of Homosexuality* 40 (3–4): 211–31.

Berry, Chris, and Fran Martin. 2003. "Syncretism and Synchronicity: Queer 'n' Asian Cyberspace in 1990s Taiwan and Korea." In *Mobile Cultures: New Media in Queer Asia*, edited by Chris Berry, Fran Martin, and Audrey Yue, 87–114. Durham, NC: Duke University Press.

Berry, Chris, Fran Martin, and Audrey Yue, eds. 2003. *Mobile Cultures: New Media in Queer Asia*. Durham, NC: Duke University Press.

Bertone, Chiara, and Marina Franchi. 2014. "Suffering As the Path to Acceptance: Parents of Gay and Lesbian Young People Negotiating Catholicism in Italy." *Journal of GLBT Family Studies* 10 (1–2): 58–78.

Bhambra, Gurminder K. 2007. "Sociology and Postcolonialism: Another Missing Revolution?" *Sociology* 41 (5): 871–84.

Bhambra, Gurminder K. 2014. *Connected Sociologies*. Theory for a Global Age Series. London: Bloomsbury Academic.

Binnie, Jon. 1995. "Trading Places: Consumption, Sexuality and the Production of Queer Space." In *Mapping Desire: Geographies of Sexualities*, edited by David Bell and Gill Valentine, 182–199. London: Routledge.

Boellstorff, Tom. 2005. *The Gay Archipelago: Sexuality and Nation in Indonesia*. Princeton, NJ: Princeton University Press.

Brainer, Amy. 2019. *Queer Kinship and Family Change in Taiwan*. New Brunswick, NJ: Rutgers University Press.

Brown, Gavin. 2009. "Thinking beyond Homonormativity: Performative Explorations of Diverse Gay Economies." *Environment and Planning A: Economy and Space* 41 (4): 1496–510.

Browne, Kath, Niharika Banerjea, Nick McGlynn, Sumita B., Leela Bakshi, Rukmini Banerjee, and Ranjita Biswas. 2017. "Towards Transnational Feminist Queer Methodologies." *Gender, Place and Culture* 24 (10): 1376–97.

Butler, Judith. 1990. *Gender Trouble: Feminism and the Subversion of Identity*. London: Routledge.

Butler, Judith. 1993. *Bodies That Matter: On the Discursive Limits of "Sex."* New York: Routledge.

Canaday, Margot. 2009. *The Straight State: Sexuality and Citizenship in Twentieth-century America*. Princeton, NJ: Princeton University Press.

Cao, Jin, and Lei Guo. 2016. "Chinese 'Tongzhi' Community, Civil Society, and Online Activism." *Communication and the Public* 1 (4): 504–8.

Cao, Jin, and Xinlei Lu. 2014. "A Preliminary Exploration of the Gay Movement in Mainland China: Legacy, Transition, Opportunity, and the New Media." *Signs: Journal of Women in Culture and Society* 39 (4): 840–48.

Carrillo, Hector. 2017. *Pathways of Desire: The Sexual Migration of Mexican Gay Men*. Chicago: University of Chicago Press.

Carter, Julia, and Simon Duncan. 2018. *Reinventing Couples: Tradition, Agency and Bricolage*. Basingstoke: Palgrave Macmillan.

Cass, Vivienne C. 1984. "Homosexual Identity Formation: Testing a Theoretical Mode." *Journal of Sex Research* 20 (2): 143–67.

Chakrabarty, Dipesh. 2000. *Provincializing Europe: Postcolonial Thought and Historical Difference*. Princeton, NJ: Princeton University Press.

Chan, Alan T. Y., and Shu-Kam Lee. 2014. "Education Plans, Personal Challenges and Academic Difficulties: An Empirical Study on Self-disclosure among Post-90s Teens in Hong Kong." *International Journal of Adolescence and Youth* 19 (4): 468–83.

Chan, Gerald, Pak K. Lee, and Lai-Ha Chan. 2011. *China Engages Global Governance: A New World Order in the Making?* London: Routledge.

Chan, Kam Wing, and Li Zhang. 1999. "The *Hukou* System and Rural-Urban Migration in China: Processes and Changes." *China Quarterly* 160:818–55.

Chan, Lik Sam. 2018. "Ambivalence in Networked Intimacy: Observations from Gay Men Using Mobile Dating Apps." *New Media and Society* 20 (7): 2566–81.

Chan, Phil C. W. 2007. "Same-Sex Marriage/Constitutionalism and Their Centrality to Equality Rights in Hong Kong: A Comparative-Socio-Legal Appraisal." *International Journal of Human Rights* 11 (1): 33–84. https://doi.org.10.1080/13642980601176274.

Chan, Phil C. W. 2008. "Male/Male Sex in Hong Kong: Privacy, Please?" *Sexuality and Culture* 12 (2): 88–115.

Chang, Jiang, and Hailong Ren. 2017. "Keep Silent, Keep Sinful: Mainstream Newspaper's Representation of Gay Men and Lesbians in Contemporary China." *Indian Journal of Gender Studies* 24 (3): 317–40.

Chang, Kyung-Sup. 2010. "The Second Modern Condition? Compressed Modernity as Internalized Reflexive Cosmopolitization." *British Journal of Sociology* 61 (3): 444–64.

Chao, Antonia 趙彥寧. 2000. "台灣同志研究的回顧與展望—— 一個關於文化生產的分析" [A reflection upon Taiwan's queer studies: From a viewpoint of cultural production and reproduction]. 台灣社會研究季刊 [*Taiwan: A Radical Quarterly in Social Studies*] 38:207–44.

Chao, Antonia. 2001. "Drinks, Stories, Penis, and Breasts: Lesbian Tomboys in Taiwan from 1960s to 1990s." *Journal of Homosexuality* 40 (3–4): 185–210.

Chao, Antonia. 2002. "How Come I Can't Stand Guarantee for My Own Life?: Taiwan Citizenship and the Cultural Logic of Queer Identity." *Inter-Asia Cultural Studies* 3 (3): 369–81.

Chase, Thomas. 2012. "Problems of Publicity: Online Activism and Discussion of Same-Sex Sexuality in South Korea and China." *Asian Studies Review* 36 (2): 151–70.

Chen, Kuan-Hsing, ed. 1998. *Trajectories: Inter-Asia Cultural Studies*. London: Routledge.

Chen, Kuan-Hsing. 2010. *Asia as Method: Towards Deimperialization*. Durham, NC: Duke University Press.

Chen, Li-fen. 2011. "Queering Taiwan: In Search of Nationalism's Other." *Modern China* 37 (4): 383–421.

Chen-Dedman, Adam. 2022. "Tongzhi Sovereignty: Taiwan's LGBT Rights Movement and the Misplaced Critique of Homonationalism." *International Journal of Taiwan Studies*. https://doi:10.1163/24688800-20221267.

Cheng, Sealing. 2001. "Consuming Places in Hong Kong: Experiencing Lan Kwai Fong." In *Consuming Hong Kong*, edited by Gordon Mathews and Lui Tailok, 237–62. Hong Kong: Hong Kong University Press.

Cheung, Doug H., Sin How Lim, Thomas E. Guadamuz, Stuart Koe, and Chongyi Wei. 2015. "The Potential Role of Circuit Parties in the Spread of HIV among Men Who Have Sex with Men in Asia: A Call for Targeted Prevention." *Archives of Sexual Behavior* 44:389–97.

Chi, Ta-wei 紀大偉. 2017.《同志文學史：台灣的發明》[A queer invention in Taiwan: A history of Tongzhi literature]. 台北：聯經出版 [Taipei: Linking Books].

Chiang, Howard. 2010. "Epistemic Modernity and the Emergence of Homosexuality in China." *Gender and History* 22 (3): 629–57.

Chiang, Howard, ed. 2012. *Transgender China*. New York: Palgrave Macmillan.

Chiang, Howard, and Ari Larissa Heinrich, eds. 2014. *Queer Sinophone Cultures*. London: Routledge.

Chiang, Howard, and Yin Wang, eds. 2017. *Perverse Taiwan*. London: Routledge.

Chiang, Howard, and Alvin K. Wong. 2016. "Queering the Transnational Turn: Regionalism and Queer Asias." *Gender, Place and Culture: A Journal of Feminist Geography* 23 (11): 1643–56.

Choi, Ji Young. 2018. "Historical and Theoretical Perspectives on the Rise of China: Long Cycles, Power Transitions, and China's Ascent." *Asian Perspective* 42:61–84.

Choi, Susanne Y. P., and Ming Luo. 2016. "Performative Family: Homosexuality, Marriage and Intergenerational Dynamics in China." *British Journal of Sociology* 67 (2): 260–80.

Chong, Gladys Pak Lei. 2020. "Who Wants 9-to-5 Jobs? Precarity, (In)security, and Chinese Youths in Beijing and Hong Kong." *Information Society* 36 (5): 266–78.

Chong, Gladys Pak Lei, Yiu Fai Chow, and Jeroen de Kloet. 2019. "Towards Trans-Asia: Projects, Possibilities, Paradoxes." In *Trans-Asia as Method: Theory and Practices*, edited by Jeroen de Kloet, Yiu Fai Chow, and Gladys Pak Lei Chong, 1–24. London: Rowman and Littlefield.

Chou, Wah-Shan. 2000. *Tongzhi: Politics of Same-Sex Eroticism in Chinese Societies*. New York: Haworth Press.

Chou, Wah-Shan. 2001. "Homosexuality and the Cultural Politics of Tongzhi in Chinese Societies." *Journal of Homosexuality* 40 (3–4): 27–46.

Chu, Wei-Cheng 朱偉誠. 2003. "同志‧臺灣：性公民、國族建構或公民社會" [Queer(ing) Taiwan: Sexual citizenship, nation-building or civil society]. 女學學誌 [*Taiwan Journal of Women's and Gender Studies*] 15:115–51.

Chu, Wei-Cheng, and Fran Martin, eds. 2007. "Global Queer, Local Theories." Special issue, *Inter-Asia Cultural Studies* 8 (4).

Chua, Beng Huat. 2015. "Inter-Asia Referencing and Shifting Frames of Comparison." In *The Social Sciences in the Asian Century*, edited by Carol Johnson, Vera Mackie, and Tessa Morris-Suzuki, 67–81. Canberra: Australian National University.

Chun, Allen. 1996. "Discourses of Identity in the Changing Spaces of Public Culture in Taiwan, Hong Kong and Singapore." *Theory, Culture and Society* 13 (1): 51–75.

Collett, Nigel. 2018. *A Death in Hong Kong: The MacLennan Case of 1980 and the Suppression of a Scandal*. Hong Kong: City University of Hong Kong.

Collins, Patricia Hill. 1990. *Black Feminist Thought: Knowledge, Consciousness, and the Politics of Empowerment*. Boston: Unwin Hyman.

Connell, R. W. 1995. *Masculinities*. Cambridge: Polity Press.

Connell, Raewyn. 2014. "The Sociology of Gender in Southern Perspective." *Current Sociology* 62 (4): 550–67.

Connell, Raewyn. 2015. "Meeting at the Edge of Fear: Theory on a World Scale." *Feminist Theory* 16 (1): 49–66.

Cooper, Davina. 2002. "Imagining the Place of the State: Where Governance and Social Power Meet." In *Handbook of Lesbian and Gay Studies*, edited by Diane Richardson and Steven Seidman, 231–52. London: Sage.

Crenshaw, Kimberle. 1991. "Mapping the Margins: Intersectionality, Identity Politics, and Violence against Women of Color." *Stanford Law Review* 43 (6): 1241–99.

Crossley, Nick. 2001. *The Social Body: Habit, Identity and Desire*. London: Sage.

Cruz-Malave, Arnold, and Martin F. Manalansan IV, eds. 2002. *Queer Globalization: Citizenship and the Afterlife of Colonialism*. New York: New York University Press.

Dai, Jinhua. 2018. *After the Post–Cold War: The Future of Chinese History*. Durham, NC: Duke University Press.

Damm, Jens. 2017. "From Psychoanalysis to AIDS: The Early Contradictory Approaches to Gender and Sexuality and the Recourse to American Discourses during Taiwan's Societal Transformation in the Early 1980s." In *Perverse Taiwan*, edited by Howard Chiang and Yin Wang, 64–85. London: Routledge.

Dangerous Bedfellows, ed. 1996. *Policing Public Sex: Queer Politics and the Future of AIDS Activism*. Boston: South End Press.

Davis, Deborah S., and Sarah L. Friedman, eds. 2014. *Wives, Husbands, and Lovers: Marriage and Sexuality in Hong Kong, Taiwan, and Urban China*. Hong Kong: Hong Kong University Press.

Decena, Carlos Ulises. 2008. "Tacit Subjects." *GLQ: A Journal of Lesbian and Gay Studies* 14 (2–3): 339–59.

De Kloet, Jeroen, Yiu Fai Chow, and Gladys Pak Lei Chong, eds. 2019. *Trans-Asia as Method: Theory and Practices*. London: Rowman and Littlefield.

De Kloet, Jeroen, and Anthony Y. H. Fung. 2017. *Youth Cultures in China*. Cambridge: Polity Press.

De Kloet, Jeroen, Jian Lin, and Yiu Fai Chow. 2020. "'We Are Doing Better': Biopolitical Nationalism and the COVID-19 Virus in East Asia." *Cultural Commons* 23 (4): 635–40.

D'Emilio, John. 1983. "Capitalism and Gay Identity." In *Powers of Desire*, edited by Ann Snitow, Christine Stansell, and Sharan Thompson, 100–113. New York: Monthly Review Press.

Denzin, Norman K., and Yvonna S. Lincoln. 1994. "The Fifth Moment." In *Handbook of Qualitative Research*, edited by Yvonna S. Lincoln and Norman K. Denzin, 575–86. Thousand Oaks, CA: Sage.

Derrida, Jacques. 1976. *Of Grammatology*. Translated by Gayatri Chakravorty Spivak. Baltimore, MD: John Hopkins University Press.

Dhawan, Nikita. 2013. "The Empire Prays Back: Religion, Secularity, and Queer Critique." *Boundary 2* 40 (1): 191–222.

Dikötter, Frank. 1995. *Sex, Culture and Modernity in China: Medical Science and the Construction of Sexual Identities in the Early Republican Era*. Hong Kong: Hong Kong University Press.

Duggan, Lisa. 2002. "The New Homonormativity: The Sexual Politics of Neoliberalism." In *Materializing Democracy: Toward a Revitalized Cultural Politics*, edited by Donald E. Pease, Joan Dayan, and Richard R. Flores, 175–94. Durham, NC: Duke University Press.

Duncan, Duane, Garrett Prestage, and Jeffery Grierson. 2015a. "'I'd Much Rather Have Sexual Intimacy as Opposed to Sex': Young Australian Gay Men, Sex, Relationships and Monogamy." *Sexualities* 18 (7): 798–816.

Duncan, Duane, Garrett Prestage, and Jeffery Grierson. 2015b. "Trust, Commitment, Love and Sex: HIV, Monogamy and Gay Men." *Journal of Sex and Marital Therapy* 41 (4): 345–60.

Duncombe, Jean, Kaeren Harrison, Graham Allan, and Dennis Marsden, eds. 2004. *The State of Affairs: Explorations in Infidelity and Commitment*. London: Routledge.

Eisenlohr, Patrick, Stefan Kramer, and Andreas Langenohl. 2019. "Modern Times, Disjunct Temporalities and Divergent Realities." Program note of the annual conference for Priority Program 1688, Herchen, Germany, May 15–18, 2019. https://www.aesthetische-eigenzeiten.de/workspace/dokumente/jt-5-2019-modern-times-disjunct-temporalities-and-divergent-realities-expose_1.pdf. See also the German version of the book published after the conference: *Parallaxen moderner Zeitlichkeit*, edited by Patrick Eisenlohr, Stefan Kramer, and Andreas Langenohl (Hannover: Wehrhahn Verlag, 2021). https://www.wehrhahn-verlag.de/public/index.php?ID_Section=1&ID_Category=1&ID_Product=1437.

Elder, Glen H., Jr. 1975. "Age Differentiation and the Life Course." *Annual Review of Sociology* 1 (1): 165–90.

Elder, Glen H., Jr., Monica Kirkpatrick Johnson, and Robert Crosnoe. 2003. "The Emergence and Development of Life Course Theory." In *Handbook of the Life Course*, edited by Jeylan T. Mortimer and Michael J. Shanahan, 3–22. New York: Kluwer Academic.

Ellis, Havelock. 1933. *Psychology of Sex*. London: Heinemann.

Eng, David L. 2001. *Racial Castration: Managing Masculinity in Asian America*. Durham, NC: Duke University Press.

Eng, David L., Jack Halberstam, and José Esteban Muñoz. 2005. "Introduction: What's Queer about Queer Studies Now?" In "What's Queer about Queer Studies Now?," edited by Jack Halberstam, José Esteban Muñoz, and David L. Eng. Special issue, *Social Text*, no. 84–85, 1–17.

Eng, David L., and Jasbir K. Puar. 2020. "Introduction: Left of Queer." *Social Text* 38 (4): 1–23.

Engebretsen, Elisabeth L. 2014. *Queer Women in Urban China: An Ethnography*. London: Routledge.

Engebretsen, Elisabeth L. 2016. "Under Pressure: Lesbian-Gay Contract Marriages and Their Patriarchal Bargains." In *Transforming Patriarchy: Chinese Families in the Twenty-First Century*, edited by Goncalo Santos and Stevan Harrell, 163–81. Seattle: University of Washington Press.

Engebretsen, Elisabeth L. 2019. "'As Long as My Daughter Is Happy': 'Familial Happiness' and Parent Support-Narratives for LGBTQ Children." In *Chinese Discourses on Happiness*, edited by Gerda Wielander, 86–105. Hong Kong: Hong Kong University Press.

Engebretsen, Elisabeth L., and William F. Schroeder, eds. 2015. *Queer/Tongzhi China: New Perspectives on Research, Activism and Media Cultures*. Copenhagen: NIAS Press.

Epprecht, Marc. 2004. *Hungochani: The History of a Dissident Sexuality in Southern Africa*. Montreal: McGill-Queen's University Press.

Escobar, Arturo. 2020. *Pluriversal Politics: The Real and the Possible*. Durham, NC: Duke University Press.

Evans, David T. 1993. *Sexual Citizenship: The Material Construction of Sexualities*. London: Routledge.

Evans, Harriet. 1995. "Defining Difference: The 'Scientific' Construction of Sexuality and Gender in the People's Republic of China." *Signs: Journal of Women in Culture and Society* 20 (2): 357–94.

Evans, Harriet. 1997. *Women and Sexuality in China: Discourses of Female Sexuality and Gender Since 1949*. Cambridge: Polity.

Family Council. 2021. "Introduction." Hong Kong SAR Government. Accessed June 21, 2022. https://www.familycouncil.gov.hk/en/home/home_intro.html.

Fang, Gang 方剛. 1995.《同性戀在中國》[Homosexuality in China]. 香港: 天地圖書 [Hong Kong: Cosmos Books].

Farrer, James. 2002. *Opening Up: Youth Sex Culture and Market Reform in Shanghai*. Chicago: University of Chicago Press.

Fei, Xiaotong. 1992. *From the Soil: The Foundations of Chinese Society*. Translated by Gary G. Hamilton and Wang Zheng. Berkeley: University of California Press.

Ferguson, Roderick A. 2004. *Aberrations in Black: Toward a Queer of Color Critique*. Minneapolis: University of Minnesota Press.

Fields, Jessica. 2001. "Normal Queers: Straight Parents Respond to Their Children's 'Coming Out.'" *Symbolic Interaction* 24 (2): 165–87.

Fleischauer, Stefan. 2007. "The 228 Incident and the Taiwan Independence Movement's Construction of a Taiwanese Identity." *China Information* 21 (3): 373–401.

Florida, Richard L. 2002. *The Rise of the Creative Class…and How It's Transforming Work, Leisure, and Community, and Everyday Life*. New York: Basic Books.

Fong, Brian C. H. 2021. "Rethinking China's Influence across Surrounding Jurisdictions: A Concentric Center-Periphery Framework." In *China's Influence and the Center-Periphery Tug of War in Hong Kong, Taiwan and Indo-Pacific*, edited by Brian C. H. Fong, Jieh-min Wu, and Andrew J. Nathan, 3–23. London: Routledge.

Fong, Brian C. H., Jieh-min Wu, and Andrew J. Nathan, eds. 2021. *China's Influence and the Center-Periphery Tug of War in Hong Kong, Taiwan and Indo-Pacific*. London: Routledge.

Fong, Vanessa. 2004. *Only Hope: Coming of Age under China's One Child Policy*. Stanford, CA: Stanford University Press.

Foucault, Michel. 1980. *The History of Sexuality*. Volume 1: *An Introduction*. Translated by Robert Hurley. New York: Vintage.

Foucault, Michel. 1982. "The Subject and Power." In *Michel Foucault: Beyond Structuralism and Hermeneutics*, edited by Hubert L. Dreyfus and Paul Rabinow, 208–26. Chicago: University of Chicago Press.

Fraser, Suzanne. 2008. "Getting Out in the 'Real World': Young Men, Queer and Theories of Gay Community." *Journal of Homosexuality* 55 (2): 245–64.

Fu, Li-yeh 傅立葉. 2010. "從性別觀點看台灣的國家福利體制" [The model of the state welfare in Taiwan: Analysis from a gender perspective]. 台灣社會研究季刊 [*Taiwan: A Radical Quarterly in Social Studies*] 80:207–23.

Fu, Xiaoxing 富曉星. 2012. 《空間、文化、表演：東北A市男同性戀群體的人類學觀察》 [Space culture performance: Anthropological observations on male homosexual community in City A in Dongbei]. 北京：光明日報出版社 [Beijing: Guangming Ribao Chubanshe].

Fung, Kwok-kin. 2017. "Neoliberalization and Community Development Practices in Hong Kong." *Community Development Journal* 52 (1): 55–75.

Fuss, Diana. 1989. *Essentially Speaking: Feminism, Nature and Difference*. London: Routledge.

Gagnon, John, and William Simon. 1974. *Sexual Conduct: The Social Sources of Human Sexuality*. London: Routledge.

Gao, Ge. 1995. "Comparative Research on Hooliganism." *Chinese Sociology and Anthropology* 27 (3): 64–78.

Ghaziani, Amin. 2011. "Post-Gay Collective Identity Construction." *Social Problems* 58 (1): 99–125.

Giddens, Anthony. 1991. *Modernity and Self-Identity: Self and Society in the Late Modern Age*. Cambridge: Polity Press.

Giddens, Anthony. 1992. *The Transformation of Intimacy: Sexuality, Love and Eroticism in Modern Societies*. Cambridge: Polity Press.

Gilbert, Jeremy. 2013. *Common Ground: Democracy and Collectivity in an Age of Individualism*. London: Pluto Press.

Go, Julian. 2016. *Postcolonial Thoughts and Social Theory*. New York: Oxford University Press.

Go, Julian. 2020. "Race, Empire, and Epistemic Exclusion: Or the Structures of Sociological Thought." *Sociological Theory* 38 (2): 79–100.

Gong, Jin. 2021. "Queering the World Factory: The Study of Gay Migrant Workers in a South China Industrial Zone." PhD diss., Department of Sociology, University of Hong Kong.

Gopinath, Gayatri. 1998. "Homo Economics: Queer Sexualities in a Transnational Frame." In *Burning Down the House*, edited by Rosemary Marangoly George, 102–23. Boulder, CO: Westview Press.

Gopinath, Gayatri. 2005. *Impossible Desires: Queer Desires and South Asian Public Cultures*. Durham, NC: Duke University Press.

Grafsky, Erika L. 2014. "Becoming the Parent of a GLB Son or Daughter." *Journal of GLBT Family Studies* 10 (1–2): 36–57.

Green, Adam Isaiah. 2002. "Gay but Not Queer: Toward a Post-queer Study of Sexuality." *Theory and Society* 31 (4): 521–45.

Grewal, Inderpal, and Caren Kaplan, eds. 1994. *Scattered Hegemonies: Postmodernity and Transnational Feminist Practices*. Minneapolis: University of Minnesota.

Grewal, Inderpal, and Caren Kaplan. 2001. "Global Identities: Theorizing Transnational Studies of Sexuality." *GLQ: A Journal of Lesbian and Gay Studies* 7 (4): 663–79.

Guang, Lei. 2003. "Rural Taste, Urban Fashion: The Cultural Politics of Rural/Urban Difference in Contemporary China." *Positions: East Asia Cultures Critique* 11 (3): 613–46.

Guo, Ting. 2016. "Translating Homosexuality into Chinese: A Case Study of Pan Guangdan's Translation of Havelock Ellis' *Psychology of Sex: A Manual for Students* (1933)." *Asia Pacific Translation and Intercultural Studies* 3 (1): 47–61.

Guo, Xiaofei 郭曉飛. 2007.《中國法視野下的同性戀》[Homosexuality under Chinese law]. 北京: 知識產權出版社 [Beijing: Zhishi Chanquan Chubanshe].

Hakim, Jamie. 2018. "The Rise of Chemsex: Queering Collective Intimacy in Neoliberal London." *Cultural Studies* 33 (2): 249–75. https://doi.org.10.1080/09502386.2018.1435702.

Halberstam, Judith. 2005. *In a Queer Time and Place: Transgendered Bodies, Subcultural Lives*. New York: New York University Press.

Halberstam, Judith. 2011. *The Queer Art of Failure*. Durham, NC: Duke University Press.

Hall, Stuart. 1992. "The West and the Rest: Discourse and Power." In *Formations of Modernity*, edited by Stuart Hall and Bram Gidben, 85–95. Cambridge: Polity.

Halperin, David M., and Valerie Traub. 2009. *Gay Shame*. Chicago: University of Chicago Press.

Hammack, Philip L., and Bertram J. Cohler, eds. 2009. *The Story of Sexual Identity: Narrative Perspectives on the Gay and Lesbian Life Course*. Oxford: Oxford University Press.

Hammack, Phillip L., and Bertram J. Cohler. 2011. "Narrative, Identity, and the Politics of Exclusion: Social Change and the Gay and Lesbian Life Course." *Sexuality Research and Social Policy* 8 (3): 162–82.

Han, C. Winter. 2015. *Geisha of a Different Kind: Race and Sexuality in Gaysian America*. New York: New York University Press.

Hannerz, Ulf. 1996. *Transnational Connections: Culture, People, Places*. London: Routledge.

Hansen, Mette Halskov, and Rune Svarverud, eds. 2010. *iChina: The Rise of the Individual in Modern Chinese Society*. Copenhagen: NIAS Press.

Haritaworn, Jin, Chin-ju Lin, and Christian Klesse. 2006. "Poly/logue: A Critical Introduction to Polyamory." *Sexualities* 9 (5): 515–29.

He, Na, and Roger Detels. 2005. "The HIV Epidemic in China: History, Response, and Challenge." *Cell Research* 15 (11–12): 825–32.

He, Xiaopei, and Susie Jolly. 2002. "Chinese Tongzhi Women Organizing in the 1990s." *Inter-Asia Cultural Studies* 3 (3): 479–91.

Heaphy, Brian. 2007. *Late Modernity and Social Change: Reconstructing Social and Personal Life*. London: Routledge.

Heaphy, Brian, Catherine Donovan, and Jeffery Weeks. 2004. "A Different Affair? Openness and Nonmonogamy in Same Sex Relationships." In *The State of Affairs: Explorations in Infidelity and Commitment*, edited by Jean Duncombe, Kaeren Harrison, Graham Allan, and Dennis Marsden, 167–86. London: Lawrence Erlbaum Associates.

Herdt, Gilbert. 1981. *Guardian of the Flutes*. Volume 1: *Idioms of Masculinity*. Chicago: University of Chicago Press.

Herrmann-Pillath, Carsten. 2016. "Fei Xiaotong's Comparative Theory of Chinese Culture." *Copenhagen Journal of Asian Studies* 34 (1): 25–57.

Hershatter, Gail. 2007. *Women in China's Long Twentieth Century*. Berkeley: University of California Press.

Hildebrandt, Timothy. 2011. "Same-Sex Marriage in China? The Strategic Promulgation of a Progressive Policy and Its Impact on LGBT Activism." *Review of International Studies* 13 (3): 1313–33.

Hill, Richard Child, Bae-Gyoon Park, and Asato Saito. 2012. "Introduction." In *Locating Neoliberalism in East Asia: Neoliberalizing Spaces in Developmental States*, edited by Bae-Gyoon Park, Richard Child Hill, and Asato Saito, 1–26. Malden, MA: Blackwell.

Hinsch, Bret. 1990. *Passions of the Cut Sleeve: The Male Homosexual Tradition in China*. Berkeley: University of California Press.

Ho, Danny Kwok-Leung. 2004. "Citizenship as a Form of Governance: A Historical Overview." In *Remaking Citizenship in Hong Kong*, edited by Agnes S. Ku and Ngai Pun, 19–36. Oxon: Routledge Curzon.

Ho, Josephine Chuen-juei. 2008. "Is Global Governance Bad for East Asian Queers?" *GLQ: A Journal of Lesbian and Gay Studies*, 14 (4), 457–79.

Ho, Josephine Chuen-juei 何春蕤. 2017.《性/別治理》[Gender governance in Taiwan]. 台灣: 國立中央大學性/別研究室 [Taiwan: Center for the Study of Sexualities, National Central University].

Ho, Josephine Chuen-juei 何春蕤, Yin-Bin Ning 甯應斌, and Naifei Ding 丁乃非. 2005. "近年台灣重大性／別事件" [Major issues of Gender and Sexuality in Taiwan in Recent Years]. In《性政治入門：台灣性運演講集（2005）》[Introduction to Politics of sexuality: Lectures on sex rights movement in Taiwan], edited by Chuen-juei Ho 何春蕤, Naifei Ding 丁乃非, and Yin-Bin Ning 甯應斌, 41–98. 台灣: 中央大學性/別研究室 [Taiwan: Center for the Study of Sexualities, National Central University].

Ho, Loretta Wing-wah. 2010. *Gay and Lesbian Subculture in Urban China*. London: Routledge.

Ho, Michelle H. S., and Evelyn Blackwood, eds. 2022. "Queer Asias: Genders and Sexualities across Borders and Boundaries." Special issue, *Sexualities*. https://doi.org/10.1177/13634607221092153.

Ho, Ming-sho. 2019a. *Challenging Beijing's Mandate of Heaven: Taiwan's Sunflower Movement and Hong Kong's Umbrella Movement*. Philadelphia: Temple University Press.

Ho, Ming-sho. 2019b. "Taiwan's Road to Marriage Equality: Politics of Legalizing Same-Sex Marriage." *China Quarterly* 238:482–503.

Ho, Petula Sik Ying. 1997. "Politicising Identity: Decriminalisation of Homosexuality and the Emergence of Gay Identity in Hong Kong." PhD diss., University of Essex.

Ho, Petula Sik Ying. 2011. "Recognition Struggle: One Woman's Politics of Iconogenesis." *Asian Journal of Women's Studies* 17 (1): 7–33.

Ho, Petula Sik Ying, Stevi Jackson, Siyang Cao, and Chi Kwok. 2018. "Sex with Chinese Characteristics: Sexuality Research in/on 21st Century China." *Journal of Sex Research* 55 (4–5): 486–521.

Ho, Petula Sik Ying, and Adolf Kat-tat Tsang. 2000. "Negotiating Anal Intercourse in Inter-racial Gay Relationships in Hong Kong." *Sexualities* 3 (3): 299–323.

Ho, Petula Sik Ying, and Adolf Kat-tat Tsang. 2004. "Beyond Being Gay: The Proliferation of Political Identities in Colonial Hong Kong." In *Gendering Hong Kong*, edited by Anita K. W. Chan and W. L. Wong, 667–89. Hong Kong: Oxford University Press.

Ho, Petula Sik Ying, and Adolf Ka Tat Tsang. 2012. *Sex and Desire in Hong Kong*. Hong Kong: Hong Kong University Press.

Hobbs, Mitchell, Stephen Owen, and Livia Gerber. 2017. "Liquid Love? Dating Apps, Sex, Relationships and the Digital Transformation of Intimacy." *Journal of Sociology* 53 (2): 271–84.

Holt, Martin. 2011. "Gay Men and Ambivalence about 'Gay Community': From Gay Community Attachment to Personal Communities." *Culture, Health and Society* 13 (8): 854–71.

Hong Kong Government. 1963. *Hong Kong Report for the Year 1962*. Hong Kong: Hong Kong Government Press.

Howe, Neil, and William Strauss. 2000. *Millennials Rising: The Next Great Generation*. New York: Vintage Books.

Hsiao, Hsin-Huang Michael, and Yu-Yuan Kuan. 2016. "The Development of Civil Society Organizations in Post-authoritarian Taiwan (1988–2014)." In *Routledge*

Handbook of Contemporary Taiwan, edited by Gunter Schubert, 253–67. London: Routledge.

Hu, Hsien Chin. 1944. "The Chinese Concepts of 'Face.'" *American Anthropologist* 46 (1): 45–64.

Huang, Hans Tao-ming. 2011. *Queer Politics and Sexual Modernity in Taiwan*. Hong Kong: Hong Kong University Press.

Huang, Ke-hsien. 2017. "'Culture War' in a Globalized East: How Taiwanese Conservative Christianity Turned Public during the Same-Sex Marriage Controversy and a Secularist Backlash." *Review of Religion and Chinese Society* 4 (1): 108–36.

Huang, Mingle 黃明樂. 2009.《港孩》[Hong Kong children]. 香港: 明窗出版社 [Hong Kong: Ming chuang chu ban she].

Huang, Shuzhen, and Daniel C. Brouwer. 2018. "Coming Out, Coming Home, Coming With: Models of Queer Sexuality in Contemporary China." *Journal of International and Intercultural Communication* 11 (2): 97–116.

Huang, Yingying 黃盈盈, and Suiming Pan 潘绥銘, eds. 2009.《性，研究ing》[Sex, researching]. 高雄: 萬有出版社 [Gaoxiong: Wanyou Chubanshe].

Huang, Yingting, Suiming Pan, Peng Tao, and Yanning Gao. 2009. "Teaching Sexualities at Chinese Universities: Context, Experience, and Challenges." *International Journal of Sexual Health* 21 (4): 282–95.

Hung, Lucifer 洪凌. 2015. "排除與補殘— 從晚近同婚倡議探究臺灣性別政治鬥爭" [Exclusion and compensation: Analyzing same-sex marriage propaganda and relative power struggles within Taiwan gender politics]. 應用倫理評論 [*Applied Ethic Review*] 58:175–205.

Ingram, Gordon Brent, Anne-Marie Bouthillette, and Yolanda Retter, eds. 1997. *Queers in Space: Communities, Public Spaces, Sites of Resistance*. Seattle, WA: Bay Press.

International Rehabilitation Council for Torture Victims (IRCT). 2020. *It's Torture, Not Therapy: A Global Overview of Conversion Therapy; Practices, Perpetrators, and the Role of States*. Copenhagen: IRCT. https://irct.org/publications/thematic-reports/146.

Iwabuchi, Koichi. 2014. "De-westernisation, Inter-Asian Referencing and Beyond." *European Journal of Cultural Studies* 17 (1): 44–57.

Jackson, Peter A. 2003. "Gay Capitals in Global Gay History: Cities, Local Markets, and the Origins of Bangkok's Same-Sex Cultures." In *Post-colonial Urbanism: Southeast Asia Cities and Global Processes*, edited by Ryan Bishop, John Phillips, and Wei Wei Yeo, 151–63. London: Routledge.

Jackson, Stevi, and Petula Sik Ying Ho. 2020. *Women Doing Intimacy: Gender, Family and Modernity in Britain and Hong Kong*. London: Palgrave Macmillan.

Jackson, Stevi, and Sue Scott. 2004. "The Personal Is Still Political: Heterosexuality, Feminism and Monogamy." *Feminism and Psychology* 14 (1): 151–57.

Jagose, Annamarie. 1996. *Queer Theory: An Introduction*. New York: New York University Press.

Jamieson, Lynn. 2004. "Intimacy, Negotiated Nonmonogamy, and the Limits of the Couple." In *The State of Affairs: Explorations in Infidelity and Commitment*, edited by Jean Duncombe, Kaeren Harrison, Graham Allan, and Dennis Marsden, 35–57. London: Lawrence Erlbaum Associates.

Jeffreys, Elaine, ed. 2006. *Sex and Sexuality in China*. New York: Routledge.

Jeffreys, Elaine. 2007. "Querying Queer Theory: Debating Male-Male Prostitution in the Chinese Media." *Critical Asian Studies* 39 (1): 151–75.

Jeffreys, Elaine, and Haiqing Yu. 2015. *Sex in China*. Cambridge: Polity.

Jhang, Jhu-Cin. 2018. "Scaffolding in Family Relationships: A Grounded Theory of Coming Out to Family." *Family Relations* 67 (1): 161–75.

Jheng, Ying-jie 鄭英傑. 2018. "從「草莓族」到「蒲公英族」：臺灣青(少)年文化圖像的 轉向及其教育啟示" [From "Strawberry Generation" to "Youth Precariat": The transformation of Taiwanese youth culture and its educational implications] 教育研究月刊 [Journal of Education Research] 296:90–107.

Johnson, Mark, Peter Jackson, and Gilbert Herdt. 2000. "Critical Regionalities and the Study of Gender and Sexual Diversity in South East and East Asia." *Culture, Health and Sexuality* 2 (4): 361–75.

Jones, Rodney. 2007. "Imagined Comrades and Imaginary Protections: Identity, Community and Sexual Risk among Men Who Have Sex with Men in China." *Journal of Homosexuality* 53 (3): 83–115.

Kam, Lucetta Yip-Lo. 2013. *Shanghai Lalas: Female Tongzhi Communities and Politics in Urban China*. Hong Kong: Hong Kong University Press.

Kam, Lucetta Yip-Lo. 2015. "The Demand for a 'Normal' Life: Marriage and Its Discontents in Contemporary China." In *Routledge Handbook of Sexuality Studies in East Asia*, edited by Mark McLelland and Vera Mackie, 77–86. London: Routledge.

Kang, Dredge Byung'Chu. 2017. "Eastern Orientations: Thai Middle-Class Gay Desire for 'White Asians.'" *Culture, Theory and Critique* 58 (2): 182–208.

Kang, Wenqing. 2009. *Obsession: Male Same-Sex Relations in China, 1900–1950*. Hong Kong: Hong Kong University Press.

Kang, Wenqing. 2012. "The Decriminalization and Depathologization of Homosexuality in China." In *China in and beyond the Headlines*, edited by Timothy B. Weston and Lionel M. Jensen, 231–48. Lanham, MD: Rowman and Littlefield.

Kao, Ying Chao. 2018. "Organizing Transnational Moral Conservativism: How US Christian and Taiwanese 'Pro-family' Movements Converge, Diverge and Collide." PhD diss., Department of Sociology, Rutgers University.

Kao, Ying Chao. 2021. "The Coloniality of Queer Theory: The Effects of "Homonormativity" on Transnational Taiwan's Path to Equality." *Sexualities*. https://doi.org/10.1177/13634607211047518.

Kao, Ying Chao, and Herng-Dar Bih. 2014. "Masculinity in Ambiguity: Constructing Taiwanese Masculine Identities between Great Powers." In *Masculinities in a Global Era*, edited by Joseph Gelfer, 175–91. New York: Springer.

Ke, Fei 喀飛. 2016a. "台灣同運現場：那一夜 常德街" [The firsthand observation of the Tongzhi movement in Taiwan: That night in Chang-de street]. 酷時代 [Age of Queer], March 17. http://ageofqueer.com/archives/9223.

Ke, Fei 喀飛. 2016b. "台灣同運現場：誰剝光了男同性戀？AG健身中心事件" [The firsthand observation of the Tongzhi movement in Taiwan: Who stripped homosexual? Event in AG gym]. 酷時代 [Age of Queer], May 19. http://ageofqueer.com/archives/10522.

Ke, Fei 喀飛. 2021.《台灣同運三十：一位平權運動參與者的戰鬥發聲》[The 30-year crusade of LGBT rights movements in Taiwan: Viewpoints from an activist]. 台灣：一葦文思 [Taiwan: Gate Books].

Kehl, Katharina. 2020. "Homonationalism Revisited: Race, Rights, and Queer Complexities." *Lambda Nordica* 25 (2): 17–38.

Kim-Puri, H. J. 2005. "Conceptualizing Gender-Sexuality-State-Nation: An Introduction." *Gender and Society* 19 (2): 137–59.

King, Gary, Jennifer Pan, and Margaret E. Roberts. 2013. "How Censorship in China Allows Government Criticism but Silences Collective Expression." *American Political Science Review* 107 (2): 326–43.

Kitchin, Rob. 2020. "Civil Liberties or Public Health, or Civil Liberties and Public Health? Using Surveillance Technologies to Tackle the Spread of COVID-19." *Space and Polity* 24 (3): 362–81.

Kong, Shiu-ki 江紹祺. 2014.《男男正傳：香港年長男同志口述史》[Oral history of older gay men in Hong Kong]. 香港：進一步 [Hong Kong: Stepforward Multimedia].

Kong, Travis S. K. 2002. "The Seduction of the Golden Boy: The Body Politics of Hong Kong Gay Men." *Body and Society* 8 (1): 29–48. https://doi.org10.1177/1357034X02008001002.

Kong, Travis S. K. 2005. "Queering Masculinity in Hong Kong Movies." In *Masculinities and Hong Kong Cinema*, edited by Laikwan Pang and Day Wong, 57–80. Hong Kong: Hong Kong University Press.

Kong, Travis S. K. 2011. *Chinese Male Homosexualities: Memba, Tongzhi and Golden Boy*. London: Routledge.

Kong, Travis S. K. 2012a. "A Fading Tongzhi Heterotopia: Hong Kong Older Gay Men's Use of Spaces." *Sexualities* 15 (8): 896–916. https://doi.org.10.1177/1363460712459308.

Kong, Travis S. K. 2012b. "Reinventing the Self under Socialism: The Case of Migrant Male Sex Workers ('Money Boys') in China." *Critical Asian Studies* 44 (3): 283–308.

Kong, Travis S. K. 2016. "The Sexual in Chinese Sociology: Homosexuality Studies in Contemporary China." *Sociological Review* 64 (3): 495–514.

Kong, Travis S. K. 2017. "Sex and Work on the Move: Money Boys in Post-socialist China." *Urban Studies* 54 (3): 678–94.

Kong, Travis S. K. 2018. "Gay and Grey: Participatory Action Research in Hong Kong." *Qualitative Research* 18 (3): 257–72.

Kong, Travis S. K. 2019a. *Oral Histories of Older Gay Men in Hong Kong: Unspoken but Unforgotten*. Hong Kong: Hong Kong University Press.

Kong, Travis S. K. 2019b. "Transnational Queer Sociological Analysis of Sexual Identity and Civic-Political Activism in Hong Kong, Taiwan and Mainland China."

British Journal of Sociology 70 (5): 1904–25. https://doi.org.10.1111/1468–4446 .12697.

Kong, Travis S. K. 2020. "The Pursuit of Masculinity by Young Gay Men in Neoliberal Hong Kong and Shanghai." *Journal of Youth Studies* 23 (8): 1004–21.

Kong, Travis S. K. 2021. "Be a Responsible and Respectable Man: Two Generations of Chinese Gay Men Accomplishing Masculinity in Hong Kong." *Men and Masculinities* 24 (1): 64–83.

Kong, Travis S. K. 2022. "Toward a Transnational Queer Sociology: Historical Formation of Tongzhi Identities and Cultures in Hong Kong and Taiwan (1980s–1990s) and China (Late 1990s–early 2000s)." *Journal of Homosexuality* 69 (3): 474–98.

Kong, Travis S. K., Hsiao-Wei Kuan, Sky H. L. Lau, and Sara L. Friedman. 2021. "LGBT Movements in Taiwan, Hong Kong, and China." In *Oxford Encyclopedia of LGBT Politics and Policy*, edited by D. Haider-Markel. Oxford: Oxford University Press. https://doi.org/10.1093/acrefore/9780190228637.013.1275.

Kong, Travis S. K., Sky H. L. Lau, and Amory H. W. Hui. 2019. "Tongzhi." In *Global Encyclopedia of Lesbian, Gay, Bisexual, Transgender, and Queer (LGBTQ) History*, edited by Howard Chiang, 1603–8. Farmington Hills, MI: Charles Scribner's Sons.

Kong, Travis S. K., Sky H. L. Lau, and Eva C. Y. Li. 2015. "The Fourth Wave? A Critical Reflection on the Tongzhi Movement in Hong Kong." In *The Routledge Handbook of Sexuality Studies in East Asia*, edited by Mark McLelland and Vera Mackie, 188–201. London: Routledge.

Kong, Travis S. K., Ken Plummer, and Dan Mahoney. 2002. "Queer(y)ing the Interview: From Criminalised Homosexuals to Post-modern Queers." In *The Handbook of Interviewing*, edited by Jaber Gubrium and James A. Holstein, 239–58. London: Sage.

Koo, Anita C., and Thomas W. P. Wong. 2009. "Family in Flux: Benchmarking Family Changes in Hong Kong Society." Special issue, *Social Transformations in Chinese Societies* 4:17–56.

Kramer, Jerry Lee. 1995. "Bachelor Farmers and Spinsters: Gay and Lesbian Identities and Communities in Rural North Dakota." In *Mapping Desire: Geographies of Sexualities*, edited by David Bell and Gill Valentine, 200–213. London: Routledge.

Ku, Agnes S., and Ngai Pun, eds. 2004. *Remaking Citizenship in Hong Kong*. Oxon: Routledge Curzon.

Kuan, Hsiao-wei. 2019a. "LGBT Rights in Taiwan—The Interaction between Movements and the Law." In *Taiwan and International Human Rights: A Story of Transformation*, edited by J. A. Cohen, W. P. Alford, and C. F. Lo, 593–608. New York: Springer.

Kuan, Hsiao-wei 官曉薇. 2019b. "臺灣民主化後同志人權保障之變遷——法律與社會運動的觀點" [The development of LGBT rights in democratic Taiwan: An analysis from the perspective of law and social movements]. 中研院法學期刊 [*Academia Sinica Law Journal*], no. 1, 551–615.

Kuan, Hsiao-wei 官曉薇. 2019c. "婚姻平權與法律動員——釋字第 748 號解釋前之立法與訴訟行動" [Marriage equality and legal mobilization: The litigation and legislative actions before judicial Yuan Interpretation No. 748]. 台灣民主季刊 [*Taiwan Democracy Quarterly*] 16 (1): 1–44.

Lan, Pei Chia. 2014. "Compressed Modernity and Glocal Entanglement: The Contested Transformation of Parenting Discourses in Postwar Taiwan." *Current Sociology* 62 (4): 531–49.

Lancaster, Roger N. 1988. "Subject Honor and Object Shame: The Construction of Male Homosexuality and Stigma in Nicaragua." *Ethnology* 27 (2): 111–25.

Langlois, Anthony J. 2018. "International Political Theory and LGBTQ Rights." In *The Oxford Handbook of International Political Theory*, edited by Chris Brown and Robyn Eckersley, 370–82. Oxford: Oxford University Press.

Lau, Siu-kai. 1982. *Society and Politics in Hong Kong*. Hong Kong: Chinese University Press.

Law, Wing Sang. 1998. "Managerializing Colonialism." In *Trajectories: Inter-Asia Cultural Studies*, edited by Kuan-Hsing Chen, 109–21. London: Routledge.

Law, Wing Sang. 2017. "Decolonisation Deferred: Hong Kong Identity in Historical Perspective." In *Citizenship, Identity and Social Movements in the New Hong Kong: Localism after the Umbrella Movement*, edited by Lam Waiman and Luke Cooper, 13–33. London: Routledge.

Lee, Ching Kwan. 2007. *Against the Law: Labor Protests in China's Rustbelt and Sunbelt*. Berkeley and Los Angeles: University of California Press.

Lee, Francis L. F., and Joseph M. Chan. 2018. *Media and Protest Logics in the Digital Era: The Umbrella Movement in Hong Kong*. New York: Oxford University Press.

Lee, Pei Wen 李佩雯. 2018. "當「他們」也是「我們」：已出櫃同志與原生家庭之跨群體溝通關係維繫研究" [Intergroup relational maintenance among post come-out homosexual individuals and their original family members]. 傳傳播研究與實踐 [*Journal of Communication Research and Practice*] 8 (1): 65–101.

Lee, Po-Han. 2017. "Queer Activism in Taiwan: An Emergent Rainbow Coalition From the Assemblage Perspective." *Sociological Review* 65 (4): 682–98.

Leong, Russell, ed. 1996. *Asian American Sexualities: Dimensions of the Gay and Lesbian Experience*. London: Routledge.

Lethbridge, Henry J. 1976. "The Quare Fellow: Homosexuality and the Law in Hong Kong." *Hong Kong Law Journal* 6 (3): 292–326.

Leung, Helen Hok-Sze. 2007. "Archiving Queer Feelings in Hong Kong." *Inter-Asia Cultural Studies* 8 (4): 559–71.

Leung, Helen Hok-Sze. 2008. *Undercurrents: Queer Culture and Postcolonial Hong Kong*. Hong Kong: Hong Kong University Press.

Leung, Janet T. Y., and Daniel T. L. Shek. 2018. "Families in Transition in Hong Kong: Implications to Family Research and Practice." *International Public Health Journal* 10 (2): 143–55.

Leung, Vivian W. Y., Ching Man Lam, and Yan Liang. 2020. "Parents' Expectations of Familial Elder Care under the Neoliberal Hong Kong Society." *Journal of Family Issues* 41 (4): 437–59.

Levine, Martin. 1979. "Gay Ghetto." *Journal of Homosexuality* 4 (4): 363–77.

Lewin, Ellen, and William L. Leap, eds. 1996. *Out in the Field: Reflections of Lesbian and Gay Anthropologists*. Urbana: University of Illinois Press.

Li, Chunling. 2021. *China's Youth: Increasing Diversity amid Persistent Inequality*. Washington, DC: Brookings Institution Press.

Li, Yinhe. 2006. "Regulating Male Same-Sex Relationships in the People's Republic of China." In *Sex and Sexuality in China*, edited by Elaine Jeffreys, 82–101. London: Routledge.

Li, Yinhe 李銀河, and Xiaobo Wang 王小波. 1992.《他們的世界—— 中國男同性戀群落透視》[Their world: Looking into the male homosexual community in China]. 中國: 山西人民出版社 [China: Shanxi People's Press].

Li, Yitan, and Enyu Zhang. 2017. "Changing Taiwanese Identity and Cross-Strait Relations: A Post 2016 Taiwan Presidential Election Analysis." *Journal of Chinese Political Science* 22 (1): 17–35.

Licoppe, Christian, Carole Anne Rivière, and Julien Morel. 2016. "Grindr Casual Hook-Ups as Interactional Achievements." *New Media and Society* 18 (11): 2540–58.

Lim, Eng-Beng. 2014. *Brown Boys and Rice Queens: Spellbinding Performance in the Asias*. New York: New York University Press.

Lim, Song-Hwee. 2008. "How to Be Queer in Taiwan: Translation, Appropriation, and the Construction of a Queer Identity in Taiwan." In *AsiaPacifiQueer: Rethinking Genders and Sexualities*, edited by Fran Martin, Peter A. Jackson, Mark McLelland, and A. Yue, 235–50. Urbana: University of Illinois Press.

Lin, Dennis Chwen-der 林純德. 2015. "「同志權益與性解放無關」?: 真愛聯盟事件中的同運含蓄政略" [Gay rights have nothing to do with sex education? Gay reticent politics in the True Love Alliance event]. 台灣社會研究季刊 [*Taiwan: A Radical Quarterly in Social Studies*] 101:201–36.

Lin, Qiqing. 2019. "One Baby, Two Fathers: The Rise of Gay Men Turning to Surrogacy." Sixth Tone, January 14. https://www.sixthtone.com/news/1003427/one -baby%2C-two-fathers-the-rise-of-gay- men-turning-to-surrogacy.

Lin, Thung-Hong 林宗弘, Ching-Shu Hung 洪敬舒, Chien-Hung Li 李健鴻, Chao-Ching Wang 王兆慶, and Feng-Yi Chang 張烽益. 2011.《崩世代》[The collapsing generation]. 台北: 台灣勞工陣線 [Taipei: Taiwan Labour Front.].

Lin, Tung-Fa 林桶法. 2018. "戰後初期到 1950 年代 臺灣人口移出與移入" [The migration of Taiwanese population in early post-war stage in 1950]. 臺灣學通訊 [*Newsletter of Taiwan Studies*] 103:4–7.

Lin, Xiaodong, and Máirtín Mac an Ghaill. 2017. "(Re)masculinizing '*Suzhi Jiaoyu*' (Education for Quality): Aspirational Values of Modernity in Neoliberal China." In *Masculinity and Aspiration in an Era of Neoliberal Education*, edited by Garth Stahl, Joseph Nelson, and Derron Wallace, 147–65. London: Routledge.

Liu, Jen-peng, and Naifei Ding. 2005. "Reticent Poetics, Queer Politics." *Inter-Asia Cultural Studies* 6 (1): 30–55.

Liu, Petrus. 2015. *Queer Marxism in Two Chinas*. Durham, NC: Duke University Press.

Liu, Petrus, and Lisa Rofel, eds. 2010. "Beyond the Strai(gh)ts: Transnationalism and Queer Chinese Politics." Special issue, *Positions: East Asia Cultures Critique* 18 (2).

Liu, Tingting, and Chris K. K. Tan. 2020. "On the Transactionalisation of Conjugal Bonds: A Feminist Materialist Analysis of Chinese Xinghun Marriages." *Anthro-*

pological Forum: A Journal of Social Anthropology and Comparative Sociology 30 (4): 443–63.

Liu, Tingting, Yinan Wang, and Zhongxuan Lin. 2021. "The Cruel Optimism of Digital Dating: Heart-Breaking Mobile Romance among Rural Migrant Workers in South China." *Information, Communication and Society.* https://doi.org.10.1080 /1369118X.2021.1874039.

Liu, Wen 劉文. 2021. "非西方、亞洲或中美冷戰結構? 重置酷兒臺灣的戰(暫)時主體" [Non-Western sexuality, queer Asia, or Cold War geopolitics? Repositioning queer Taiwan in the temporal turn]. 臺灣文學研究集刊 [*NTU Studies in Taiwan Literature*] 26:3–35.

Liu, Wen, and Charlie Yi Zhang. 2022. "Homonationalism as a Site of Contestation and Transformation: On Queer Subjectivities and Homonationalism across Sinophone Societies." In *Homonationalism, Femonationalism and Ablenationalism: Critical Pedagogies Contextualised*, edited by Angeliki Sifaki, C. L. Quinan, and Katarina Loncarevic, 31–47. London: Routledge.

Liu, Xuekun. 2021. "Homonationalist and Homocolonialist Discourses in Hong Kong's Anti-extradition Protests: Online Evaluations and Representations of LGBT Rights." *Discourse, Context and Media* 40. https://doi.org/10.1016/j.dcm.2021.100465.

Lizada, Miguel Antonio Nograles. 2021. "Post-1997 Gay Cinema of Thailand, Hong Kong, and the Philippines." PhD diss., Department of Comparative Literature, University of Hong Kong.

Lo, Ming-Cheng M., and Hsin-Yi Hsieh. 2020. "The 'Societalization' of Pandemic Unpreparedness: Lessons from Taiwan's COVID Response." *American Journal of Cultural Sociology* 8 (3): 384–404.

Louie, Kam. 2002. *Theorising Chinese Masculinity: Society and Gender in China.* Cambridge: Cambridge University Press.

Love, Heather. 2021. *Underdogs: Social Deviance and Queer Theory.* Chicago: University of Chicago Press.

Lugones, Maria. 2007. "Heterosexism and the Colonial/Modern Gender System." *Hypatia* 22(1): 186–219.

Ma, Eric Kit-Wai. 2012. "Compressed Modernity in South China." *Global Media and Communication* 8 (3): 289–308.

Lui, Tailok 呂大樂. 2007.《四代香港人》 [Four generations of Hong Kong people]. 香港: 進一步 [Hong Kong: Stepforward Multimedia].

Luk, Ka Wing. 2020. "Rethinking Adulthood: The Housing Transition of the Current Younger Generation in Hong Kong." PhD diss., Department of Sociology, University of Hong Kong.

Malinowski, Bronislaw. 1922. *Argonauts of the Western Pacific: An Account of Native Enterprise and Adventure in the Archipelagos of Melanesian New Guinea.* London: Routledge/Kegan Paul.

Manalansan, Martin F., IV. 2003. *Global Divas: Filipino Gay Men in the Diaspora.* Durham, NC: Duke University Press.

Mannheim, Karl. 1952. *Essays on the Sociology of Knowledge.* London: Routledge/ Kegan Paul.

Marshall, Daniel, Peter Aggleton, Rob Cover, Mary Lou Rasmussen, and Benjamin Hegarty. 2019. "Queer Generations: Theorizing a Concept." *International Journal of Cultural Studies* 22 (4): 558–76.

Martin, Fran. 2003. *Situating Sexualities: Queer Representation in Taiwanese Fictions, Film and Public Culture*. Hong Kong: Hong Kong University Press.

Martin, Fran. 2009. "That Global Feeling: Sexual Subjectivities and Imagined Geographies in Chinese-Language Lesbian Cyberspaces." In *Internationalizing Internet Studies: Beyond Anglophone Paradigms*, edited by George Goggin and Mark McLelland, 285–301. London: Routledge.

Martin, Fran. 2015. "Transnational Queer Sinophone Cultures." In *Routledge Handbook of Sexuality Studies in East Asia*, edited by Mark McLelland and Vera Mackie, 35–48. London: Routledge.

Martin, Fran, Peter Jackson, Mark McLelland, and Audrey Yue, eds. 2008. *AsiaPacifiQueer: Rethinking Genders and Sexualities*. Urbana: University of Illinois Press.

Massad, Joseph. 2002. "Re-orienting Desire: The Gay International and the Arab World." *Public Culture* 14 (2): 361–85.

Massad, Joseph. 2007. *Desiring Arabs*. Chicago: University of Chicago Press.

Mathews, Gordon. 1997. "Heunggongyahn: On the Past, Present, and Future of Hong Kong Identity." *Bulletin of Concerned Asian Scholars* 29 (3): 3–13.

McCrindle, Mark. 2014. *The ABC of XYZ: Understanding the Global Generations*. Sydney: McCrindle Research.

McIntosh, Mary. 1968. "The Homosexual Role." *Social Problems* 16 (2): 182–92.

McLelland, Mark, and Vera Mackie, eds. 2015. *Routledge Handbook of Sexuality Studies in East Asia*. London: Routledge.

Mead, Margaret. 1952. *Sex and Temperament in Three Primitive Societies*. London: Routledge.

Meghji, Ali. 2021. *Decolonizing Sociology: An Introduction*. Cambridge: Polity.

Mendoza, Victor Roman. 2009. "Terrorist Assemblages: Homonationalism in Queer Times (Review)." *Journal of Asian American Studies* 12 (1): 128–32.

Miao, Weishan, and Lik Sam Chan. 2020. "Social Constructivist Account of the World's Largest Gay Social App: Case Study of Blued in China." *Information Society* 36 (4): 214–25.

Millner-Larsen, Nadja, and Gavin Butt. 2018. "Introduction: The Queer Common." *GLQ: A Journal of Lesbian and Gay Studies* 24 (4): 399–419.

Moussawi, Ghassan, and Salvador Vidal-Ortiz. 2020. "A Queer Sociology: On Power, Race, and Decentering Whiteness." *Sociological Forum* 35 (4): 1272–89.

Mutchler, Matt G. 2000. "Young Gay Men's Stories in the States: Scripts, Sex, and Safety in the Time of AIDS." *Sexualities* 3 (1): 31–54.

Nash, Catherine J., and Andrew Gorman-Murray. 2014. "LGBT Neighbourhoods and 'New Mobilities': Towards Understanding Transformations in Sexual and Gendered Urban Landscapes." *International Journal of Urban and Regional Research* 38 (3): 756–72.

National Bureau of Statistics of China. 2022. *China Population Census Yearbook 2020: The Seventh National Population Census*. Beijing: China Statistics Press.

Ng, Eve, and Xiomeng Li. 2020. "A Queer 'Socialist Brotherhood': The *Guardian* Web Series, Boys' Love Fandom, and the Chinese State." *Feminist Media Studies* 20 (4): 479–95.

Nguyen, Tan Hoang. 2014. *A View from the Bottom: Asian American Masculinity and Sexual Representation*. Durham, NC: Duke University Press.

Ning, Yin-Bin 卡維波. 2018. "台灣同性婚姻的三方爭議" [The three perspectives on the controversy of Taiwanese same-sex marriage]. 人間思想 [*Renjian Thought Review*] 17:78–91.

Ong, Aihwa. 1999. *Flexible Citizenship: The Cultural Logics of Transnationality*. Durham, NC: Duke University Press.

Ong, Aiwha. 2011. "Introduction." In *World Cities: Asian Experiments and the Art of Being Global*, edited by Ananya Roy and Aihwa Ong, 1–25. Oxford: Wiley-Blackwell.

Ortmann, Stephen. 2017. "The Development of Hong Kong Identity: From Local to National Identity." In *Citizenship, Identity and Social Movements in the New Hong Kong: Localism after the Umbrella Movement*, edited by Wai-Man Lam and Luke Cooper, 114–31. London: Routledge.

Oswin Natalie. 2008. "Critical Geographies and the Uses of Sexuality: Deconstructing Queer Space." *Progress in Human Geography* 32 (1): 89–103.

Otmazgin, Nissim. 2016. "A New Cultural Geography of East Asia: Imagining a 'Region' through Popular Culture." *Asia-Pacific Journal* 7 (5). https://apjjf.org/2016/07/Otmazgin.html.

Pan, Guangdan 潘光旦. 1986. 《性心理學》 [Psychology of sex]. 北京: 三聯書店 [Beijing: Sanlian Shudian].

Pan, Suiming. 2006. "Transformation in the Primary Life Cycle: The Origins and Nature of China's Sexual Revolution." In *Sex and Sexuality in China*, edited by Elaine Jeffreys, 21–42. New York: Routledge.

Parsons, Talcott. 1942. "Age and Sex in the Social Structure of the United States." *American Sociological Review* 7 (5): 604–16.

Patton, Cindy. 1998. "Stealth Bombers of Desire: The Globalization of 'Alterity' in Emerging Democracies." In *Bulletin of Queer Politics and Queer Theory*, edited by Antonia Chao, 301–23. Taiwan: Center for the Study of Sexualities.

Philpot, Steven P., Duane Duncan, Jeanne Ellard, Benjamin R. Bavinton, Jeffrey Grierson, and Garrett Prestage. 2017. "Negotiating Gay Men's Relationships: How Are Monogamy and Non-monogamy Experienced and Practiced over Time?" *Culture, Health and Sexuality* 20 (8): 915–28.

Plummer, Ken. 1975. *Sexual Stigma: An Interactionist Account*. London: Routledge/Kegan Paul.

Plummer, Ken. 1983. *Documents of Life: An Introduction to the Problems and Literature of a Humanistic Method*. London: Unwin Hyman.

Plummer, Ken, ed. 1992. *Modern Homosexualities: Fragments of Lesbian and Gay Experience*. London: Routledge.

Plummer, Ken. 1995. *Telling Sexual Stories: Power, Change and Social Worlds*. London: Routledge.

Plummer, Ken. 1998. "Afterword: The Past, Present, and Futures of the Sociology of Same-Sex Relations." In *Social Perspectives in Lesbian and Gay Studies:*

A Reader, edited by Peter M. Nardi and Beth E. Schneider, 605–14. London: Routledge.

Plummer, Ken. 2003. *Intimate Citizenship: Private Decisions and Public Dialogues*. Montreal: McGill-Queen's University Press.

Plummer, Ken. 2010. "Generational Sexualities, Subterranean Traditions and the Hauntings of the Sexual World: Some Preliminary Remarks." *Symbolic Interaction* 33 (2): 163–90.

Plummer, Ken. 2012. "Critical Sexualities Studies." In *The Wiley Blackwell Companion to Sociology*, edited by George Ritzer, 243–68. Oxford: Blackwell Publishing.

Plummer, Ken. 2015. *Cosmopolitan Sexualities: Hope and the Humanist Imagination*. Cambridge: Polity.

Puar, Jasbir K. 2002. "A Transnational Feminist Critique of Queer Tourism." *Antipode* 34 (5): 935–46.

Puar, Jasbir K. 2007. *Terrorist Assemblages: Homonationalism in Queer Times*. Durham, NC: Duke University Press.

Puar, Jasbir K. 2010. "Israel's Gay Propaganda War." *Guardian*, July 1. https://www.theguardian.com/commentisfree/2010/jul/01/israels-gay-propaganda-war/.

Puar, Jasbir K. 2013. "Rethinking Homonationalism." *International Journal of Middle East Studies* 45 (2): 336–39.

Puar, Jasbir K. 2022. "Whither Homonationalism?" In *Homonationalism, Femonationalism and Ablenationalism: Critical Pedagogies Contextualised*, edited by Angeliki Sifaki, C. L. Quinan, and Katarina Loncarevic, 2–8. London: Routledge.

Pun, Ngai. 2005. *Made in China: Women Factory Workers in a Global Workplace*. Durham, NC: Duke University Press.

Qiao, Dongping, and Qianwen Xie. 2017. "Public Perceptions of Child Physical Abuse in Beijing." *Child and Family Social Work* 22:213–25.

Rahman, Momin. 2010. "Queer as Intersectionality: Theorizing Gay Muslim Identities." *Sociology* 44 (5): 944–61.

Rahman, Momin. 2014. "Queer Rights and the Triangulation of Western Exceptionalism." *Journal of Human Rights* 13 (3): 274–89.

Rainie, Lee, and Barry Wellman. 2012. *Networked: The New Social Operating System*. Cambridge, MA: MIT Press.

Reiter, Bernd, ed. 2018. *Constructing the Pluriverse: The Geopolitics of Knowledge*. Durham, NC: Duke University Press.

Renninger, Bryce J. 2019. "Grindr Killed the Gay Bar, and Other Attempts to Blame Social Technologies for Urban Development: A Democratic Approach to Popular Technologies and Queer Sociality." *Journal of Homosexuality* 66 (12): 1736–55.

Richardson, Diane. 2000. "Constructing Sexual Citizenship: Theorizing Sexual Rights." *Critical Social Policy* 20 (1): 105–35.

Richardson, Diane. 2005. "Desiring Sameness? The Rise of a Neoliberal Politics of Normalization." *Antipode* 37 (3): 515–35.

Richardson, Diane. 2015. "Neoliberalism, Citizenship and Activism." In *Ashgate Research Companion to Lesbian and Gay Activism*, edited by David Paternotte and Manon Tremblay, 259–71. London: Routledge.

Richardson, Diane. 2017. "Rethinking Sexual Citizenship." *Sociology* 51 (2): 208–24.

Ringrose, Jessica, and Emma Renold. 2010. "Normative Cruelties and Gender Deviants: The Performative Effects of Bully Discourses for Girls and Boys in School." *British Educational Research Journal* 36 (4): 573–96.

Risor, Helene, and Ignacia Arteaga Perez. 2018. "Disjunctive Belongings and the Utopia of Intimacy: Violence, Love and Friendship among Poor Urban Youth in Neoliberal Chile." *Identities: Global Studies in Culture and Power* 25 (2): 228–44.

Ritchie, Jason. 2015. "Pinkwashing, Homonationalism, and Israel–Palestine: The Conceits of Queer Theory and the Politics of the Ordinary." *Antipode* 47 (3): 616–34.

Robinson, Victoria. 1997. "My Baby Just Cares for Me: Feminism, Heterosexuality and Non-monogamy." *Journal of Gender Studies* 6 (2): 143–57.

Roen, Katrina. 2019. "Rethinking Queer Failure: Trans Youth Embodiments of Distress." *Sexualities* 22 (1–2): 48–64.

Rofel, Lisa. 1999. *Other Modernities: Gendered Yearnings in China after Socialism.* Berkeley: University of California Press.

Rofel, Lisa. 2007. *Desiring China: Experiments in Neoliberalism, Sexuality, and Public Culture.* Durham, NC: Duke University Press.

Rofel, Lisa. 2010. "The Traffic in Money Boys." *Positions: East Asian Cultures Critique* 18 (2): 425–58.

Rofel, Lisa. 2011. "Queer Studies, Materialism, and Crisis: A Roundtable Discussion." *GLQ: A Journal of Lesbian and Gay Studies* 18 (1): 127–47.

Rofel, Lisa. 2012. "Grassroots Activism: Non-normative Sexual Politics in Postsocialist China." In *Unequal China: The Political Economy and Cultural Politics of Inequality*, edited by Wanning Sun and Yingjie Guo, 154–67. London: Routledge.

Roth, Kenneth. 2020. "China's Global Threat to Human Rights." Human Rights Watch. Accessed July 6, 2022. https://www.hrw.org/world-report/2020/country-chapters/global.

Rowe, Matthew S., and Gary W. Dowsett. 2008. "Sex, Love, Friendship, Belonging and Place: Is There a Role for 'Gay Community' in HIV Prevention Today?" *Culture, Health and Society* 10 (4): 329–44.

Ruan, Fang Fu. 1991. *Sex in China: Studies in Sexology in Chinese Culture.* New York: Plenum Press.

Ruan, Fang Fu, and Vern L. Bullough. 1992. "Lesbianism in China." *Archives of Sexual Behavior* 21 (3): 217–26.

Ruan, Fang Fu, and Y. M. Tsai. 1987. "Male Homosexuality in the Traditional Chinese Literature." *Journal of Homosexuality* 14 (3–4): 21–33.

Ryan, Gery W., and H. Russell Bernard. 2000. "Data Management and Analysis Methods." In *Handbook of Qualitative Research*, edited by Norman K. Denzin and Yovanna S. Lincoln, 769–802. Thousand Oaks, CA: Sage.

Said, Edward W. 1978. *Orientalism: Western Conceptions of the Orient.* London: Penguin.

Samara, Tony Roshan. 2015. "Politics and the Social in World-Class Cities: Building a Shanghai Model." *Urban Studies* 52 (15): 2906–21.

Samshasha 小明雄. 1997.《中國同性愛史錄》[History of homosexuality in China]. 香港：
粉紅三角出版社 [Hong Kong: Rosa Winkel Press].

Sang, Tsz-Lan Deborah. 1999. "Translating Homosexuality: The Discourse of
Tongxing'ai in Republican China." In *Tokens of Exchange: The Problem of Trans-
lation in Global Circulation*, edited by Lydia He Liu, 276–304. Durham, NC:
Duke University Press.

Sang, Tsz-Lan Deborah. 2003. *The Emerging Lesbian: Female Same-Sex Desire in
Modern China*. Chicago: University of Chicago Press.

Savin-Williams, Ritch C. 2005. *The New Gay Teenager*. Cambridge, MA: Harvard
University Press.

Schalet, Amy T. 2011. *Not under My Roof: Parents, Teens, and the Culture of Sex*.
Chicago: University of Chicago Press.

Schotten, C. Heike. 2016. "Homonationalism: From Critique to Diagnosis; or, We Are
All Homonational Now." *International Feminist Journal of Politics* 18 (3): 351–70.

Sedgwick, Eve K. 1990. *Epistemology of the Closet*. Berkeley: University of California
Press.

Seidman, Steven. 1996a. "Empire and Knowledge: More Troubles, New Opportunities for Sociology (Book Review)." *Contemporary Sociology* 25 (3): 31–316.

Seidman, Steven, ed. 1996b. *Queer Theory/Sociology*. Oxford: Basil Blackwell.

Seidman, Steven. 2002. *Beyond the Closet: The Transformation of Gay and Lesbian
Life*. New York: Routledge.

Seidman, Steven. 2005. "From Outsider to Citizen." In *Regulating Sex: The Politics
of Intimacy and Identity*, edited by Elizabeth Bernstein and Laurie Schaffner,
225–46. London: Routledge.

Sheller, Mimi, and John Urry. 2006. "The New Mobilities Paradigm." *Environment
and Planning A: Economy and Space* 38 (2): 207–26.

Shi, Jenpeng. 2021. "Parenting in an Uncertain Future: The Experiences of Parents in
the 'PFLAG China' Community." PhD diss., Department of Sociology, University
of Essex.

Shieh, Wen-Yi 謝文宜, Wen-Long Chen 陳雯隆, and Hsiu-Yun Tseng 曾秀雲. 2017. "台
灣同志長期伴侶關係的正向經營策略" [A study of the positive strategies used in long-
term same-sex couple relationship in Taiwan]. 臺灣性學學刊 [*Formosan Journal of
Sexology*] 23 (1): 53–79.

Shieh, Wen-Yi 謝文宜, and Hsiu-Yun Tseng 曾秀雲. 2015. "臺灣同志伴侶的家庭圖像" [A
study on same-sex couples' family images in Taiwan]. 臺大社工學刊 [*NTU Social
Work Review*] 31:1–54.

Shih, Shu-mei. 2013. "Introduction: What Is Sinophone Studies?" In *Sinophone
Studies: A Critical Reader*, edited by Shu-mei Shih, Chien-hsin Tsai, and Brian
Bernards, 1–15. New York: Columbia University Press.

Sifaki, Angeliki, C. L. Quinan, and Katarina Loncarevic, eds. 2022. *Homonationalism, Femonationalism and Ablenationalism: Critical Pedagogies Contextualised*.
London: Routledge.

Sinfield, Alan. 1996. "Diaspora and Hybridity: Queer Identities and the Ethnicity
Model." *Textual Practice* 10 (2): 271–93.

Skocpol, Theda. 1979. *States and Social Revolutions: A Comparative Analysis of France, Russia, and China.* Cambridge: Cambridge University Press.

Smart, Carol. 2007. *Personal Life: New Directions in Sociological Thinking.* Cambridge: Polity.

So, Alvin Y. 2002. "Social Protests, Legitimacy Crisis, and the Impetus toward Soft Authoritarianism in the Hong Kong SAR." In *The First Tung Chee-hwa Administration: The First Five Years of the Hong Kong Special Administration Region,* edited by Siu-kai Lau, 399–418. Hong Kong: Chinese University Press.

Solinger, Dorothy. 1999. *Contesting Citizenship in Urban China: Peasant, Migrants, the State, and the Logic of the Market.* Berkeley: University of California Press.

Somerville, Siobhan. 2014. "Queer." In *Keywords for American Cultural Studies,* edited by Glenn Hendler and Bruce Burgett, 203–7. New York: New York University Press.

Sommer, Matthew H. 1997. "The Penetrated Male in Late Imperial China: Judicial Construction and Social Stigma." *Modern China* 23 (2): 140–80. https://doi.org.10.1177/009770049702300202.

Spires, Anthony J. 2011. "Contingent Symbiosis and Civil Society in an Authoritarian State: Understanding the Survival of China's Grassroots NGOs." *American Journal of Sociology* 117 (1): 1–45.

Spires, Anthony J. 2019. "Regulation as Political Control: China's First Charity Law and Its Implications for Civil Society." *Nonprofit and Voluntary Sector Quarterly* 49 (3): 571–88.

Stacey, Judith, and Barrie Thorne. 1985. "The Missing Feminist Revolution in Sociology." *Social Problems* 32 (4): 301–16.

Standing, Guy. 2011. *The Precariat: The New Dangerous Class.* London: Bloomsbury.

Stein, Arlene, and Ken Plummer. 1994. "'I Can't Even Think Straight': 'Queer Theory' and the Missing Sexual Revolution in Sociology." *Sociological Theory* 12 (2): 178–87.

Strauss, Anselm L., and Juliet M. Corbin. 1997. *Grounded Theory in Practice.* Thousand Oaks, CA: Sage.

Stychin, Carl F. 1998. *A Nation by Rights: National Cultures, Sexual Identity Politics, and the Discourse of Rights.* Philadelphia: Temple University Press.

Sun, Yuezhu. 2011. "Parenting Practices and Chinese Singleton Adults." *Ethnology* 50 (4): 333–50.

Svab, Alenka, and Roman Kuhar. 2014 "The Transparent and Family Closets: Gay Men and Lesbians and Their Families of Origin." *Journal of GLBT Family Studies* 10 (1–2): 15–35.

Taiwan Tongzhi Hotlines 台灣同志諮詢熱線. 2010.《彩虹熟年巴士》[Rainbow elderly bus]. 台北:基本書坊 [Taipei: Gbooks].

Taiwan Tongzhi Hotlines 台灣同志諮詢熱線. 2018.《2017年台灣同志(LGBTI)人權政策檢視報告》[2017 Taiwan LGBTI rights policy review]. 台北: 台灣同志諮詢熱線 [Taipei: Taiwan Tongzhi Hotlines]. https://hotline.org.tw/sites/hotline.org.tw/files/20180103_Ren_Quan_Bao_Gao_A4_Zhong_Wen_Ban_pages.pdf.

Tan, K. Cohen, and Shuxin Cheng. 2020. "Sang Subculture in Post-reform China." *Global Media and China* 5 (1): 86–99.

Tang, Can 唐灿, and Jiang Zhang 張建. 2013.《家庭問題與政府: 責任促進家庭發展的國內外比較研究》[Family development and government responsibilities: A comparative study of policy efforts in China and abroad] 北京: 社會科學文獻出版社 [Beijing: Shehui kexue wenxian chubanshe].

Tang, Denise Tse-Shang. 2011. *Conditional Spaces: Hong Kong Lesbian Desires and Everyday Life*. Hong Kong: Hong Kong University Press.

Tapley, Heather. 2012. "Mapping the Hobosexual: A Queer Materialism." *Sexualities* 15 (3–4): 373–90.

Tedeschi, Miriam, Ekaterina Vorobeva, and Jussi S. Jauhiainen. 2020. "Transnationalism: Current Debates and New Perspectives." *Geojournal*. https://doi.org/10.1007/s10708-020-10271-8.

Therborn, Göran. 2004. *Between Sex and Power: Family in the World, 1900–2000*. London: Routledge.

Therborn, Göran. 2011. *The World: A Beginner's Guide*. Cambridge: Polity.

Tian, Ian Liujia. 2019. "Graduated In/Visibility: Reflections on Ku'er Activism in (Post)socialist China." *QED: A Journal in GLBTQ Worldmaking* 6 (3): 56–75.

Torkelson, Jason. 2012. "A Queer Vision of Emerging Adulthood: Seeing Sexuality in the Transition to Adulthood." *Sexuality Research and Social Policy* 9 (2): 132–42.

Troidon, Richard R. 1988. *Gay and Lesbian Identity: A Sociological Analysis*. Lanham, MD: Rowman and Littlefield.

Tsang, Donald. 2006. "Big Market, Small Government." Government of the Hong Kong SAR. Accessed September 18, 2021. http://www.ceo.gov.hk/archive/2012/eng/press/oped.htm.

Tseng, Bowen 曾柏文. 2014. "太陽花運動: 論述軸線的空間性" [The Sunflower Movement: The spatiality of discursive axes]. 思想 [*Reflexion*] 27:129–48.

Valentine, Gill. 1993. "(Hetero)sexing Space: Lesbian Perceptions and Experiences of Everyday Spaces." *Environment and Planning D: Society and Space* 11 (4): 395–413.

Valocchi, Stephen. 2005. "Not Yet Queer Enough: The Lessons of Queer Theory for the Sociology of Gender and Sexuality." *Gender and Society* 19 (6): 750–70.

van Eeden-Moorefield, Brad, Kevin Malloy, and Kristen Benson. 2016. "Gay Men's (Non)monogamy Ideals and Lived Experience." *Sex Roles* 75 (1): 43–55.

van Gulik, Robert Hans. 1961. *Sexual Life in Ancient China: A Preliminary Survey of Chinese Sex and Society from ca. 1500 B.C. till 1644 A.D.* Leiden: Brill.

Walker, Christopher, and Jessica Ludwig. 2017. "From 'Soft Power' to 'Sharp Power': Rising Authoritarian Influence in the Democratic World." In *Sharp Power: Rising Authoritarian Influence*, edited by Juan Pablo Cardenal, Jacek Kucharczyk, Grigorij Mesežnikov, and Gabriela Pleschová, 8–25. Washington, DC: International Forum for Democratic Studies, National Endowment in Democracy.

Wang, Chih-ming. 2017a. "Affective Rearticulations: Cultural Studies in and from Taiwan." *Cultural Studies* 31 (6): 740–63.

Wang, Chih-ming. 2017b. "'The Future That Belongs to Us': Affective Politics, Neoliberalism and the Sunflower Movement." *International Journal of Cultural Studies* 20 (2): 177–92.

Wang, Frank T. Y. 王增勇. 2011. "家庭照顧者做為一種改革長期照顧的社會運動" [Reforming long term care through the movement of family caregivers]. 台灣社會研究季刊 [*Taiwan: A Radical Quarterly in Social Studies*] 85:396–414.

Wang, Frank T. Y. 王增勇. 2014. "福利造家?：國家對家庭照顧實踐的規訓" [Making family by social welfare? The discipline of the family care practices from the state]. In《21世紀的家：臺灣的家何去何從?》[Family in the 21st century: Where is the Taiwanese family headed?], edited by Ying-Kuei Huang 黃應貴 et al., 35–65. 台北：群學 [Taipei: Socio Publishing].

Wang, Frank T. Y., Herng-Dar Bih, and David J. Brennan. 2009. "Have They Really Come Out? Gay Men and Their Parents in Taiwan." *Culture, Health and Sexuality* 11 (3): 285–96.

Wang, Georgette, and Zhong-Bo Liu. 2010. "What Collective? Collectivism and Relationalism from a Chinese Perspective." *Chinese Journal of Communication* 3 (1): 42–63.

Wang, Shuaishuai. 2019a. "Live Streaming, Intimate Situations, and the Circulation of Same-Sex Affect: Monetizing Affective Encounters on Blued." *Sexualities* 23 (5–6): 934–50.

Wang, Shuaishuai. 2019b. "Living with Censorship: The Political Economy and Cultural Politics of Chinese Gay Dating Apps." PhD diss., Department of Media Studies, University of Amsterdam.

Wang, Shu-Yung 王舒芸. 2014. "門裡門外誰照顧，平價普及路迢迢?臺灣嬰兒照顧政策之體制內涵分析" [The analysis of infant care policies and debates in Taiwan]. 台灣社會研究季刊 [*Taiwan: A Radical Quarterly in Social Studies*] 96:49–93.

Wang, Shu-Yung 王舒芸, and Pin Wang 王品. 2014. "台灣照顧福利的發展與困境：1990–2012" [The development and predicament of Taiwan care welfare: 1990–2012]. In《台灣婦女處境白皮書：2014年》[White book of the situation of Taiwanese women], edited by Jau-Hwa Chen 陳瑤華, 29–75. 台北：女書文化 [Taipei: Fembooks Publishing].

Wang, Stephanie Yingyi. 2019. "When Tongzhi Marry: Experiments of Cooperative Marriage between Lalas and Gay Men in Urban China." *Feminist Studies* 45 (1): 13–35.

Wang, Ying-Ting, and Wen-Shan Yang. 2019. "Changes and Trends in Family Structure in Taiwan, 1990–2010." *Journal of Family Issues* 40 (14): 1896–911.

Warner, Leah, Tugce Kurtis, and Akanksha Adya. 2020. "Navigating Criticisms of Intersectional Approaches: Reclaiming Intersectionality for Global Social Justice and Well-Being." *Women and Therapy* 43 (3–4): 262–77.

Warner, Michael, ed. 1993. *Fear of a Queer Planet: Queer Politics and Social Theory.* Minneapolis: University of Minnesota Press.

Warner, Michael. 1999. *The Trouble with Normal: Sex, Politics, and the Ethics of Queer Life.* New York: Free Press.

Watson, Lesley. 2017. "Situating the Self in Global Context: Reconceptualizing Transnational and Cosmopolitan Identities." *Sociology Compass* 12, no. 7, e12592. https://doi.org/10.1111/soc4.12592.

Weeks, Jeffrey. 1981. *Sex, Politics and Society: The Regulation of Sexuality since 1800.* London: Longman.

Weeks, Jeffrey. 1985. *Sexuality and Its Discontents: Meanings, Myths and Modern Sexualities*. London: Routledge.

Weeks, Jeffrey, Brian Heaphy, and Catherine Donovan, C. 2001. *Same-Sex Intimacies: Families of Choice and Other Life Experiments*. London: Routledge.

Wei, John. 2020. *Queer Chinese Cultures and Mobilities: Kinship, Migration, and Middle Classes*. Hong Kong: Hong Kong University Press.

Wei, Wei 魏偉. 2015.《酷讀中國社會：城市空間，流行文化和社會政策》[Queering Chinese society: Urban space, popular culture and social policy]. 廣西師範大學出版 [Guangxi: Normal University Press].

Wei, Wei. 2021. "Queering the Rise of China: Gay Parenthood, Transnational ARTS, and Dislocated Reproductive Rights." *Feminist Studies* 47 (2): 312–40.

Wei, Wei, and Yunxiang Yan. 2021. "Rainbow Parents and the Familial Model of Tongzhi (LGBT) Activism in Contemporary China." *Chinese Sociological Review*. https://doi.org/10.1080/21620555.2021.1981129.

Weston, Kath. 1993. "Lesbian/Gay Studies in the House of Anthropology." *Annual Review of Anthropology* 22:339–67.

Wharton, Amy S. 2006. "'The Missing Feminist Revolution in Sociology': Twenty Years Later; Looking Back, Looking Ahead." *Social Problems* 53 (4): 443.

Whittle, Stephen. 1994. "Consuming Differences: The Collaboration of the Gay Body with the Cultural State." In *The Margins of the City: Gay Men's Urban Lives*, edited by Stephen Whittle, 27–41. Aldershot: Ashgate.

Whyte, Martin King. 1997. "The Fate of Filial Obligations in Urban China." *China Journal* 38:1–31.

Wielander, Gerda. 2019. *Chinese Discourses on Happiness*. Hong Kong: Hong Kong University Press.

Williams, Raymond. 1977. *Marxism and Literature*. Oxford: Oxford University Press.

Wilson, Ara. 2006. "Queering Asia." *Intersections: Gender, History and Culture in the Asian Context* 14 (3). Accessed July 6, 2021. http://intersections.anu.edu.au /issue14/wilson.html.

Winer, Canton, and Catherine Bolzendahl. 2020. "Conceptualizing Homonationalism: (Re)formulation, Application, and Debates of Expansion." *Sociology Compass* 15 (1). https://doi.org/10.1111/soc4.12853.

Wong, Angela Wai Ching. 2013. "The Politics of Sexual Morality and Evangelical Activism in Hong Kong." *Inter-Asia Cultural Studies* 14 (3): 340–60.

Wong, Day. 2004 "(Post-)identity Politics and Anti-normalization: (Homo)sexual Rights Movement." In *Remaking Citizenship in Hong Kong*, edited by Agnes S. Ku and Pun Ngai, 195–214. London: Routledge.

Wong, Day. 2007. "Rethinking the Coming Home Alternative: Hybridization and Coming Out Politics in Hong Kong's Anti-homophobia Parades." *Inter-Asia Cultural Studies* 8 (4): 600–16.

Wong, Day. 2016. "Sexology and the Making of Sexual Subjects in Contemporary China." *Journal of Sociology* 52 (1): 68–82.

Wong, Hung. 2012. "Changes in Social Policy in Hong Kong Since 1997: Old Wine in New Bottles?" In *Contemporary Hong Kong Government and Politics*, edited by

Wai-man Lam, Percy Luen-tim Lui, and Wilson Wong, 277–96. Hong Kong: Hong Kong University Press.

Wong, James K., and Alvin Y. So. 2020. "The Re-making of Developmental Citizenship in Post-handover Hong Kong." *Citizenship Studies* 24 (7): 934–49.

Wong, Victor, and Tat Chor Au-Yeung. 2019. "Autonomous Precarity or Precarious Autonomy? Dilemmas of Young Workers in Hong Kong." *Economic and Labour Relations Review* 30 (2): 241–61.

Woolwine, David. 2000. "Community in Gay Male Experience and Moral Discourse." *Journal of Homosexuality* 38 (4): 5–37.

Worth, Heather, Jun Jing, Karen McMillan, Chunyan Su, Xiaoxing Fu, Yuping Zhang, Zhao Rui, Angela Kelly-Hanku, Jia Cui, and Youchun Zhang. 2019. "'There Was No Mercy at All': Hooliganism, Homosexuality and the Opening-Up of China." *International Sociology* 34 (1): 38–57.

Wu, Chia-ling. 2018. "From Single Motherhood to Queer Reproduction Access Politics of Assisted Conception in Taiwan." In *Gender, Health, and History in Modern East Asia*, edited by Angela Ki-che Leung and Izumi Nakayama, 92–114. Hong Kong: Hong Kong University Press.

Wu, Fengshi. 2017. "An Emerging Group Name 'Gongyi': Ideational Collectivity in China's Civil Society." *China Review* 17 (2): 123–50.

Wu, Jieh-min. 2021. "More Than Sharp Power: Chinese Influence Operations in Taiwan, Hong Kong and Beyond." In *China's Influence and the Center-Periphery Tug of War in Hong Kong, Taiwan and Indo-Pacific*, edited by Brian C. H. Fong, Jieh-min Wu, and Andrew J. Nathan, 24–44. London: Routledge.

Wu, Jing. 2003. "From 'Long Yang' and 'Dui Shi' to Tongzhi: Homosexuality in China." *Journal of Gay and Lesbian Psychotherapy* 7 (1–2): 117–43.

Wu, Shangwei. 2020. "Domesticating Dating Apps: Non-single Chinese Gay Men's Dating App Use and Negotiations of Relational Boundaries." *Media, Culture and Society* 43 (3): 515–31.

Yan, Yunxiang. 2003. *Private Life under Socialism: Love, Intimacy, and Family Change in a Chinese Village, 1949–1999*. Stanford, CA: Stanford University Press.

Yan, Yunxiang. 2010. "The Chinese Path to Individualization." *British Journal of Sociology* 61 (3): 489–512.

Yan, Yunxiang. 2016. "Intergenerational Intimacy and Descending Familism in Rural North China." *American Anthropology* 118 (2): 244–57.

Yan, Yunxiang. 2017. "Doing Personhood in Chinese Culture: The Desiring Individual, Moralist Self and Relational Person." *Cambridge Journal of Anthropology* 35 (2): 1–17.

Yan, Yunxiang. 2018. "Neo-familism and the State in Contemporary China." *Urban Anthropology* 47 (3–4): 181–224.

Yan, Yunxiang, ed. 2021. *Chinese Families Upside Down: Intergenerational Dynamics and Neo-familism in the Early 21st Century*. Leiden: Brill.

Yau, Albert C. H., and Travis S. K. Kong. 2021. "Male Sex Work and Masculinities in Hong Kong and Mainland China: 'One Country, Two Men.'" In *The Routledge*

Handbook of Male Sex Work, Culture, and Society, edited by John Geoffrey Scott, Christian Grov, and Victor Minichiello, 555–70. London: Routledge.

Yau, Ching, ed. 2010. *As Normal as Possible: Negotiating Sexuality and Gender in Mainland China and Hong Kong*. Hong Kong: Hong Kong University Press.

Yeh, Chung-Yang 葉崇揚, Yi-Chun Chou 周怡君, and Yu-Hsuan Yang 楊佑萱. 2020. "家庭主義的分歧? 台灣民眾對兒童及老人照顧的福利態度分析" [Divergent familialism? Public attitude towards childcare and eldercare in Taiwan]. 臺大社會工作學刊 [*NTU Social Work Review*] 41:1–56.

Yeh, Kuang-hui 葉光輝. 2009. "華人孝道雙元模型研究的回顧與前瞻" [The dual filial piety model in Chinese culture: Retrospect and prospects]. 本土心理學研究[*Indigenous Psychological Research in Chinese Societies*] 32:101–48.

Yeh, Kuang-hui, Chin-chun Yi, Wei-chun Tsao, and Po-san Wan. 2013. "Filial Piety in Contemporary Chinese Societies: A Comparative study of Taiwan, Hong Kong, and China." *International Sociology* 28 (3): 277–96.

Yeo, Tien Ee Dominic, and Tsz Hin Fung. 2018. "'Mr. Right Now': Temporality of Relationship Formation on Gay Mobile Apps." *Mobile Media and Communication* 6 (1): 3–18.

Yip, Andrew K. T. 1997. "Gay Male Christian Couples and Sexual Exclusivity." *Sociology* 31 (2): 289–306.

Yuan, Mingming. 2020. "Ideological Struggle and Cultural Intervention in Online Discourse: An Empirical Study of Resistance through Translation in China." *Perspectives Studies in Translation Theory and Practice* 28 (4): 625–43.

Yue, Audrey. 2011. "Critical Regionalities in Inter-Asia and the Queer Diaspora." *Feminist Media Studies* 11 (1): 131–38.

Yue, Audrey, and Helen Hok-sze Leung. 2017. "Notes towards the Queer Asian City: Singapore and Hong Kong." *Urban Studies* 54 (3): 747–64.

Zhang, Li. 2001. *Strangers in the City: Reconfigurations of Space, Power, and Social Networks within China's Floating Population*. Stanford, CA: Stanford University Press.

Zhang, Li, and Aihwa Ong, eds. 2008. *Privatizing China: Socialism from Afar*. Ithaca, NY: Cornell University Press.

Zhao, Jing Jamie, Ling Yang and Maud Lavin. 2017. "Introduction." In *Boys' Love, Cosplay and Androgynous Idols: Queer Fan Cultures in Mainland China, Hong Kong, and Taiwan*, edited by Maud Lavin, Ling Yang and Jing Jamie Zhao, xi–xxxiii. Hong Kong: Hong Kong University Press.

Zhou, Min, and Tianyang Hu. 2020. "Social Tolerance of Homosexuality: A Quantitative Comparison of Mainland China, Singapore, and Taiwan." *Chinese Sociological Review* 52 (1): 27–55.

Zhu, Jingshu. 2017. "'Unqueer' Kinship? Critical Reflections on 'Marriage Fraud' in Mainland China." *Sexualities* 21 (7): 1075–91.

Page numbers in italics indicate photographs or tables.

121–22; neoliberalism in, 55, 106, 118–19, 156; one-child policy, 68–69, 72, 186n11; One China, 1, 6–7, 43, 137, 148–49, 154–56, 168; pink economy in, 47–48, 102; post-Mao reform era, 46; power and influence, 155–56; PRC vs ROC, 5–6; privatization in, 118–19, 156; prostitution in, 49; research on, 26; rise of, 5–9; same-sex love in Ancient, 27; socialism of, 165, 176n4; the state in, 55, 106; subjecthood in, 129; and Taiwan, 6–7, 151–52, 155–56, 160; *tongzhi* identity in, 45–53; *tongzhi* world in, 45–53, 128, 157; and United States, 5; victimhood caused by, 131. *See also* Xi Jinping

China, People's Republic of (PRC): conception of China, 137; family under, 68; homosexuality under, 46; political history of, 7, 28, 43, 46; vs ROC, 5; and Sunflower Movement, 181n23. *See also* China, mainland; one-child policy

China Queer Film Festival Tour, 51

China, Republic of (ROC), 5–6, 28, 39. *See also* Taiwan

Chinese Classification of Mental Disorders (*CCMD*), 46

Chinese Communist Party (CCP), 7, 46, 68–69, 155

Chineseness, 3, 137, 142–43, 148, 168, 169

Chinese New Year, 70, 120

Chinese Psychiatric Association, 8

Chinese Tongzhi Conference, 32, 167

Chong, Gladys Pak Lei, 18

Chou, Wah-Shan, 13, 62

Chow, Yiu Fai, 18

Christianity, 8, 30, 38–39, 43, 64, 135. *See also* evangelicalism

cinema, New Queer, 40

circuit parties, 8, 105, 161, 166

citizenship: depoliticized, 112; good, 135; in Hong Kong, 112, 158–59; protest, 158; sexual, 8, 161; *suzhi* (in mainland China), 101, 147, 151, 157; in Taiwan, 160–61. *See also* protests; sexual citizenship

City Magazine (Hong Kong), 32

civil society, as site of governance/resistance, 23, 27, 33

classical sociology, 10. *See also* sociology

closet, the, 64, 65–67, 71, 73, 77, 84. *See also* coming out

Coalition for Marriage Equality (Taiwan), 44

Cody (research participant), 97–98, 100–101, 171

Cold War, 28–29, 140, 141, 154, 169, 190n1

collapsing generation (Lin et al.), 20. *See also* generations

collective action, 49, 146. *See also* protests; resistance

collective intimacy, 89, 107. *See also* intimacy

colonialism: and academic work, 170; comparative research on, 18; and filial piety, 74; and gender, 170; heteronormativity privileged by, 130; homo-, 131, 133, 145; and Hong Kong, 29, 74, 153, 158, 165; political suppression from, 31; of sociology (decolonializing), 178n19; subjectivity, 7, 37–38; and Taiwan, 37–38

coming out: about, xiv, 23–24, 62–85; Chinese context for, 63–68, 168; coming home, 67; coming with, 67; double closet of, 65–66; and family, 56, 71; and filial piety, 71–73, 77, 81, 83; generational strategies, 73; and homonormativity, 12; in Hong Kong, 74–78; and identity politics, 68; and interviews, 22; in mainland China, 68–73; models for, 63–64, 67, 187n17; queer agency, 64; as relational politics, 24, 62–85, 162; scaffolding dynamic of, 66, 71–72; stages of, 71; in Taiwan, 78–82; to *tongzhi* world, 86. *See also* closet, the

commons, the, 90

community: about, 4; gay, 88–89, 107; personal, 90; in *tongzhi* world, 86–87. *See also* gay scene; queer community and commons; *tongzhi* world

community building, 57, 107

compensated dating, 114, 189n12. *See also* relationships

compressed modernity (Chang), 86, 97, 106. *See also* modernities

comrade, 32. *See also* entries beginning with *tongzhi*

comrade literature, 48

conduct-based rights, 27. *See also* sexual citizenship

Confucianism: cultural heritage of, xv, 26; and family values, 4, 56, 147, 151; and HIV/AIDS prevention, 51; and nationalism, 156. *See also* Chineseness; religious groups; spirituality

Connell, Raewyn, 91, 170, 192n4

consent, ages of, 34–35

Constitutional Interpretation No. 748 (Taiwan), 134

consumerism and consumption, 87, 107

contract marriage, 53. *See also* marriage

cosmopolitanism, 33, 52, 87, 107, 159

COVID-19: in Hong Kong, 113, 115–18; in mainland China, 119; and romantic relationships/sexual contact, 76, 117–18; in Taiwan, 3, 124; travel delayed/hastened by, 70–71, 73, 148; and writing of this book, 155, 171

Criminal Law of 1997 (mainland China), 47

critical regionalism, 13–14

critical sexualities studies, 12. *See also* sexuality studies

cruel optimism (Berlant): the good life, 158, 161–62; love and sex as, 108–12, 127–29; and masculinity, 188n3; monogamy as, 24. *See also* optimism

cruising, 98, 100, 111, 122, 125, 158

Cui Zi'en, 48

Da-an Sports Center (Taiwan), 103

Dai Jinhua, 5, 154

Dajin (research participant), 124–26, 162

Daniel (research participant), 116–18, 142–45, 160

Danlan (website), 51

Darwinism (social), 28

Decena, Carlos Ulises, 186n10

de Kloet, Jeroen, 18

democracy: belief in, 28; in mainland China, 2, 28, 147; in Hong Kong, 36, 112, 141, 144; in Taiwan, 6, 20, 41, 126–27, 135, 137, 160. *See also* protests; Sunflower Movement; tongzhi movement: as sociodemocratic movement

depression, 72, 115. *See also* mental health/illness

developmentalism, 55, 87, 107, 112, 119, 129. *See also* neoliberalism

deviance, 10–11, 28

Ding, Naifei, 62, 67

discourse and materiality, 17–18

discrepant modernity (Rofel), 86, 97, 106. *See also* modernities

disjunctive modernities (Appadurai), 86, 97, 106. *See also* modernities

Domestic and Cohabitation Relationship Violence Ordinance (Hong Kong), 35

Doudou (research participant), 72–73, 150, 158, 171

Dowsett, Gary W., 107

drugs. *See* chemfun and chemsex

Duggan, Lisa. *See* homonormativity

Durkheim, Emile, 10

economics, 1, 2, 5, 6, 14, 56, 149, 158, 191n1. *See also* pink economy

election reform, 135

Elements (*tongzhi* social group, Hong Kong), 93–95

Ellis, Havelock, 28

endocrine therapy, 38. *See also* aversion therapy

Engebretsen, Elisabeth L., 62, 85

essentialism, 9, 13, 16, 63, 191n3

Eternal Summer (Chen), 114

Eurocentrism, 11, 170

evangelicalism: and HKSAR government, 34–35, 54, 141; involvement in legislation, 35, 182n8, 182n8; in Taiwan, 34–35, 43, 54, 135, 141; transnational, 8, 56. *See also* Christianity; spirituality

Evangelista, John Andrew, 192n5

exceptionalism, 132, 133, 135, 153

extradition law amendment bill protests (ELAB protests). *See* antiextradiction bill protests

face: *lian*, 72; *mianzi*, 66, 82–83

Facebook, 2, 104–5, 187n1

familial heteronormativity, 63. *See also* family; heteronormativity

familialism, explicit (Taiwan), 79

familism, 74, 162

family: about, 4; biopolitics of, 67; Chinese context of, 24, 62–68; and coming out, 56, 71; as confining *tongzhi* generations, 47; and Confucianism, 4, 56, 147, 151; coresidence (Hong Kong), 76, 118; cultural values of, 56; filial piety as organizing, 38; generational composition of, 79; governance over gay lives, 30, 82; heteropatriarchal ideals, 26, 34–35; in Hong Kong, xiii, 30, 34–35, 74–78, 128; in mainland China, 46, 68–69, 71; neo-familism, 65; and neoliberalism, 62–63, 65, 71, 76–77, 81–82, 162; nuclear, 68; organizational structure, 38; privatiza-tion of, 74; and selfhood, 84, 162; and the state, 69, 79, 82; structures, 74; in Taiwan, 78–79, 81; three-generation, 68

Family Support Agreement (mainland China), 69

Fan Popo, 48

Fei Xiaotong, 187n18

female homosexuality, 28–29. *See also* same-sex love

feminine gender expression, 70, 103, 113–14, 177n12, 184n30

feminism, xvi, 15–16, 39, 50

Feminist Five, 50–51

filial piety: about, 38, 47; in mainland China, 68–69; and colonial governance, 74; and coming out, 71–73, 77, 81, 83; as cultural asset, 82; heterosexual marriage as part of, 68; in Hong Kong, 77; redefining of, 66, 73, 77; in Taiwan, 79, 81; and *tongzhi* identity, 65

Fong, Brian C. H., 7

Foucault, Michel, *The History of Sexuality*, 13

freedom of speech, 7, 58, 143. *See also* democ-racy; protest

Fudan University (mainland China), *50*

fujoshi (female fans of BL novels, Japanese), 98

GagaOOlala (video streaming site), 41

Gao Yanning, 184n34

gay: use of term, 14–15. *See also* homo-sexuality; queer; *tongzhi*

gay- and lesbian-themed movies, 95, 182n13, 184n27

gay bars, 88–89, *93*, 94, 97, 99

gay business model, 55–56, 166

Gay Chat (gay student organization, Taiwan), 40

Gay Counselors Association (Taiwan), 40

Gay Games (Hong Kong), 8, 36, 145

gayness: rejection of Western, 167–68; trans-national imagination of, 101; Western constructions of, 4, 8

gay scene: in Asia, 94–95; in mainland China, 8, 47, 100, 122; depoliticized, 91; in Hong Kong, 93–94; in neighborhoods, 89; in Taiwan, 106, 128–29; traditional vs in present, 88–89; in Western world, 86, 88. *See also tongzhi* world

Gay Teachers' Alliance (Taiwan), 40

gaze, the, 13, 17, 90

gender, xvi, 11, 35–36, 83, 170

gender and sexuality studies, 41, 50, 102

Gender Equity Education Act (Taiwan), 43, 81, 103, 134, 160

Gender Sexuality Rights Association Taiwan, 40

generational sexualities, xiii, 19–23, 30–31

generations: 22K, 123; collapsing (youth, Lin et al.), 123, 127; and family composition, 79; terms for, 19–20, 79, 92

Generation Y, 20

Generation Z, 20

Geng Le, 51

geopolitics, xvi–xvii, 154, 156

Giddens, Anthony, 110

G&L (magazine, Taiwan), 41

globalization: critiquing, 165–69; homogeni-zation from, 13; and post-'90s *tongzhi* generation, 5–9; vs transnationalism, 9, 15

global queering (Altman), 13. *See also* queering

Go, Julian, 18

Gong nui (Hong girl), 114, 189n13

gongyi work, 50–51

Grindr (app), 88–89, 94–95

grounded-theory approach, 23. *See also* methodology

Growlr (app), 104

Gtopia (circuit party), 8. *See also* circuit parties

guai baobao (good gay), 135, 161

guaitai (freak), 40. *See also* queer; *tongzhi*

Guangdong (mainland China), 124, 166

Guangzhou (mainland China), 47

gym bodies, 92, 94, 96, 114, 125

Hakim, Jamie, 89
Hakka people, 136
Hall, Stuart, 10
Han Chinese, 20–21, 37–38, 136–37, 168
hanren (ethnic Han Chinese), 168
hanxu (implicit/reserved, Liu and Ding), 67
Hao (research participant), 3, 80–82, 138–40,
    162, 171, 187n17
happiness, 65, 85
Happiness 42 (gay bar, Shanghai), 100.
    See also gay bars
Happy (research participant), 96
Haritaworn, Jin, 134, 154
hegemony, scattered (Grewal and Kaplan), 17
Hehe Secrets (Hong Kong), 95, 187n1
Heinrich, Ari Larissa, 168
Herdt, Gilbert, 177n12
hetero/homosexual binary, 11, 65
heteronormativity: challenges to, 77–78;
    colonialism as privileging, 130; vs
    domination, other forms of, 17; familial,
    63; hierarchy produced by, 37; and mas-
    culinity, 188n1; reflections by research
    participants, 70; and same-sex desires,
    83; and sexual citizenship, 37; and youth
    sexuality, 127–28
heteropatriarchy, 26
Hiro (research participant), 79–82, 162,
    187nn16–17
HIV/AIDS: anxieties around, 44, 75; and Con-
    fucianism, 51; and *gongyi* work, 51; and
    nationalism, 51; negative images of, 33;
    policy in mainland China, 147; preven-
    tion/treatment, 51; and queer commu-
    nity, 88; research on, 40; transmission, 31
HKSAR government: distrust in, 144, 146;
    and evangelical Christianity, 34–35, 54,
    141; and neoliberalism, 74, 112; and pink
    economics, 54. *See also* Hong Kong
Ho, Denise, 36
Ho, Vivian, *35*
Hoklo people, 136
homocolonialism, 131, 133, 145
homoeroticism, 27–28
homonationalism: about, 25, 131–34; in
    mainland China, 25, 55, 138–39, 147–51,
    153; with Chinese characteristics, 131,
    150–51; failed, 141; in Hong Kong, 25,

55, 131, 141, 151; Kong's work on, 190n1;
    as pinkwashing, 152; pragmatic, 25, 55,
    61, 131, 147–51, 153, 156, 158; in Taiwan,
    22, 25, 55, 130, 134–40, 151; and United
    States, 132–33, 151–53; use by victims,
    151–52; and victimhood, 131
homonormative masculinity: about, 24,
    58, 162; difficulty of achieving, 105; as
    governing gay/*tongzhi* world, 87, 91–92;
    vs heteronormativity, 37; in Hong Kong,
    96; in mainland China, 102, 121; under
    neoliberalism, 63, 76, 81, 87, 107; in
    research participants, 96, 121, 162; in Tai-
    wan, 105; in *tongzhi* movement vs pink
    economy, 102; and youth sexuality, 108
homonormativity: and coming-out model, 12;
    economic familism, 191n1; in the family,
    162; and homonationalism, 132–35; vs
    homonormative masculinity, 24, 37, 87;
    as sexual citizenship model, 91
homosexuality: activism around, 31–32, 40,
    118; ambivalence toward, 45, 54–55;
    -as-minority theory, 11; comparative
    analysis, *60–61*; (de)criminalization of,
    xiii–xiv, 7–8, 31, 54, 156; disapproval for,
    70; etymology, 28; female, 28, 29; gov-
    ernmental attitude toward, 49, 152, 156;
    in Hong Kong, xiii–xiv, 131; identity for-
    mation, 63; laws around, 131; in mainland
    China, 29, 55; medical/mental illness
    model of, xii–xiv, 7–8, 28, 30, 38, 46, 47,
    166; in modern China, 27–29; morality
    of, 28; and nationalism, 54–55, 136–40,
    153; pathologization, 46; public debate
    on, 30–31; and rejection of marriage, 71;
    and religion, 30, 56; as social deviance,
    xiii–xiv, 30; societal expectations of, 71;
    in sociology, 10; sociology of, 9–19, 170;
    and the state, 131–32; subject formation,
    32; in Taiwan, 8, 38, 40–41, 54, 81, 130,
    160–61; as unhealthy lifestyle, xiii–xiv,
    30, 39; use of term, 51; Western model
    (critique of), 167, 171. *See also* gay; queer;
    tongzhi
homosociality, 101
homotransnationalism, 134, 154
Hong Kong: about, 29–37; and Beijing
    government (mainland China), 75, 131,

141, 144, 158–59; and Britain, 6; Christianity in, 30; citizenship, 112, 158–59; colonialism in, 29, 74, 153, 158, 165; coming out in, 74–78; COVID-19 in, 113, 115–18; democracy in, 36, 112, 141, 144; developmental politics of, 112; education in, 76; family in, xii, 30, 34–35, 74–78, 118, 128; gay/*tongzhi* world in, 106, 159; generational terms in, 20; histories of, 21; homonationalism in, 25, 55, 131, 141, 151; identity, 2–3, 6, 131, 141–46, 159, 168; immigrants/refugees in, 29; industrialization/urbanization of, 6, 29; Lan Kwai Fong, 8, 31; love and sex in, 128; market economy in, 56; nationalism in, 142–43, 152–53, 160; neoliberalism in, 55–56; pink economy in, 21, 31, 54, 92; Pride demonstrations, 8, 33, 95, 145–46; rebranding of, 29, 141–42; refugees/migrants in, xiii; religious backlash to *tongzhi* movement, 43–44, 56; research on, 26; same-sex marriage in, 36, 141; subjecthood in, 129; and Taiwan, 139–40; *tongzhi* identity in, 33–36; *tongzhi* rights in, 141; urbanization, 6, 29. *See also* Gay Games (Hong Kong); HKSAR government; Pink Dot (Hong Kong); protests
Hong Kong Alliance for Family, 34
Hong Kong Children (Huang), 20
Hong Kong Lesbian and Gay Film Festival (HKLGFF), 32–33, 35
Hong Kong Ten Percent Club (*tongzhi* social group), 182n12
hooliganism, 8, 46–47, 52, 91
Horizons (*tongzhi* social group, Hong Kong), 182n12
Ho Sik Ying, 191n7
housing: in Hong Kong, xiii, xiv, 30, 75, 92, 113; in mainland China, 119; public, 75, 113
Huang, Hans Tao-ming, 26
Huang, Ke-hsien, 44
Huang, Yingying, 48
huaqiao (diasporic ethnic Chinese), 168
huijia feihun ("destroy the family and abolish matrimony"), 135
hukou system (household registration), 122

I am (circuit party), 8. *See also* circuit parties
I can I BB (Qi Pa Shuo) (TV show, mainland China), 48
identity: about, 4; -based rights (Richardson), 27; collective, 90; concealing, 66–67; essentializing, 16, 63; formation, 30–31, 34–53, 63, 83–84; global gay (Altman), 177n13; Hongkonger vs *Zhongguoren*, 2; and imagined community, 90; in lesbian/gay studies, 63; nonnormative sexual, 9, 131; politics, 62, 63, 68; positive gay, 45, 103, 161, 163; transnationalism as form of, 14; unified notions of, 178n17; Western theory on, xv. *See also* intersectionality; sexual citizenship
imagined community, 90. *See also* community
imagined geographies, 90
imperialism: in China, 7; and homocolonialism, 133; and sociology, 10; of United States, 5
individualism, 64, 66, 89
industrialization, 6, 29, 39, 166
insider/outsider dichotomy, 22. *See also* binaristic thinking
Instagram, 95–96, 105
International Day Against Homophobia, Transphobia and Biphobia (IDAHOT), 8, 33–34, 182n14
International NGO Law (2017, mainland China), 49
International Women's Day, 50
Internet, gay spaces on, 97, 122
intersectionality, 11, 16–17, 22, 87, 178n18
interviews, 20–23, 178n21. *See also* methodology
intimacy, xv, 4, 89, 107
in-vitro fertilization, 53. *See also* birthing methods
iPhones vs Huawei/Xiaomi, 2
Isle Margin (journal, Taiwan), 41, 184n25
Isvara (*tongzhi* social group, Hong Kong), 182n12
Italy, family-centered culture, 64
Iwabuchi, Koichi, 19

Jack'd (app), 99
Japan, 37, 55, 106, 136

Jay (research participant), 124–25, 162, 171

Jianggu (research participant), 139, 162

Jin Xing Show (TV show, mainland China), 48

jobs: "good," 2, 128. *See also* cruel optimism (Berlant)

John (research participant), 76–78, 160, 171

Kam, Lucetta Yip-Lo, 62

Kang, Dredge Byung'Chu, 91

Kangxi Lai Le (TV program, Taiwan), 41, 101

Kaohsiung Pride (Taiwan), *42. See also* Pride demonstrations

Kim-Puri, H. J., 15–16

King, Gary, 49

KMT government: China, conception of, 6, 136–37, 139; and colonial history of Taiwan, 37–38; homosexuality under, 38, 54; and martial law, 38, 136, 160; 2.28 incident, 190n2. *See also* Taiwan

Knee, Eric, 88

knowledge, xvi, xvi–xvii, 170–71

Korea, 43–44, 55, 56, 106

Kuaxingbie Zhongxin (Trans Center, mainland China), 48

ku'er: use of term, 32, 40, 182n11. *See also* queer

Kurtis, Tugce, 17, 178n18

Kwan, Stanley, 48

labor precarity, 120–22, 123–24

lala (lesbian), 2

La La Dancehall (Shanghai), 97. *See also* Shanghai (mainland China)

Lancaster, Roger N., 177n12

land prices, 30, 92, 113. *See also* housing

Lan Kwai Fong (Hong Kong), 8, 31, 92

Lan Yu (Kwan), 48

Law, Wing Sang, 142

Lee Teng-Hui, 137

Leonard (research participant), 96

lesbians. *See* female homosexuality

Leung Chun Kwong v. the Secretary for the Civil Service and Commissioner of Inland Revenue, 183n21

Leung, Helen Hok-Sze, 19, 89

Leung T. C. William Roy v. Secretary for Justice, 34–35

LGBT Civil Rights Alliance (Taiwan), 40

LGBT+, use of term, 176n5

Li, Yinhe, 62

lian (face), 72. *See also* face

life-course approach, 20

life stories and generational sexualities, 19–23

Lin, Dennis Chwen-der, 39–40

Lin, Thung-Hong, 20

LINE (online chat group), 95, 105

Li Ning, 49

literature: classical Chinese, 32; homosexuality in (Taiwan), 40–41; and sociology, xvi

Liu, Jen-peng, 62

Liu, Petrus, 26

Liu, Wen, 190n1

liumangzui (hooliganism). *See* hooliganism

Li Yuanzhen, 39

Lizada, Miguel Antonio Nograles, 128

local essentialism, 13, 16. *See also* essentialism

London (UK), 86–87

loss of face, 66, 82–83. *See also* face

love: for China, 139, 149; in China/Hong Kong, 128; as cruel optimism, 127–29; parental, 156; same-sex, 27–28, 166–67. *See also* monogamy; relationships

Love, Heather, 11

Lucca (gay bar, Shanghai), 99. *See also* gay bars

Lu Hsiu-lien, 39

Lu Xinlei, 97

MacLennan, John, 31

male brothels, 47–48. *See also* prostitution

Malinowski, Bronislaw, 177n12

Manalansan, Martin F., IV., 12

Maoism, 7, 46, 118–19, 156

market economy, 23, 27, 33, 56

marriage: and filial piety, 68; in mainland China, 71; as norm, 72; opposition to, 36; *pianhun* (fraudulent), 66–67, 71, 73, 78, 121, 157; as public, 78; rejection by younger generations, 53, 71; as structuring society, 157; *xinghun* (contract/fake), 67, 71, 73, 78, 121–22, 157. *See also* same-sex marriage martial law: Christianity under, 38; cultural aspects, 56, 130, 136–37; overturning and repressive legacy, 20, 57, 160; and *tongzhi* movement, 183n24; 2.28 incident, 190n2

Martin, Fran, 13, 26

Marx, Karl, 10

Marxism, xvi, 39, 45, 165–66. *See also* theory

masculinity: in Chinese societies, 91–92; and cruel optimism, 188n3; gay, 163; and heteronormativity, 188n1; neoliberal, 76, 81; political activism as norm of gay, 118; straight, 83; in Taiwan, 125; Western theory on, xv. *See also* homonormative masculinity

Massad, Joseph, 133, 177n13

massage parlors, 41, 47–48. *See also* prostitution

masturbation, 38, 114, 121, 126. *See also* sexual acts

materialism, queer, 11

materiality and discourse, 17–18

Mathews, Gordon, 6

Ma Ying-jeou, 43, 135

Mead, Margaret, 177n12

Meghji, Ali, 178n19

mental health/illness: homosexuality model, xii–xiv, 7–8, 28, 30, 38, 46, 47, 166; in research participants, 72, 115

mental hygiene movement (Taiwan), 38

methodology: grounded-theory approach, 23; interviews, 20–23, 178n21; life-course approach, 20; queer Asia as, 18–19; of this book, 15, 20–23, 170, 179n22. *See also* transnational queer sociology

mianzi (face), 66, 72, 82, 83. *See also* face

migration flows, 97. *See also* rural to urban migration

military service, 125, 190n16

Millennials, 20

Mingming, 48

mingyuan (socialite/celebrity), 101, 125

modeling, 18, 166

modernities: Arab-Israeli, 152; Asian, 89; in China, 97; forms of, 16; in Hong Kong, 29; polychronic, 4; Taiwanese, 37–38; in *tongzhi* communities, 106; Western, 153

money boys, 52, 97. *See also* prostitution

monkey (gay community term), 98

monogamy: as conflict in relationships, 114; as cruel optimism, 24, 108–12; as ideal in mainland China, 121–22; masturbation as substitution for, 121; negotiating, 163; as normative, 135; open relationships, 116–17; vs polyamory, 127

monster parenting, 75, 77. *See also* parents and parenting

muscle bears (gay community term), 94

muscularity. *See* gym bodies

nanshen (male god), 2, 114–15, 189n11

National Central University (Taiwan), 41

nationalism: Chinese, 2, 28, 37–38; and Confucianism, 156; and HIV/AIDS prevention, 51; and homosexuality, 54–55, 136–40, 153; in Hong Kong, 142–43, 152–53, 160; identifications with, 134; nationhood and nation building, 41, 68–69, 90; on queerness, 151; Taiwanese, 123, 136–40, 161

National Security Law (Hong Kong), 57

National Work Group for Combating Pornography and Illegal Publications (NWGCPP, mainland China), 46

neofamilism, 65. *See also* family

neoliberalism: in Asia, 55, 162; in mainland China, 55, 106, 118–19, 156; developmental, 55; ethics of care, 118; and family, 62–63, 65, 71, 76–77, 81–82, 162; and futurity, 123; gender roles under, 83; the good under, 128; and (homonormative) masculinity, 63, 76, 81, 87, 107; in Hong Kong, 55–56, 74, 112; individuality under, 62–63; privatization under, 74; and queer normativity, 91; self-reliance, 41, 47, 74, 83, 112; success prioritized by, 162; in Taiwan, 55, 123, 127; and *tongzhi* community, 36–37, 97. *See also* cruel optimism (Berlant); globalization

networked individualism, 89. *See also* individualism

networked intimacy, 89. *See also* intimacy

New Age spirituality, 114–15

new queer studies, 12. *See also* queer studies

New York (US), 86–87

in Taiwan, 44; Tiananmen protests, 20; Umbrella Movement, 6; against work culture, 157. *See also* activism; citizenship

Puar, Jasbir, 12, 55, 132, 151. *See also* homonationalism

public housing, 75, 113. *See also* housing

public space, 57, 82, 97

Qing dynasty, 27

QQ (instant-message software), 120

QT v. Director of Immigration, 183n21

qualitative sociology, 19, 22. *See also* sociology

queer: as adjective, 14; agency, 64; as attitude, 14; as practice, 14; vs queer studies, 15; vs queer theory, 15; as regulatory, 132; translations, 40; use of term, 14–15, 32, 163, 167, 176n5, 182n11; as verb, 14. *See also* gay; homonationalism; homosexuality; *tongzhi*

queer Asian studies, xv, 9, 13–15

queer cinema, 40

Queer & Class (Taiwan), 40

queer community and commons, 87–88

Queer Comrades (webcast, mainland China), 48

queer cultural production, 57

queer diasporic studies, 13–14

queer hybridization model, 13

queering: adulthood, 128; global (Altman), 13; transnational turn (Chiang and Wong), 19

queer intelligentsia/elite, 32, 55–56

queer materialism, 11

queer-of-color critique, 13–14

queer pedagogy, xiv

queer politics, 13. See also *tongzhi* activism

queer spaces, 97

queer studies, new, 12

queer theory, xiv, xv–xvi, 9–19

Rahman, Momin, 133

Rainie, Lee, 89

rape/sodomy, codes against, 27, 181n1. *See also* buggery

Red House (Taipei, Taiwan), 8, 102

regionalism, 19

relational politics, coming out as, 24, 62–85, 162. *See also* politics

relationship-based rights, 27. *See also* sexual citizenship

relationships: compensated dating, 114; importance of, 108; long-distance, 139; monogamy as conflict in, 114; open, 116–18; politics and partner choice, 3, 115, 117, 139, 159

religious groups, 43–44, 56

Renmin University (Beijing), 48, 167

Renninger, Bryce J., 88–89

Renold, Emma, 108, 188n1

reproductive rights, 140

resistance: about, 4; guerrilla-style, 51; sites of, 23, 27, 33, 36. *See also* activism; protests

Richardson, Diane, 12, 91

Ringrose, Jessica, 108, 188n1

rise of China, xv, 5–9, 154, 168; discourse, 4, 168

Roberts, Margaret E., 49

Rofel, Lisa, 16, 51–52, 119, 171

romantic relationships, 3, 163. *See also* monogamy

Rowe, Matthew S., 107

rural to urban migration, 69–70, 97, 101, 119, 121–22

same-sex love: in ancient China, 27; cultural specificity of, 26; female, 28; *tongxinglian*, 166–67

same-sex marriage: in Hong Kong, 36, 141; legislation, 8, 44, 134–35; relationships outside, 30; in Taiwan, 3, 38–39, 134–35, *136*, 140, 160

Samshasha, 32

San Francisco (US), 86–87

Satsanga (*tongzhi* social group, Hong Kong), 182n12

scattered hegemonies (Grewal and Kaplan), 17

Schotten, C. Heike, 133

self, the, 63, 64, 84, 162, 187n18

self-help, 32, 57, 95, 102, 159, 161

Seoul (South Korea), 8

sex: biological understanding of, 46; as cruel optimism, 127–29; cultural understandings of, 177n12; etymology, 28

sexology, 10, 28, 38

sexual acts: anal sex, 46, 94–95, 126; bare-
back sex, 94–95; chemfun and chemsex,
94–96, 116; masturbation, 38, 114, 121,
126; oral sex, 114, 126
sexual addiction, 38
sexual citizenship: conduct-based rights
(Richardson), 27; homonormativity as model for, 91; identity-based
rights (Richardson), 27; morals, 45;
relationship-based rights (Richardson),
27; and sexual identity, 12; Taiwanese,
161; and *tongzhi* activism, 8, 27
sexual emancipation model, 12, 86–87, 89,
165
sexual exceptionalism, 132, 135, 153
sexual identity, xiii, 2, 11, 12, 87. *See also* gay;
homosexuality; queer; *tongzhi*
sexuality: biological understanding of, 46;
(un)changeability of, 72; decolonizing,
xv, 169–71; oppression of, 17; parental
acceptance of, 73; as produced, 10;
self-acceptance, 70; and the state, 130;
Western model of, 13; youth, 108, 127–28
sexuality studies, 12
Sexual Offences Act (United Kingdom, 1967),
29
Sexual Orientation Discrimination Ordinance (SODO, Hong Kong), 34
sexual subjectivity, 7. *See also* subjectivity
sexual violence, 181n1
Sham, Jimmy, 36
Shanghai (mainland China): about, 1, 21, 47,
69; economy in, 119; gay/*tongzhi* scene
in, 8, 21, 97, 100; loneliness of life in,
101; Pride, 8, 48, 97, 99, 100
shangliang fengsu ("virtuous customs,"
Taiwan), 8
Shang Yin (webTV drama series), 48–49, 100
Shenzhen (mainland China), 1, 47, 121, 166
Shitou, 48
Singapore, 43–44, 55, 56
Sinophone studies, 168
Skocpal, Theda, 18
So, Alvin Y., 112
social constructionism, 11, 63
social Darwinism, 28
socialism, 7, 46, 101, 118, 130, 165, 176n4
social mobility, 113, 123

Social Order Maintenance Law (Taiwan),
8, 38
sociology: banning of, 46; classical, 10; criticism of, 170; decolonizing, 178n19; and
empire's development, 10; feminism in,
xv–xvi; history of discipline, 10; homosexuality in, 10; and imperialism, 10;
and literature, xvi; mobilities paradigm
(Sheller and Urry), 15; nonnormative
sexual identity in, 9; and postcolonial
literature, xvi; and poststructuralism,
xvi; qualitative, 19, 22; and queer theory,
9–19, 169–70; symbolic interactionism
in, 11; transnational feminist and queer,
xv–xvi, 15–16; use of term, 15. *See also*
transnational queer sociology
SongKran (circuit party), 8. *See also* circuit
parties
South Korea, 43–44, 55, 56, 106
sovereignty, 6
space, politics of, 87
sperm donation, 53. *See also* assisted reproductive technology (ART); birthing methods
spirituality, 114–15. *See also* religious groups
Spring Festival, 67
Stacey, Judith, xv–xvi
state, the: in mainland China, 55, 106; vs civil
society, 57–58; and family, 69, 79, 82;
feminism, 39; as governance and resistance site, 23, 27, 33; and (homo)sexual-
ity, 130, 131–32; as identity-shaping, 54,
58; unifying vs heterogeneous, 131–32;
use of term, 175n1
Stein, Arlene, xvi
stories, 19, 171. *See also* life stories and generational sexualities
straightness, as racial norm (Puar), 132
strawberry generation (Taiwan), 20
subjectivity, 7, 27, 37–38
Sunflower Movement: and PRC, 181n23
Sunflower Movement (Taiwan): about, xv,
103, 126, 135, 181n23; optimism of, 109,
123–24, 128; and Taiwanese identity, 137
sunshine (gay community term), 96
Sun Zhongxin, 185n34
surrogacy, 53. *See also* birthing methods
surveillance, 7, 17, 49, 139, 153
suzhi (quality) citizens, 101, 147, 151, 157

Sydney (Australia), 87
symbolic interaction and labeling theory, 63, 176n10, 178n17

Taipei (Taiwan), 3, 8, 21, 105
Taipei City (Taiwan), 41
Taipei Golden Horse International Film Festival, 40
Taipei New Park (228 Peace Memorial Park), 38, 40
Taiwan: and Beijing government (mainland China), 138–39, 160; and mainland China, 6–7, 151–52, 155–56, 160; Christianity in, 38–39, 43, 135; citizenship in, 160–61; civil rights movement in, 41; colonial history of, 37–38; and colonialism, 37–38; COVID-19 in, 3, 124; democracy in, 6, 20, 41, 126–27, 135, 137, 160; demographics, 78–79, 136; economic growth, 43, 135; evangelicalism in, 34–35, 54, 141; family in, 78–79, 81; feminism in, 39; gay world in, 106, 128–29; gender discrimination, 43; generational terms in, 20; historical aspects, 37; homonationalism in, 25, 55, 130, 134–40, 151; homosexuality in, 8, 38, 40–41, 54, 160–61; and Hong Kong, 139–40; independence, 3, 7; industrialization in, 39; intellectual culture of, 38; market economy in, 56; martial law, 56–57; military system, 190n16; nationalism, 123, 136–40, 161; nation building, 41; neoliberalism in, 55, 123, 127; perceptions of, 143–44; pink economy in, 41, 73, 102; policing in, 8, 38, 152; post-'90s generation in, 161; Pride demonstrations in, 42–43, 45, 79–80, 103–4, 134; pride in, 42–43, 45, 79–80, 103–4, 134; pro-gay government, 43; religious backlash to *tongzhi* movement, 56; vs Republic of China, 137; research on, 26; same-sex marriage in, 3, 38–39, 134–35, 136, 140, 160; subjecthood in, 129; *tongzhi* identity formation in, 37–45; *tongzhi* rights in, 134–35; *tongzhi* world in, 102–5, 161; urbanization, 39; Western/global affiliations, 135, 165; women's movements, 39. *See also* KMT government; Sunflower Movement (Taiwan); Taiwanese identity

Taiwan Alliance to Promote Civil Partnership Rights (TAPCPR), 44
Taiwanese identity: vs Chinese identity, 137; vs Hongkonger identity, 168–69; and nationalism, 123, 136–40, 161; in youth, 130, 138. *See also* Taiwan
Taiwan International Queer Film Festival, 41
Tang, Denise Tse-Shang, 62
temporality, strange (Halberstam), 127–28
Thailand, 55, 106
theory, 13, 23, 39, 170. *See also* Marxism; Western theory
Thorne, Barrie, xv–xvi
Tian, Ian Liujia, 46, 185n38
Tiananmen protests, 20, 147
Tinder (app), 94–95
Tokyo (Japan), 8
tongxinglian (same-sex love), 28, 166–67
Tongxinglian Qinyou Hui. *See* PFLAG China (Parents and Friends of Lesbians and Gays, Tongxinglian Qinyou Hui)
tongzhi (comrade), use of term, xiii–xiv, 14, 32, 166–67, 191n3. *See also* gay; homosexuality; queer
tongzhi (first generation), 58, 181n7
tongzhi activism, 8, 36, 149
tongzhi community and communities: emergence of, 8; engagement with, 89–90; and neoliberalism, 36–37, 97; normativity in, 91; and *tongzhi* identity, 86
tongzhi generations, 53–59
Tongzhi Hotlines (Taiwan), 40
tongzhi identity: in mainland China, 45–53; the closet in, 65–66; as enlightened/liberated, 153; and filial piety, 65; and government, 34; and hetero/homonormativities, 44–45; in Hong Kong, 33–36; research on, 26; and social institutions, 58; sociomaterialist analysis of, 33–34; in Taiwan, 45; and *tongzhi* community, 86
tongzhi movement: vs democratic movement(s), 158; and economic development, 149; opposition to, 8, 43; as sociodemocratic movement, 39, 138, 144–46; (in)visibility of, 57–58
Tongzhi Shangwu (mainland China), 48
Tongzhi Space Action Network (Taiwan), 40
tongzhi stories (comrade literature), 48

Xiaofei (research participant), 69–73, 149–50, 158
Xiaoyu (research participant), 147–50
Xi Jinping, xv, 7, 49, 55, *61*, 155
Ximending neighborhood (Taipei City, Taiwan), 41
xing (sex), 28
xinghun marriages (contract/fake), 67, 71, 73, 78, 121–22, 157. *See also* marriage
xin tongzhi dianying (New Queer Cinema), 40
Xinxin (research participant), 98–101

Yeh Yung-chih, 103, 184n30
Yeh Yung-chih, mother of, *42*
yellow-ribbon camp, 2, 112–13, 115, 117, 144–45, 158–59. *See also* blue-ribbon camp

Yifan (research participant), 1–2, 120–23, 149, 158, 171
youth: ambiguity of, 127, 163; as a "collapsing generation" (Lin et al.), 123; radicalism of politics, 113, 118; sexuality, 108, 127–28. *See also* sexuality
Yoyo (research participant), 75, 77–78, 160
Yue, Audrey, 19, 89

ZANK (app), 48–49, 185n39
Zhang, Charlie Yi, 190n1
Zhang, Li, 118
Zhiheshe (student society, China), *50*
Zhong G (code for CCP), 139
Zhongguoren (Chinese national), 2, 137, 168
Zhonghuaminguoren (National of the Republic of China), 137